THE BALKANS

PREFACE

The authors of this volume have not worked in conjunction. Widely separated, engaged on other duties, and pressed for time, we have had no opportunity for interchange of views. Each must be held responsible, therefore, for his own section alone. If there be any discrepancies in our writings (it is not unlikely in so disputed a field of history) we can only regret an unfortunate result of the circumstances. Owing to rapid change in the relations of our country to the several Balkan peoples, the tone of a section written earlier may differ from that of another written later. It may be well to state that the sections on Serbia and Bulgaria were finished before the decisive Balkan developments of the past two months. Those on Greece and Rumania represent only a little later stage of the evolution. That on Turkey, compiled between one mission abroad and another, was the latest to be finished.

If our sympathies are not all the same, or given equally to friends and foes, none of us would find it possible to indite a Hymn of Hate about any Balkan people. Every one of these peoples, on whatever side he be fighting to-day, has a past worthy of more than our respect and interwoven in some intimate way with our history. That any one of them is arrayed against us to-day is not to be laid entirely or chiefly at its own door. They are all fine peoples who have not obtained their proper places in the sun. The best of the Osmanli nation, the Anatolian peasantry, has yet to make its physical and moral qualities felt under civilized conditions. As for the rest—the Serbs and the Bulgars, who have enjoyed brief moments of barbaric glory in their past, have still to find themselves in that future which shall be to the Slav. The Greeks, who were old when we were not as yet, are younger now than we. They are as incalculable a factor in a political forecast as another Chosen Race, the Jews. Their past is the world's glory: the present in the Near East is theirs more than any people's: the future—despite the laws of corporate being and decline, dare we say they will have no part in it? Of Rumania what are we to think? Her mixed people has had the start of the Balkan Slavs in modern civilization, and evidently her boundaries must grow wider yet. But the limits of her possible expansion are easier to set than those of the rest.

We hope we have dealt fairly with all these peoples. Mediaeval history, whether of the East or the West, is mostly a record of bloodshedding and cruelty; and the Middle Age has been prolonged to our own time in most parts of the Balkans, and is not yet over in some parts. There are certain things salutary to bear in mind when we think or speak of any part of that country to-day. First, that less than two hundred years ago, England had its highwaymen on all roads, and its smuggler dens and caravans, Scotland its caterans, and Ireland its moonlighters. Second, that religious fervour has rarely mitigated and generally increased our own savagery. Thirdly, that our own policy in Balkan matters has been none too wise, especially of late. In permitting the Treaty of Bucarest three years ago, we were parties to making much of the trouble that has ensued, and will ensue again. If we have not been able to write about the Near East under existing circumstances altogether *sine ira et studio*, we have tried to remember that each of its peoples has a case.

D.G. HOGARTH.
November, 1915.

CONTENTS

BULGARIA AND SERBIA.
By NEVILL FORBES

BULGARIA.

SERBIA.

GREECE.
By ARNOLD J. TOYNBEE

RUMANIA:
HER HISTORY AND POLITICS

TURKEY.
By D. G. HOGARTH

BULGARIA AND SERBIA.

1.

Introductory

The whole of what may be called the trunk or *massif* of the Balkan peninsula, bounded on the north by the rivers Save and Danube, on the west by the Adriatic, on the east by the Black Sea, and on the south by a very irregular line running from Antivari (on the coast of the Adriatic) and the lake of Scutari in the west, through lakes Okhrida and Prespa (in Macedonia) to the outskirts of Salonika and thence to Midia on the shores of the Black Sea, following the coast of the Aegean Sea some miles inland, is preponderatingly inhabited by Slavs. These Slavs are the Bulgarians in the east and centre, the Serbs and Croats (or Serbians and Croatians or Serbo-Croats) in the west, and the Slovenes in the extreme north-west, between Trieste and the Save; these nationalities compose the southern branch of the Slavonic race. The other inhabitants of the Balkan peninsula are, to the south of the Slavs, the Albanians in the west, the Greeks in the centre and south, and the Turks in the south-east, and, to the north, the Rumanians. All four of these nationalities are to be found in varying quantities within the limits of the Slav territory roughly outlined above, but greater numbers of them are outside it; on the other hand, there are a considerable number of Serbs living north of the rivers Save and Danube, in southern Hungary. Details of the ethnic distribution and boundaries will of course be gone into more fully later; meanwhile attention may be called to the significant fact that the name of Macedonia, the heart of the Balkan peninsula, has been long used by the French gastronomers to denote a dish, the principal characteristic of which is that its component parts are mixed up into quite inextricable confusion.

Of the three Slavonic nationalities already mentioned, the two first, the Bulgarians and the Serbo-Croats, occupy a much greater space, geographically and historically, than the third. The Slovenes, barely one and a half million in number, inhabiting the Austrian provinces of Carinthia and Carniola, have never been able to form a political state, though, with the growth of Trieste as a great port and the persistent efforts of Germany to make her influence if not her flag supreme on the shores of the Adriatic, this small people has from its geographical position and from its anti-German (and anti-Italian) attitude achieved considerable notoriety and some importance.

Of the Bulgars and Serbs it may be said that at the present moment the former control the eastern, and the latter, in alliance with the Greeks, the western half of the peninsula. It has always been the ambition of each of these three nationalities to dominate the whole, an ambition which has caused endless waste of blood and money and untold misery. If the question were to be settled purely on ethnical considerations, Bulgaria would acquire the greater part of the interior of Macedonia, the most numerous of the dozen nationalities of which is Bulgarian in sentiment if not in origin, and would thus undoubtedly attain the hegemony of the peninsula, while the centre of gravity of the Serbian nation would, as is ethnically just, move north-westwards. Political considerations, however, have until now always been against this solution of the difficulty, and, even if it solved in this sense, there would still remain the problem of the Greek nationality, whose distribution along all the coasts of the Aegean, both European and Asiatic, makes a delimitation of the Greek state on purely ethnical lines virtually impossible. It is curious that the Slavs, though masters of the interior of the peninsula and of parts of its eastern and western coasts, have never made the shores of the Aegean (the White Sea, as they call it) or the cities on them their own. The Adriatic is the only sea on the shore of which any Slavonic race has ever made its home. In view of this difficulty, namely, the interior of the peninsula being Slavonic while the coastal fringe is Greek, and of the approximately equal numerical strength of all three nations, it is almost inevitable that the ultimate solution of the problem and delimitation of political boundaries will have to be effected by means of territorial compromise. It can only be hoped that this ultimate compromise will be agreed upon by the three countries concerned, and will be more equitable than that which was forced on them by Rumania in 1913 and laid down in the Treaty of Bucarest of that year.

If no arrangement on a principle of give and take is made between them, the road to the East, which from the point of view of the Germanic powers lies through Serbia, will sooner or later inevitably be forced open, and the independence, first of Serbia, Montenegro, and Albania, and later of Bulgaria and Greece, will disappear, *de facto* if not in appearance, and both materially and morally they will become the slaves of the central empires. If the Balkan League could be reconstituted, Germany and Austria would never reach Salonika or Constantinople.

2.
The Balkan Peninsula in Classical Times
400 B.C.-A.D. 500.

In the earlier historical times the whole of the eastern part of the Balkan peninsula between the Danube and the Aegean was known as Thracia, while the western part (north of the forty-first degree of latitude) was termed Illyricum; the lower basin of the river Vardar (the classical Axius) was called Macedonia. A number of the tribal and personal names of the early Illyrians and Thracians have been preserved. Philip of Macedonia subdued Thrace in the fourth century B.C. and in 342 founded the city of

Philippopolis. Alexander's first campaign was devoted to securing control of the peninsula, but during the Third century B.C. Thrace was invaded from the north and laid waste by the Celts, who had already visited Illyria. The Celts vanished by the end of that century, leaving a few place-names to mark their passage. The city of Belgrade was known until the seventh century A.D. by its Celtic name of Singidunum. Naissus, the modern Nish, is also possibly of Celtic origin. It was towards 230 B.C. that Rome came into contact with Illyricum, owing to the piratical proclivities of its inhabitants, but for a long time it only controlled the Dalmatian coast, so called after the Delmati or Dalmati, an Illyrian tribe. The reason for this was the formidable character of the mountains of Illyria, which run in several parallel and almost unbroken lines the whole length of the shore of the Adriatic and have always formed an effective barrier to invasion from the west. The interior was only very gradually subdued by the Romans after Macedonia had been occupied by them in 146 B.C. Throughout the first century B.C. conflicts raged with varying fortune between the invaders and all the native races living between the Adriatic and the Danube. They were attacked both from Aquileia in the north and from Macedonia in the south, but it was not till the early years of our era that the Danube became the frontier of the Roman Empire.

In the year A.D. 6 Moesia, which included a large part of the modern kingdom of Serbia and the northern half of that of Bulgaria between the Danube and the Balkan range (the classical Haemus), became an imperial province, and twenty years later Thrace, the country between the Balkan range and the Aegean, was incorporated in the empire, and was made a province by the Emperor Claudius in A.D. 46. The province of Illyricum or Dalmatia stretched between the Save and the Adriatic, and Pannonia lay between the Danube and the Save. In 107 A.D. the Emperor Trajan conquered the Dacians beyond the lower Danube, and organized a province of Dacia out of territory roughly equivalent to the modern Wallachia and Transylvania, This trans-Danubian territory did not remain attached to the empire for more than a hundred and fifty years; but within the river line a vast belt of country, stretching from the head of the Adriatic to the mouths of the Danube on the Black Sea, was Romanized through and through. The Emperor Trajan has been called the Charlemagne of the Balkan peninsula; all remains are attributed to him (he was nicknamed the Wallflower by Constantine the Great), and his reign marked the zenith of Roman power in this part of the world. The Balkan peninsula enjoyed the benefits of Roman civilization for three centuries, from the first to the fourth, but from the second century onwards the attitude of the Romans was defensive rather than offensive. The war against the Marcomanni under the Emperor Marcus Aurelius, in the second half of this century, was the turning-point. Rome was still victorious, but no territory was added to the empire. The third century saw the southward movement of the Germanic peoples, who took the place of the Celts. The Goths invaded the peninsula, and in 251 the Emperor Decius was killed in battle against them near Odessus on the Black Sea (the modern Varna). The Goths reached the outskirts of Thessalonica (Salonika), but were defeated by the Emperor Claudius at Naissus (Nish) in 269; shortly afterwards, however, the Emperor Aurelian had definitively to relinquish Dacia to them. The Emperor Diocletian, a native of Dalmatia, who reigned from 284 to 305, carried out a redistribution of the imperial provinces. Pannonia and western Illyria, or Dalmatia, were assigned to the prefecture of Italy, Thrace to that of the Orient, while the whole centre of the peninsula, from the Danube to the Peloponnese, constituted the prefecture of Illyria, with Thessalonica as capital. The territory to the north of the Danube having been lost, what is now western Bulgaria was renamed Dacia, while Moesia, the modern kingdom of Serbia, was made very much smaller. Praevalis, or the southern part of Dalmatia, approximately the modern Montenegro and Albania, was detached from that province and added to the prefecture of Illyria. In this way the boundary between the province of Dalmatia and the Balkan peninsula proper ran from near the lake of Scutari in the south to the river Drinus (the modern Drina), whose course it followed till the Save was reached in the north.

An event of far-reaching importance in the following century was the elevation by Constantine the Great of the Greek colony of Byzantium into the imperial city of Constantinople in 325. This century also witnessed the arrival of the Huns in Europe from Asia. They overwhelmed the Ostrogoths, between the Dnieper and the Dniester, in 375, and the Visigoths, settled in Transylvania and the modern Rumania, moved southwards in sympathy with this event. The Emperor Valens lost his life fighting against these Goths in 378 at the great battle of Adrianople (a city established in Thrace by the Emperor Hadrian in the second century). His successor, the Emperor Theodosius, placated them with gifts and made them guardians of the northern frontier, but at his death, in 395, they overran and devastated the entire peninsula, after which they proceeded to Italy. After the death of the Emperor Theodosius the empire was divided, never to be joined into one whole again. The dividing line followed that, already mentioned, which separated the prefecture of Italy from those of Illyria and the Orient, that is to say, it began in the south, on the shore of the Adriatic near the Bocche di Cattaro, and went due north along the valley of the Drina till the confluence of that river with the Save. It will be seen that this division had consequences which have lasted to the present day. Generally speaking, the Western Empire was Latin in language and character, while the Eastern was Greek, though owing to the importance of the Danubian provinces to Rome from the military point of view, and the lively intercourse maintained between them, Latin influence in them was for a long time stronger than Greek. Its extent is proved by the fact that the people of modern Rumania are partly, and their language very largely, defended from those of the legions and colonies of the Emperor Trajan.

Latin influence, shipping, colonization, and art were always supreme on the eastern shores of the Adriatic, just as were those of Greece on the shores of the Black Sea. The Albanians even, descendants of the ancient Illyrians, were affected by the supremacy of the Latin language, from which no less than a quarter of their own meagre vocabulary is derived; though driven southwards by the Romans and northwards by the Greeks, they have remained in their mountain fastnesses to this day, impervious to any of the civilizations to which they have been exposed.

Christianity spread to the shores of the peninsula very early; Macedonia and Dalmatia were the parts where it was first established, and it took some time to penetrate into the interior. During the reign of Diocletian numerous martyrs suffered for the faith in the Danubian provinces, but with the accession of Constantine the Great persecution came to an end. As soon, however, as the Christians were left alone, they started persecuting each other, and during the fourth century the Arian controversy re-echoed throughout the peninsula.

In the fifth century the Huns moved from the shores of the Black Sea to the plains of the Danube and the Theiss; they devastated the Balkan peninsula, in spite of the tribute which they had levied on Constantinople in return for their promise of peace. After the death of Attila, in 453, they again retreated to Asia, and during the second half of the century the Goths were once more supreme in the peninsula. Theodoric occupied Singidunum (Belgrade) in 471 and, after plundering Macedonia and Greece, settled in Novae (the modern Svishtov), on the lower Danube, in 483, where he remained till he transferred the sphere of his activities to Italy ten years later. Towards the end of the fifth century Huns of various kinds returned to the lower Danube and devastated the peninsula several times, penetrating as far as Epirus and Thessaly.

3.
The Arrival of the Slavs in the Balkan Peninsula,
A.D. 500-650

The Balkan peninsula, which had been raised to a high level of security and prosperity during the Roman dominion, gradually relapsed into barbarism as a result of these endless invasions; the walled towns, such as

Salonika and Constantinople, were the only safe places, and the country became waste and desolate. The process continued unabated throughout the three following centuries, and one is driven to one of two conclusions, either that these lands must have possessed very extraordinary powers of recuperation to make it worth while for invaders to pillage them so frequently, or, what is more probable, there can have been after some time little left to plunder, and consequently the Byzantine historians' accounts of enormous drives of prisoners and booty are much exaggerated. It is impossible to count the number of times the tide of invasion and devastation swept southwards over the unfortunate peninsula. The emperors and their generals did what they could by means of defensive works on the frontiers, of punitive expeditions, and of trying to set the various hordes of barbarians at loggerheads with each other, but, as they had at the same time to defend an empire which stretched from Armenia to Spain, it is not surprising that they were not more successful. The growing riches of Constantinople and Salonika had an irresistible attraction for the wild men from the east and north, and unfortunately the Greek citizens were more inclined to spend their energy in theological disputes and their leisure in the circus than to devote either the one or the other to the defence of their country. It was only by dint of paying them huge sums of money that the invaders were kept away from the coast. The departure of the Huns and the Goths had made the way for fresh series of unwelcome visitors. In the sixth century the Slavs appear for the first time. From their original homes which were immediately north of the Carpathians, in Galicia and Poland, but may also have included parts of the modern Hungary, they moved southwards and south-eastwards. They were presumably in Dacia, north of the Danube, in the previous century, but they are first mentioned as having crossed that river during the reign of the Emperor Justin I (518-27). They were a loosely-knit congeries of tribes without any single leader or central authority; some say they merely possessed the instinct of anarchy, others that they were permeated with the ideals of democracy. What is certain is that amongst them neither leadership nor initiative was developed, and that they lacked both cohesion and organisation. The Eastern Slavs, the ancestors of the Russians, were only welded into anything approaching unity by the comparatively much smaller number of Scandinavian (Varangian) adventurers who came and took charge of their affairs at Kiev. Similarly the Southern Slavs were never of themselves able to form a united community, conscious of its aim and capable of persevering in its attainment.

The Slavs did not invade the Balkan peninsula alone but in the company of the Avars, a terrible and justly dreaded nation, who, like the Huns, were of Asiatic (Turkish or Mongol) origin. These invasions became more frequent during the reign of the Emperor Justinian I (527-65), and culminated in 559 in a great combined attack of all the invaders on Constantinople under a certain Zabergan, which was brilliantly defeated by the veteran Byzantine general Belisarius. The Avars were a nomad tribe, and the horse was their natural means of locomotion. The Slavs, on the other hand, moved about on foot, and seem to have been used as infantry by the more masterful Asiatics in their warlike expeditions. Generally speaking, the Avars, who must have been infinitely less numerous than the Slavs, were settled in Hungary, where Attila and the Huns had been settled a little more than a century previously; that is to say, they were north of the Danube, though they were always overrunning into Upper Moesia, the modern Serbia. The Slavs, whose numbers were without doubt very large, gradually settled all over the country south of the Danube, the rural parts of which, as a result of incessant invasion and retreat, had become waste and empty. During the second half of the sixth century all the military energies of Constantinople were diverted to Persia, so that the invaders of the Balkan peninsula had the field very much to themselves. It was during this time that the power of the Avars reached its height. They were masters of all the country up to the walls of Adrianople and Salonika, though they did not settle there. The peninsula seems to have been colonized by Slavs, who penetrated right down into Greece; but the Avars were throughout this time, both in politics and in war, the directing and dominating force. During another Persian war, which broke out in 622 and entailed the prolonged absence of the emperor from Constantinople, the Avars, not satisfied with the tribute extorted from the Greeks, made an alliance against them with the Persians, and in 626 collected a large army of Slavs and Asiatics and attacked Constantinople both by land and sea from the European side, while the Persians threatened it from Asia. But the walls of the city and the ships of the Greeks proved invincible, and, quarrels breaking out between the Slavs and the Avars, both had to save themselves in ignominious and precipitate retreat.

After this nothing more was heard of the Avars in the Balkan peninsula, though their power was only finally crushed by Charlemagne in 799. In Russia their downfall became proverbial, being crystallized in the saying, 'they perished like Avars'. The Slavs, on the other hand, remained. Throughout these stormy times their penetration of the Balkan peninsula had been peacefully if unostentatiously proceeding; by the middle of the seventh century it was complete. The main streams of Slavonic immigration moved southwards and westwards. The first covered the whole of the country between the Danube and the Balkan range, overflowed into Macedonia, and filtered down into Greece. Southern Thrace in the east and Albania in the west were comparatively little affected, and in these districts the indigenous population maintained itself. The coasts of the Aegean and the great cities on or near them were too strongly held by the Greeks to be affected, and those Slavs who penetrated into Greece itself were soon absorbed by the local populations. The still stronger Slavonic stream, which moved westwards and turned up north-westwards, overran the whole country down to the shores of the Adriatic and as far as the sources of the Save and Drave in the Alps. From that point in the west to the shores of the Black Sea in the east became one solid mass of Slavs, and has remained so ever since. The few Slavs who were left north of the Danube in Dacia were gradually assimilated by the inhabitants of that province, who were the descendants of the Roman soldiers and colonists, and the ancestors of the modern Rumanians, but the fact that Slavonic influence there was strong is shown by the large number of words of Slavonic origin contained in the Rumanian language.

Place-names are a good index of the extent and strength of the tide of Slav immigration. All along the coast, from the mouth of the Danube to the head of the Adriatic, the Greek and Roman names have been retained though places have often been given alternative names by the Slavonic settlers. Thrace, especially the south-eastern part, and Albania have the fewest Slavonic place-names. In Macedonia and Lower Moesia (Bulgaria) very few classical names have survived, while in Upper Moesia (Serbia) and the interior of Dalmatia (Bosnia, Hercegovina, and Montenegro) they have entirely disappeared. The Slavs themselves, though their tribal names were known, were until the ninth century usually called collectively S(k)lavini ([Greek: Sklabaenoi]) by the Greeks, and all the inland parts of the peninsula were for long termed by them 'the S(k)lavonias' ([Greek: Sklabiniai]).

During the seventh century, dating from the defeat of the Slavs and Avars before the walls of Constantinople in 626 and the final triumph of the emperor over the Persians in 628, the influence and power of the Greeks began to reassert itself throughout the peninsula as far north as the Danube; this process was coincident with the decline of the might of the Avars. It was the custom of the astute Byzantine diplomacy to look on and speak of lands which had been occupied by the various barbarian invaders as grants made to them through the generosity of the emperor; by this means, by dint also of lavishing titles and substantial incomes to the invaders' chiefs, by making the most of their mutual jealousies, and also by enlisting regiments of Slavonic mercenaries in the imperial armies, the supremacy of Constantinople was regained far more effectively than it could have been by the continual and exhausting use of force.

BULGARIA.

4.

The Arrival of the Bulgars in the Balkan Peninsula, 600-700

The progress of the Bulgars towards the Balkan peninsula, and indeed all their movements until their final establishment there in the seventh century, are involved in obscurity. They are first mentioned by name in classical and Armenian sources in 482 as living in the steppes to the north of the Black Sea amongst other Asiatic tribes, and it has been assumed by some that at the end of the fifth and throughout the sixth century they were associated first with the Huns and later with the Avars and Slavs in the various incursions into and invasions of the eastern empire which have already been enumerated. It is the tendency of Bulgarian historians, who scornfully point to the fact that the history of Russia only dates from the ninth century, to exaggerate the antiquity of their own and to claim as early a date as possible for the authentic appearance of their ancestors on the kaleidoscopic stage of the Balkan theatre. They are also unwilling to admit that they were anticipated by the Slavs; they prefer to think that the Slavs only insinuated themselves there thanks to the energy of the Bulgars' offensive against the Greeks, and that as soon as the Bulgars had leisure to look about them they found all the best places already occupied by the anarchic Slavs.

Of course it is very difficult to say positively whether Bulgars were or were not present in the welter of Asiatic nations which swept westwards into Europe with little intermission throughout the fifth and sixth centuries, but even if they were, they do not seem to have settled down as early as that anywhere south of the Danube; it seems certain that they did not do so until the seventh century, and therefore that the Slavs were definitely installed in the Balkan peninsula a whole century before the Bulgars crossed the Danube for good.

The Bulgars, like the Huns and the Avars who preceded them, and like the Magyars and the Turks who followed them, were a tribe from eastern Asia, of the stock known as Mongol or Tartar. The tendency of all these peoples was to move westwards from Asia into Europe, and this they did at considerable and irregular intervals, though in alarming and apparently inexhaustible numbers, roughly from the fourth till the fourteenth centuries. The distance was great, but the journey, thanks to the flat, grassy, treeless, and well-watered character of the steppes of southern Russia which they had to cross, was easy. They often halted for considerable periods by the way, and some never moved further westwards than Russia. Thus at one time the Bulgars settled in large numbers on the Volga, near its confluence with the Kama, and it is presumed that they were well established there in the fifth century. They formed a community of considerable strength and importance, known as Great or White Bulgaria. These Bulgars fused with later Tartar immigrants from Asia and eventually were consolidated into the powerful kingdom of Kazan, which was only crushed by the Tsar Ivan IV in 1552. According to Bulgarian historians, the basins of the rivers Volga and Don and the steppes of eastern Russia proved too confined a space for the legitimate development of Bulgarian energy, and expansion to the west was decided on. A large number of Bulgars therefore detached themselves and began to move south-westwards. During the sixth century they seem to have been settled in the country to the north of the Black Sea, forming a colony known as Black Bulgaria. It is very doubtful whether the Bulgars did take part, as they are supposed to have done, in the ambitious but unsuccessful attack on Constantinople in 559 under Zabergan, chief of another Tartar tribe; but it is fairly certain that they did in the equally formidable but equally unsuccessful attacks by the Slavs and Avars against Salonika in 609 and Constantinople in 626.

During the last quarter of the sixth and the first of the seventh century the various branches of the Bulgar nation, stretching from the Volga to the Danube, were consolidated and kept in control by their prince Kubrat, who eventually fought on behalf of the Greeks against the Avars, and was actually baptized in Constantinople. The power of the Bulgars grew as that of the Avars declined, but at the death of Kubrat, in 638, his realm was divided amongst his sons. One of these established himself in Pannonia, where he joined forces with what was left of the Avars, and there the Bulgars maintained themselves till they were obliterated by the irruption of the Magyars in 893. Another son, Asparukh, or Isperikh, settled in Bessarabia, between the rivers Prut and Dniester, in 640, and some years later passed southwards. After desultory warfare with Constantinople, from 660 onwards, his successor finally overcame the Greeks, who were at that time at war with the Arabs, captured Varna, and definitely established himself between the Danube and the Balkan range in the year 679. From that year the Danube ceased to be the frontier of the eastern empire.

The numbers of the Bulgars who settled south of the Danube are not known, but what happened to them is notorious. The well-known process, by which the Franks in Gaul were absorbed by the far more numerous indigenous population which they had conquered, was repeated, and the Bulgars became fused with the Slavs. So complete was the fusion, and so preponderating the influence of the subject nationality, that beyond a few personal names no traces of the language of the Bulgars have survived. Modern Bulgarian, except for the Turkish words introduced into it later during the Ottoman rule, is purely Slavonic. Not so the Bulgarian nationality; as is so often the case with mongrel products, this race, compared with the Serbs, who are purely Slav, has shown considerably greater virility, cohesion, and driving-power, though it must be conceded that its problems have been infinitely simpler.

<h1 style="text-align:center">5.</h1>

The Early Years of Bulgaria and the Introduction of Christianity, 700-893

From the time of their establishment in the country to which they have given their name the Bulgars became a thorn in the side of the Greeks, and ever since both peoples have looked on one another as natural and hereditary enemies. The Bulgars, like all the barbarians who had preceded them, were fascinated by the honey-pot of Constantinople, and, though they never succeeded in taking it, they never grew tired of making the attempt.

For two hundred years after the death of Asparukh, in 661, the Bulgars were perpetually fighting either against the Greeks or else amongst themselves. At times a diversion was caused by the Bulgars taking the part of the Greeks, as in 718, when they 'delivered' Constantinople, at the invocation of the Emperor Leo, from the Arabs, who were besieging it. From about this time the Bulgarian monarchy, which had been hereditary, became elective, and the anarchy of the many, which the Bulgars found when they arrived, and which their first few autocratic rulers had been able to control, was replaced by an anarchy of the few. Prince succeeded prince, war followed war, at the will of the feudal nobles. This internal strife was naturally profitable to the Greeks, who lavishly subsidized the rival factions.

At the end of the eighth century the Bulgars south of the Danube joined forces with those to the north in the efforts of the latter against the Avars, who, beaten by Charlemagne, were again pressing south-eastwards towards the Danube. In this the Bulgars were completely successful under the leadership of one Krum, whom, in the elation of victory, they promptly elected to the throne. Krum was a far more capable ruler than they had bargained for, and he not only united all the Bulgars north and south of the Danube into one dominion, but also forcibly repressed the whims of the nobles and re-established the autocracy and the hereditary monarchy. Having finished with his enemies in the north, he turned his attention to the Greeks, with no less success. In 809 he captured from them the important city of Sofia (the Roman Sardica, known to the Slavs as Sredets), which is to-day the capital of Bulgaria. The loss of this city was a blow to the Greeks, because it was a great centre of commerce and also the point at which the commercial and strategic highways of the peninsula met and crossed. The Emperor Nikiphoros, who wished to take his revenge and recover his lost property, was totally defeated by the Bulgars and lost his life in the Balkan passes in 811. After further victories, at Mesembria (the modern Misivria) in 812 and Adrianople in 813, Krum appeared before the capital, where he nearly lost his life in an ambush while negotiating for peace. During preparations for a final assault on Constantinople he died suddenly in 815. Though Krum cannot be said to have introduced civilisation into Bulgaria, he at any rate increased its power and gave it some of the more essential organs of government. He framed a code of laws remarkable for their rigour, which was undoubtedly necessary in such a community and beneficial in its effect. He repressed civil strife, and by this means made possible the reawakening of commerce and agriculture. His successor, of uncertain identity, founded in 822 the city of Preslav (known to the Russians as Pereyaslav), situated in eastern Bulgaria, between Varna and Silistria, which was the capital until 972.

The reign of Prince Boris (852-88) is remarkable because it witnessed the definitive conversion to Christianity of Bulgaria and her ruler. It is within this period also that fell the activities of the two great 'Slavonic' missionaries and apostles, the brothers Cyril and Methodius, who are looked upon by all Slavs of the orthodox faith as the founders of their civilisation. Christianity had of course penetrated into Bulgaria (or Moesia, as it was then) long before the arrival of the Slavs and Bulgars, but the influx of one horde of barbarians after another was naturally not propitious to its growth. The conversion of Boris in 865, which was brought about largely by the influence of his sister, who had spent many years in Constantinople as a captive, was a triumph for Greek influence and for Byzantium. Though the Church was at this time still nominally one, yet the rivalry between Rome and Constantinople had already become acute, and the struggle for spheres of spiritual influence had begun. It was in the year 863 that the Prince of Moravia, anxious to introduce Christianity into his country in a form intelligible to his subjects, addressed himself to the Emperor Michael III for help. Rome could not provide any suitable missionaries with knowledge of Slavonic languages, and the German, or more exactly the Bavarian, hierarchy with which Rome entrusted the spiritual welfare of the Slavs of Moravia and Pannonia used its greater local knowledge for political and not religious ends. The Germans exploited their ecclesiastical influence in order completely to dominate the Slavs politically, and as a result the latter were only allowed to see the Church through Teutonic glasses.

In answer to this appeal the emperor sent the two brothers Cyril and Methodius, who were Greeks of Salonika and had considerable knowledge of Slavonic languages. They composed the Slavonic alphabet which is to-day used throughout Russia, Bulgaria, Serbia, and Montenegro, and in many parts of Austria-Hungary and translated the gospels into Slavonic; it is for this reason that they are regarded with such veneration by all members of the Eastern Church. Their mission proved the greatest success (it must be remembered that at this time the various Slavonic tongues were probably less dissimilar than they are now), and the two brothers were warmly welcomed in Rome by Pope Adrian II, who formally consented to the use, for the benefit of the Slavs, of the Slavonic liturgy (a remarkable concession, confirmed by

Pope John VIII). This triumph, however, was short-lived; St. Cyril died in 869 and St. Methodius in 885; subsequent Popes, notably Stephen V, were not so benevolent to the Slavonic cause; the machinations of the German hierarchy (which included, even in those days, the falsification of documents) were irresistible, and finally the invasion of the Magyars, in 893, destroyed what was left of the Slavonic Church in Moravia. The missionary brothers had probably passed through Bulgaria on their way north in 863, but without halting. Many of their disciples, driven from the Moravian kingdom by the Germans, came south and took refuge in Bulgaria in 886, and there carried on in more favourable circumstances the teachings of their masters. Prince Boris had found it easier to adopt Christianity himself than to induce all his subjects to do the same. Even when he had enforced his will on them at the price of numerous executions of recalcitrant nobles, he found himself only at the beginning of his difficulties. The Greeks had been glad enough to welcome Bulgaria into the fold, but they had no wish to set up an independent Church and hierarchy to rival their own. Boris, on the other hand, though no doubt full of genuine spiritual ardour, was above all impressed with the authority and prestige which the basileus derived from the Church of Constantinople; he also admired the pomp of ecclesiastical ceremony, and wished to have a patriarch of his own to crown him and a hierarchy of his own to serve him. Finding the Greeks unresponsive, he turned to Rome, and Pope Nicholas I sent him two bishops to superintend the ecclesiastical affairs of Bulgaria till the investiture of Boris at the hands of the Holy See could be arranged. These bishops set to work with a will, substituted the Latin for the Greek rite, and brought Bulgaria completely under Roman influence. But when it was discovered that Boris was aiming at the erection of an independent Church their enthusiasm abated and they were recalled to Rome in 867.

Adrian II proved no more sympathetic, and in 870, during the reign of the Emperor Basil I, it was decided without more ado that the Bulgarian Church should be directly under the Bishop of Constantinople, on the ground that the kingdom of Boris was a vassal-state of the basileus, and that from the Byzantine point of view, as opposed to that of Rome, the State came first and the Church next. The Moravian Gorazd, a disciple of Methodius, was appointed Metropolitan, and at his death he was succeeded by his fellow countryman and co-disciple Clement, who by means of the construction of numerous churches and monasteries did a great deal for the propagation of light and learning in Bulgaria. The definite subjection of the Bulgarian Church to that of Byzantium was an important and far-reaching event. Boris has been reproached with submitting himself and his country to Greek influence, but in those days it was either Constantinople or Rome (there was no third way); and in view of the proximity of Constantinople and the glamour which its civilization cast all over the Balkans, it is not surprising that the Greeks carried the day.

6.
The Rise and Fall of the First Bulgarian Empire, 893-972

During the reign of Simeon, second son of Boris, which lasted from 893 to 927, Bulgaria reached a very high level of power and prosperity. Simeon, called the Great, is looked on by Bulgarians as their most capable monarch and his reign as the most brilliant period of their history. He had spent his childhood at Constantinople and been educated there, and he became such an admirer of Greek civilization that he was nicknamed *Hemiargos*. His instructors had done their work so well that Simeon remained spellbound by the glamour of Constantinople throughout his life, and, although he might have laid the foundations of a solid empire in the Balkans, his one ambition was to conquer Byzantium and to be recognized as basileus—an ambition which was not to be fulfilled. His first campaign against the Greeks was not very fruitful, because the latter summoned the Magyars, already settled in Hungary, to their aid and they attacked Simeon from the north. Simeon in return called the Pechenegs, another fierce Tartar tribe, to his aid, but this merely resulted in their definite establishment in Rumania. During the twenty years of peace, which strange to say filled the middle of his reign (894-913), the internal development of Bulgaria made great strides. The administration was properly organized, commerce was encouraged, and agriculture flourished. In the wars against the Greeks which occupied his last years he was more successful, and inflicted a severe defeat on them at Anchialo (the modern Ahiolu) in 917; but he was still unable to get from them what he wanted, and at last, in 921, he was obliged to proclaim himself *basileus* and *autocrat[=o]r* of all Bulgars and Greeks, a title which nobody else recognized. He reappeared before Constantinople the same year, but effected nothing more than the customary devastation of the suburbs. The year 923 witnessed a solemn reconciliation between Rome and Constantinople; the Greeks were clever enough to prevent the Roman legates visiting Bulgaria on their return journey, and thereby administered a rebuff to Simeon, who was anxious to see them and enter into direct relations with Rome. In the same year Simeon tried to make an alliance with the Arabs, but the ambassadors of the latter were intercepted by the Greeks, who made it worth their while not to continue the journey to Bulgaria.

In 924 Simeon determined on a supreme effort against Constantinople and as a preliminary he ravaged Macedonia and Thrace. When, however, he arrived before the city the walls and the catapults made him hesitate, and he entered into negotiations, which, as usual, petered out and brought him no adequate reward for all his hopes and preparations. In the west his arms were more successful, and he subjected most of the eastern part of Serbia to his rule. From all this it can be seen that he was no diplomat, though not lacking in enterprise and ambition. The fact was that while he made his kingdom too powerful for the Greeks to subdue (indeed they were compelled to pay him tribute), yet Constantinople with its impregnable walls, well-organized army, powerful fleet, and cunning and experienced statesmen, was too hard a nut for him to crack.

Simeon extended the boundaries of his country considerably, and his dominion included most of the interior of the Balkan peninsula south of the Danube and east of the rivers Morava and Ibar in Serbia and of the Drin in Albania. The Byzantine Church greatly increased its influence in Bulgaria during his reign, and works of theology grew like mushrooms. This was the only kind of literature that was ever popular in Bulgaria, and although it is usual to throw contempt on the literary achievements of Constantinople, we should know but little of Bulgaria were it not for the Greek historians.

Simeon died in 927, and his son Peter, who succeeded him, was a lover of peace and comfort; he married a Byzantine princess, and during his reign (927-69) Greek influence grew ever stronger, in spite of several revolts on the part of the Bulgar nobles, while the capital Preslav became a miniature Constantinople. In 927 Rome recognized the kingdom and patriarchate of Bulgaria, and Peter was duly crowned by the Papal legate. This was viewed with disfavour by the Greeks, and they still called Peter only *arch[=o]n* or prince *(knyaz* in Bulgarian), which was the utmost title allowed to any foreign sovereign. It was not until 945 that they recognized Peter as *basileus*, the unique title possessed by their own emperors and till then never granted to any one else. Peter's reign was one of misfortune for his country both at home and abroad. In 931 the Serbs broke loose under their leader [)C]aslav, whom Simeon had captured but who effected his escape, and asserted their independence. In 963 a formidable revolt under one Shishman undermined the whole state fabric. He managed to subtract Macedonia and all western Bulgaria, including Sofia and Vidin, from Peter's rule, and proclaimed himself independent *tsar (tsar* or *caesar* was a title often accorded by Byzantium to relatives of the emperor or to distinguished men of Greek or other nationality, and though it was originally the equivalent of the highest title, it had long since ceased to be so: the emperor's designations were *basileus* and *autocrat[=o]r*). From this time there were two Bulgarias—eastern and western. The eastern half was now little more than a Byzantine province, and the western became the centre of national life and the focus of national aspirations.

Another factor which militated against the internal progress of Bulgaria was the spread of the Bogomil heresy in the tenth century. This remarkable doctrine, founded on the dualism of the Paulicians, who had become an important political force in the eastern empire, was preached in the Balkan peninsula by one Jeremiah Bogomil, for the rest a man of uncertain identity, who made Philippopolis the centre of his activity. Its principal features were of a negative character, and consequently it was very difficult successfully to apply force against them. The Bogomils recognized the authority neither of Church nor of State; the validity neither of oaths nor of human laws. They refused to pay taxes, to fight, or to obey; they sanctioned theft, but looked upon any kind of punishment as unjustifiable; they discountenanced marriage and were strict vegetarians. Naturally a heresy so alarming in its individualism shook to its foundations the not very firmly established Bulgarian society. Nevertheless it spread with rapidity in spite of all persecutions, and its popularity amongst the Bulgarians, and indeed amongst all the Slavs of the peninsula, is without doubt partly explained by political reasons. The hierarchy of the Greek Church, which supported the ruling classes of the country and lent them authority at the same time that it increased its own, was antipathetic to the Slavs, and the Bogomil heresy drew much strength from its nationalistic colouring and from the appeal which it made to the character of the Balkan Slavs, who have always been intolerant of government by the Church. But neither the civil nor the ecclesiastical authorities were able to cope with the problem; indeed they were apt to minimize its importance, and the heresy was never eradicated till the arrival on the scene of Islam, which proved as attractive to the schismatics as the well-regulated Orthodox Church had been the reverse.

The third quarter of the tenth century witnessed a great recrudescence of the power of Constantinople under the Emperor Nikiphoros Phokas, who wrested Cyprus and Crete from the Arabs and inaugurated an era of prosperity for the eastern empire, giving it a new lease of vigorous and combative life. Wishing to reassert the Greek supremacy in the Balkan peninsula his first act was to refuse any further payment of tribute to the Bulgarians as from 966; his next was to initiate a campaign against them, but in order to make his own success in this enterprise less costly and more assured he secured the co-operation of the Russians under Svyatoslav, Prince of Kiev; this potentate's mother Olga had visited Constantinople in 957 and been baptized (though her son and the bulk of the population were still ardent heathens), and commercial intercourse between Russia and Constantinople by means of the Dnieper and the Black Sea was at that time lively. Svyatoslav did not want pressing, and arriving with an army of 10,000 men in boats, overcame northern Bulgaria in a few days (967); they were helped by Shishman and the western Bulgars, who did not mind at what price Peter and the eastern Bulgars were crushed. Svyatoslav was recalled to Russia in 968 to defend his home from attacks by the Tartar Pechenegs, but that done, he made up his mind to return to Bulgaria, lured by its riches and by the hope of the eventual possession of Constantinople.

The Emperor Nikiphoros was by now aware of the danger he had imprudently conjured up, and made a futile alliance with eastern Bulgaria; but in January 969 Peter of Bulgaria died, and in December of the same year Nikiphoros was murdered by the ambitious Armenian John Tzimisces,* who thereupon became emperor. Svyatoslav, seeing the field clear of his enemies, returned in 970, and in March of that year sacked and occupied Philippopolis. The Emperor John Tzimisces, who was even abler both as general and as diplomat than his predecessor, quietly pushed forward his warlike preparations, and did not meet the Russians

---

*   John the Little.

till the autumn, when he completely defeated them at Arcadiopolis (the modern Lule-Burgas). The Russians retired north of the Balkan range, but the Greeks followed them. John Tzimisces besieged them in the capital Preslav, which he stormed, massacring many of the garrison, in April 972. Svyatoslav and his remaining troops escaped to Silistria (the Durostorum of Trajan) on the Danube, where again, however, they were besieged and defeated by the indefatigable emperor. At last peace was made in July 972, the Russians being allowed to go free on condition of the complete evacuation of Bulgaria and a gift of corn; the adventurous Svyatoslav lost his life at the hands of the Pechenegs while making his way back to Kiev. The triumph of the Greeks was complete, and it can be imagined that there was not much left of the earthenware Bulgaria after the violent collision of these two mighty iron vessels on the top of it. Eastern Bulgaria (i.e. Moesia and Thrace) ceased to exist, becoming a purely Greek province; John Tzimisces made his triumphal entry into Constantinople, followed by the two sons of Peter of Bulgaria on foot; the elder was deprived of his regal attributes and created *magistros*, the younger was made a eunuch.

7.
The Rise and Fall of 'Western Bulgaria' and the Greek Supremacy, 963-1186

Meanwhile western Bulgaria had not been touched, and it was thither that the Bulgarian patriarch Damian removed from Silistria after the victory of the Greeks, settling first in Sofia and then in Okhrida in Macedonia, where the apostate Shishman had eventually made his capital. Western Bulgaria included Macedonia and parts of Thessaly, Albania, southern and eastern Serbia, and the westernmost parts of modern Bulgaria. It was from this district that numerous anti-Hellenic revolts were directed after the death of the Emperor John Tzimisces in 976. These culminated during the reign of Samuel (977-1014), one of the sons of Shishman. He was as capable and energetic, as unscrupulous and inhuman, as the situation he was called upon to fill demanded. He began by assassinating all his relations and nobles who resented his desire to re-establish the absolute monarchy, was recognized as *tsar* by the Holy See of Rome in 981, and then began to fight the Greeks, the only possible occupation for any self-respecting Bulgarian ruler. The emperor at that time was Basil II (976-1025), who was brave and patriotic but young and inexperienced. In his early campaigns Samuel carried all before him; he reconquered northern Bulgaria in 985, Thessaly in 986, and defeated Basil II near Sofia the same year. Later he conquered Albania and the southern parts of Serbia and what is now Montenegro and Hercegovina. In 996 he threatened Salonika, but first of all embarked on an expedition against the Peloponnese; here he was followed by the Greek general, who managed to surprise and completely overwhelm him, he and his son barely escaping with their lives.

From that year (996) his fortune changed; the Greeks reoccupied northern Bulgaria, in 999, and also recovered Thessaly and parts of Macedonia. The Bulgars were subjected to almost annual attacks on the part of Basil II; the country was ruined and could not long hold out. The final disaster occurred in 1014, when Basil II utterly defeated his inveterate foe in a pass near Seres in Macedonia. Samuel escaped to Prilip, but when he beheld the return of 15,000 of his troops who had been captured and blinded by the Greeks he died of syncope. Basil II, known as Bulgaroctonus, or Bulgar-killer, went from victory to victory, and finally occupied the Bulgarian capital of Okhrida in 1016. Western Bulgaria came to an end, as had eastern Bulgaria in 972, the remaining members of the royal family followed the emperor to the Bosphorus to enjoy comfortable captivity, and the triumph of Constantinople was complete.

From 1018 to 1186 Bulgaria had no existence as an independent state; Basil II, although cruel, was far from tyrannical in his general treatment of the Bulgars, and treated the conquered territory more as a protectorate than as a possession. But after his death Greek rule became much more oppressive. The Bulgarian patriarchate (since 972 established at Okhrida) was reduced to an archbishopric, and in 1025 the see was given to a Greek, who lost no time in eliminating the Bulgarian element from positions of importance throughout his diocese. Many of the nobles were transplanted to Constantinople, where their opposition was numbed by the bestowal of honours. During the eleventh century the peninsula was invaded frequently by the Tartar Pechenegs and Kumans, whose aid was invoked both by Greeks and Bulgars; the result of these incursions was not always favourable to those who had promoted them; the barbarians invariably stayed longer and did more damage than had been bargained for, and usually left some of their number behind as unwelcome settlers.

In this way the ethnological map of the Balkan peninsula became ever more variegated. To the Tartar settlers were added colonies of Armenians and Vlakhs by various emperors. The last touch was given by the arrival of the Normans in 1081 and the passage of the crusaders in 1096. The wholesale depredations of the latter naturally made the inhabitants of the Balkan peninsula anything but sympathetically disposed towards their cause. One of the results of all this turmoil and of the heavy hand of the Greeks was a great increase in the vitality of the Bogomil heresy already referred to; it became a refuge for patriotism and an outlet for its expression. The Emperor Alexis Comnenus instituted a bitter persecution of it, which only led to its growth and rapid propagation westwards into Serbia from its centre Philippopolis.

The reason of the complete overthrow of the Bulgarian monarchy by the Greeks was of course that the nation itself was totally lacking in cohesion and organization, and could only achieve any lasting success when an exceptionally gifted ruler managed to discount the centrifugal tendencies of the feudal nobles, as Simeon and Samuel had done. Other discouraging factors wore the permeation of the Church and State by Byzantine influence, the lack of a large standing army, the spread of the anarchic Bogomil heresy, and the fact that the bulk of the Slav population had no desire for foreign adventure or national aggrandizement.

8.
The Rise and Fall of the Second Bulgarian Empire, 1186-1258

From 1186 to 1258 Bulgaria experienced temporary resuscitation, the brevity of which was more than compensated for by the stirring nature of the events that crowded it. The exactions and oppressions of the Greeks culminated in a revolt on the part of the Bulgars, which had its centre in Tirnovo on the river Yantra in northern Bulgaria—a position of great natural strength and strategic importance, commanding the outlets of several of the most important passes over the Balkan range. This revolt coincided with the growing weakness of the eastern empire, which, surrounded on all sides by aggressive enemies—Kumans, Saracens, Turks, and Normans—was sickening for one of the severe illnesses which preceded its dissolution. The revolt was headed by two brothers who were Vlakh or Rumanian shepherds, and was blessed by the archbishop Basil, who crowned one of them, called John Asen, as *tsar* in Tirnovo in 1186. Their first efforts against the Greeks were not successful, but securing the support of the Serbs under Stephen Nemanja in 1188 and of the Crusaders in 1189 they became more so; but there was life in the Greeks yet, and victory alternated with defeat. John Asen I was assassinated in 1196 and was succeeded after many internal discords and murders by his relative Kaloian or Pretty John. This cruel and unscrupulous though determined ruler soon made an end of all his enemies at home, and in eight years achieved such success abroad that Bulgaria almost regained its former proportions. Moreover, he re-established relations with Rome, to the great discomfiture of the Greeks, and after some negotiations Pope Innocent III recognized Kaloian as *tsar* of the Bulgars and Vlakhs (roi de Blaquie et de Bougrie, in the words of Villehardouin), with Basil as primate, and they were both duly consecrated and crowned by the papal legate at Tirnovo in 1204. The French, who had just established themselves in Constantinople during the fourth crusade, imprudently made an enemy of Kaloian instead of a friend, and with the aid of the Tartar Kumans he defeated them several times, capturing and brutally murdering Baldwin I. But in 1207 his career was cut short; he was murdered while besieging Salonika by one of his generals who was a friend of his wife. After eleven years of further anarchy he was succeeded by John Asen II. During the reign of this monarch, which lasted from 1218 till 1241, Bulgaria reached the zenith of its power. He was the most enlightened ruler the country had had, and he not only waged war successfully abroad but also put an end to the internal confusion, restored the possibility of carrying on agriculture and commerce, and encouraged the foundation of numerous schools and monasteries. He maintained the tradition of his family by making his capital at Tirnovo, which city he considerably embellished and enlarged.

Constantinople at this time boasted three Greek emperors and one French. The first act of John Asen II was to get rid of one of them, named Theodore, who had proclaimed himself *basileus* at Okhrida in 1223. Thereupon he annexed the whole of Thrace, Macedonia, Thessaly, and Epirus to his dominions, and made Theodore's brother Manuel, who had married one of his daughters, viceroy, established at Salonika. Another of his daughters had married Stephen Vladislav, who was King of Serbia from 1233-43, and a third married Theodore, son of the Emperor John III, who reigned at Nicaea, in 1235. This daughter, after being sought in marriage by the French barons at Constantinople as a wife for the Emperor Baldwin II, a minor, was then summarily rejected in favour of the daughter of the King of Jerusalem; this affront rankled in the mind of John Asen II and threw him into the arms of the Greeks, with whom he concluded an alliance in 1234. John Asen II and his ally, the Emperor John III, were, however, utterly defeated by the French under the walls of Constantinople in 1236, and the Bulgarian ruler, who had no wish to see the Greeks re-established there, began to doubt the wisdom of his alliance. Other Bulgarian tsars had been unscrupulous, but the whole foreign policy of this one pivoted on treachery. He deserted the Greeks and made an alliance with the French in 1237, the Pope Gregory IX, a great Hellenophobe, having threatened him with excommunication; he went so far as to force his daughter to relinquish her Greek husband. The following year, however, he again changed over to the Greeks; then again fear of the Pope and of his brother-in-law the King of Hungary brought him back to the side of Baldwin II, to whose help against the Greeks he went with a large army into Thrace in 1239. While besieging the Greeks with indifferent success, he learned of the death of his wife and his eldest son from plague, and incontinently returned to Tirnovo, giving up the war and restoring his daughter to her lonely husband. This adaptable monarch died a natural death in 1241, and the three rulers of his family who succeeded him, whose reigns filled the period 1241-58, managed to undo all the constructive work of their immediate predecessors. Province after province was lost and internal anarchy increased. This remarkable dynasty came to an inglorious end in 1258, when its last representative was murdered by his own nobles, and from this time onwards Bulgaria was only a shadow of its former self.

9.
The Serbian Supremacy and the Final Collapse, 1258-1393

From 1258 onwards Bulgaria may be said to have continued flickering until its final extinction as a state in 1393, but during this period it never had any voice in controlling the destinies of the Balkan peninsula. Owing to the fact that no ruler emerged capable of keeping the distracted country in order, there was a regular *chasse-croise* of rival princelets, an unceasing tale of political marriages and murders, conspiracies and revolts of feudal nobles all over the country, and perpetual ebb and flow of the boundaries of the warring principalities which tore the fabric of Bulgaria to pieces amongst them. From the point of view of foreign politics this period is characterized generally by the virtual disappearance of Bulgarian independence to the profit of the surrounding states, who enjoyed a sort of rotativist supremacy. It is especially remarkable for the complete ascendancy which Serbia gained in the Balkan peninsula.

A Serb, Constantine, grandson of Stephen Nemanja, occupied the Bulgarian throne from 1258 to 1277, and married the granddaughter of John Asen II. After the fall of the Latin Empire of Constantinople in 1261, the Hungarians, already masters of Transylvania, combined with the Greeks against Constantine; the latter called the Tartars of southern Russia, at this time at the height of their power, to his help and was victorious, but as a result of his diplomacy the Tartars henceforward played an important part in the Bulgarian welter. Then Constantine married, as his second wife, the daughter of the Greek emperor, and thus again gave Constantinople a voice in his country's affairs. Constantine was followed by a series of upstart rulers, whose activities were cut short by the victories of King Uro[)s] II of Serbia (1282-1321), who conquered all Macedonia and wrested it from the Bulgars. In 1285 the Tartars of the Golden Horde swept over Hungary and Bulgaria, but it was from the south that the clouds were rolling up which not much later were to burst over the peninsula. In 1308 the Turks appeared on the Sea of Marmora, and in 1326 established themselves at Brussa. From 1295 to 1322 Bulgaria was presided over by a nobleman of Vidin, Svetoslav, who, unmolested by the Greeks, grown thoughtful in view of the approach of the Turks, was able to maintain rather more order than his subjects were accustomed to. After his death in 1322 chaos again supervened.

One of his successors had married the daughter of Uro[)s] II of Serbia, but suddenly made an alliance with the Greeks against his brother-in-law Stephen Uro[)s] III and dispatched his wife to her home. During the war which ensued the unwonted allies were utterly routed by the Serbs at Kustendil in Macedonia in 1330.

From 1331 to 1365 Bulgaria was under one John Alexander, a noble of Tartar origin, whose sister became the wife of Serbia's greatest ruler, Stephen Du[)s]an; John Alexander, moreover, recognized Stephen as his suzerain, and from thenceforward Bulgaria was a vassal-state of Serbia. Meanwhile the Turkish storm was gathering fast; Suleiman crossed the Hellespont in 1356, and Murad I made Adrianople his capital in 1366. After the death of John Alexander in 1365 the Hungarians invaded northern Bulgaria, and his successor invoked the help of the Turks against them and also against the Greeks. This was the beginning of the end. The Serbs, during an absence of the Sultan in Asia, undertook an offensive, but were defeated by the Turks near Adrianople in 1371, who captured Sofia in 1382. After this the Serbs formed a huge southern Slav alliance, in which the Bulgarians refused to join, but, after a temporary success against the Turks in 1387, they were vanquished by them as the result of treachery at the famous battle of Kosovo in 1389. Meanwhile the Turks occupied Nikopolis on the Danube in 1388 and destroyed the Bulgarian capital Tirnovo in 1393, exiling the Patriarch Euthymus to Macedonia. Thus the state of Bulgaria passed into the hands of the Turks, and its church into those of the Greeks. Many Bulgars adopted Islam, and their descendants are the Pomaks or Bulgarian Mohammedans of the present day. With the subjection of Rumania in 1394 and the defeat of an improvised anti-Turkish crusade from western Europe under Sigismund, King of Hungary, at Nikopolis in 1396 the Turkish conquest was complete, though the battle of Varna was not fought till 1444, nor Constantinople entered till 1453.

10.

The Turkish Dominion and the Emancipation, 1393-1878

From 1393 until 1877 Bulgaria may truthfully be said to have had no history, but nevertheless it could scarcely have been called happy. National life was completely paralysed, and what stood in those days for national consciousness was obliterated. It is common knowledge, and most people are now reasonable enough to admit, that the Turks have many excellent qualities, religious fervour and military ardour amongst others; it is also undeniable that from an aesthetic point of view too much cannot be said in praise of Mohammedan civilization. Who does not prefer the minarets of Stambul and Edirne* to the architecture of Budapest, notoriously the ideal of Christian south-eastern Europe? On the other hand, it cannot be contended that the Pax Ottomana brought prosperity or happiness to those on whom it was imposed (unless indeed they submerged their identity in the religion of their conquerors), or that its Influence was either vivifying or generally popular.

To the races they conquered the Turks offered two alternatives—serfdom or Turkdom; those who could not bring themselves to accept either of these had either to emigrate or take to brigandage and outlawry in the mountains. The Turks literally overlaid the European nationalities of the Balkan peninsula for five hundred years, and from their own point of view and from that of military history this was undoubtedly a very splendid achievement; it was more than the Greeks or Romans had ever done. From the point of view of humanitarianism also it is beyond a doubt that much less human blood was spilt in the Balkan peninsula during the five hundred years of Turkish rule than during the five hundred years of Christian rule which preceded them; indeed it would

---

*   The Turkish names for Constantinople and Adrianople.

have been difficult to spill more. It is also a pure illusion to think of the Turks as exceptionally brutal or cruel; they are just as good-natured and good-humoured as anybody else; it is only when their military or religious passions are aroused that they become more reckless and ferocious than other people. It was not the Turks who taught cruelty to the Christians of the Balkan peninsula; the latter had nothing to learn in this respect.

In spite of all this, however, from the point of view of the Slavs of Bulgaria and Serbia, Turkish rule was synonymous with suffocation. If the Turks were all that their greatest admirers think them the history of the Balkan peninsula in the nineteenth century would have been very different from what it has been, namely, one perpetual series of anti-Turkish revolts.

Of all the Balkan peoples the Bulgarians were the most completely crushed and effaced. The Greeks by their ubiquity, their brains, and their money were soon able to make the Turkish storm drive their own windmill; the Rumanians were somewhat sheltered by the Danube and also by their distance from Constantinople; the Serbs also were not so exposed to the full blast of the Turkish wrath, and the inaccessibility of much of their country afforded them some protection. Bulgaria was simply annihilated, and its population, already far from homogeneous, was still further varied by numerous Turkish and other Tartar colonies.

For the same reasons already mentioned Bulgaria was the last Balkan state to emancipate itself; for these reasons also it is the least trammelled by prejudices and by what are considered national predilections and racial affinities, while its heterogeneous composition makes it vigorous and enterprising. The treatment of the Christians by the Turks was by no means always the same; generally speaking, it grew worse as the power of the Sultan grew less. During the fifteenth century they were allowed to practise their religion and all their vocations in comparative liberty and peace. But from the sixteenth century onwards the control of the Sultan declined, power became decentralized, the Ottoman Empire grew ever more anarchic and the rule of the provincial governors more despotic.

But the Mohammedan conquerors were not the only enemies and oppressors of the Bulgars. The role played by the Greeks in Bulgaria during the Turkish dominion was almost as important as that of the Turks themselves. The contempt of the Turks for the Christians, and especially for their religion, was so great that they prudently left the management of it to them, knowing that it would keep them occupied in mutual altercation. From 1393 till 1767 the Bulgarians were under the Greco-Bulgarian Patriarchate of Okhrida, an organization in which all posts, from the highest to the lowest, had to be bought from the Turkish administration at exorbitant and ever-rising prices; the Phanariote Greeks (so called because they originated in the Phanar quarter at Constantinople) were the only ones who could afford those of the higher posts, with the result that the Church was controlled from Constantinople. In 1767 the independent patriarchates were abolished, and from that date the religious control of the Greeks was as complete as the political control of the Turks. The Greeks did all they could to obliterate the last traces of Bulgarian nationality which had survived in the Church, and this explains a fact which must never be forgotten, which had its origin in the remote past, but grew more pronounced at this period, that the individual hatred of Greeks and Bulgars of each other has always been far more intense than their collective hatred of the Turks.

Ever since the marriage of the Tsar Ivan III with the niece of the last Greek Emperor, in 1472, Russia had considered itself the trustee of the eastern Christians, the defender of the Orthodox Church, and the direct heir of the glory and prestige of Constantinople; it was not until the eighteenth century, however, after the consolidation of the Russian state, that the Balkan Christians were championed and the eventual possession of Constantinople was seriously considered. Russian influence was first asserted in Rumania after the Treaty of Kuchuk-Kainardji, in 1774. It was only the Napoleonic war in 1812 that prevented the Russians from extending their territory south of the Danube, whither it already stretched. Serbia was partially free by 1826, and Greece achieved complete independence in 1830, when the Russian troops, in order to coerce the Turks, occupied part of Bulgaria and advanced as far as Adrianople. Bulgaria, being nearer to and more easily repressed by Constantinople, had to wait, and tentative revolts made about this time were put down with much bloodshed and were followed by wholesale emigrations of Bulgars into Bessarabia and importations of Tartars and Kurds into the vacated districts. The Crimean War and the short-sighted championship of Turkey by the western European powers checked considerably the development at which Russia aimed. Moldavia and Wallachia were in 1856 withdrawn from the semi-protectorate which Russia had long exercised over them, and in 1861 formed themselves into the united state of Rumania. In 1866 a German prince, Charles of Hohenzollern, came to rule over the country, the first sign of German influence in the Near East; at this time Rumania still acknowledged the supremacy of the Sultan.

During the first half of the nineteenth century there took place a considerable intellectual renascence in Bulgaria, a movement fostered by wealthy Bulgarian merchants of Bucarest and Odessa. In 1829 a history of Bulgaria was published by a native of that country in Moscow; in 1835 the first school was established in Bulgaria, and many others soon followed. It must be remembered that not only was nothing known at that time about Bulgaria and its inhabitants in other countries, but the Bulgars had themselves to be taught who they were. The Bulgarian people in Bulgaria consisted entirely of peasants; there was no Bulgarian upper or middle or 'intelligent' or professional class; those enlightened Bulgars who existed were domiciled in other countries; the Church was in the hands of the Greeks, who vied with the Turks in suppressing Bulgarian nationality.

The two committees of Odessa and Bucarest which promoted the enlightenment and emancipation of Bulgaria were dissimilar in composition and in aim; the members of the former were more intent on educational and religious reform, and aimed at the gradual and peaceful regeneration of their country by these means; the latter wished to effect the immediate political emancipation of Bulgaria by violent and, if necessary, warlike means.

It was the ecclesiastical question which was solved first. In 1856 the Porte had promised religious reforms tending to the appointment of Bulgarian bishops and the recognition of the Bulgarian language in Church and school. But these not being carried through, the Bulgarians took the matter into their own hands, and in 1860 refused any longer to recognize the Patriarch of Constantinople. The same year an attempt was made to bring the Church of Bulgaria under that of Rome, but, owing to Russian opposition, proved abortive. In 1870, the growing agitation having at last alarmed the Turks, the Bulgarian Exarchate was established. The Bulgarian Church was made free and national and was to be under an Exarch who should reside at Constantinople (Bulgaria being still a Turkish province). The Greeks, conscious what a blow this would be to their supremacy, managed for a short while to stave off the evil day, but in 1872 the Exarch was triumphantly installed in Constantinople, where he resided till 1908.

Meanwhile revolutionary outbreaks began to increase, but were always put down with great rigour. The most notable was that of 1875, instigated by Stambulov, the future dictator, in sympathy with the outbreak in Montenegro, Hercegovina, and Bosnia of that year; the result of this and of similar movements in 1876 was the series of notorious Bulgarian massacres in that year. The indignation of Europe was aroused and concerted representations were urgently made at Constantinople. Midhat Pasha disarmed his opponents by summarily introducing the British constitution into Turkey, but, needless to say, Bulgaria's lot was not improved by this specious device. Russia had, however, steadily been making her preparations, and, Turkey having refused to discontinue hostilities against Montenegro, on April 24, 1877, war was declared by the Emperor Alexander II, whose patience had become exhausted; he was joined by Prince Charles of Rumania, who saw that by doing so he would be rewarded by the complete emancipation of his country, then still a vassal-state of Turkey, and its erection into a kingdom. At the beginning of the war all went well for the Russians and Rumanians, who were soon joined by large numbers of Bulgarian insurgents; the Turkish forces were scattered all over the peninsula. The committee of Bucarest transformed itself into a provisional government, but the Russians, who had undertaken to liberate the country, naturally had to keep its administration temporarily in their own hands, and refused their recognition. The Turks, alarmed at the early victories of the Russians, brought up better generals and troops, and defeated the Russians at Plevna in July. They failed, however, to dislodge them from the important and famous Shipka Pass in August, and after this they became demoralized and their resistance rapidly weakened. The Russians, helped by the Bulgarians and Rumanians, fought throughout the summer with the greatest gallantry; they took Plevna, after a three months' siege, in December, occupied Sofia and Philippopolis in January 1878, and pushed forward to the walls of Constantinople.

The Turks were at their last gasp, and at Adrianople, in March 1878, Ignatiyev dictated the terms of the Treaty of San Stefano, by which a principality of Bulgaria, under the nominal suzerainty of the Sultan, was created, stretching from the Danube to the Aegean, and from the Black Sea to Albania, including all Macedonia and leaving to the Turks only the district between Constantinople and Adrianople, Chalcidice, and the town of Salonika; Bulgaria would thus have regained the dimensions it possessed under Tsar Simeon nine hundred and fifty years previously.

This treaty, which on ethnological grounds was tolerably just, alarmed the other powers, especially Great Britain and Germany, who thought they perceived in it the foundations of Russian hegemony in the Balkans, while it would, if put into execution, have blighted the aspirations of Greece and Serbia. The Treaty of Berlin, inspired by Bismarck and Lord Salisbury, anxious to defend, the former, the interests of (ostensibly) Austria-Hungary, the latter (shortsightedly) those of Turkey, replaced it in July 1878. By its terms Bulgaria was cut into three parts; northern Bulgaria, between the Danube and the Balkans, was made an autonomous province, tributary to Turkey; southern Bulgaria, fancifully termed Eastern Rumelia (Rumili was the name always given by the Turks to the whole Balkan peninsula), was to have autonomous administration under a Christian governor appointed by the Porte; Macedonia was left to Turkey; and the Dobrudja, between the Danube and the Black Sea, was adjudged to Rumania.

11.
The Aftermath, and Prince Alexander of Battenberg, 1878-86

The relations between the Russians and the Bulgarians were better before the liberation of the latter by the former than after; this may seem unjust, because Bulgaria could never have freed herself so decisively and rapidly alone, and Russia was the only power in whose interest it was to free her from the Turks, and who could translate that interest so promptly into action; nevertheless, the laws controlling the relationships of states and nationalities being much the same as those which control the relationships of individuals, it was only to be expected.

What so often happens in the relationships of individuals happened in those between Russia and Bulgaria. Russia naturally enough expected Bulgaria to be grateful for the really large amount of blood and treasure which its liberation had cost Russia, and, moreover, expected its gratitude to take the form of docility and a general acquiescence in all the suggestions and wishes expressed by its liberator. Bulgaria was no doubt deeply grateful, but never had the slightest intention of expressing its gratitude in the desired way; on the contrary, like most people who have regained a long-lost and unaccustomed freedom of action or been put under an obligation, it appeared touchy and jealous of its right to an independent judgement. It is often assumed by Russophobe writers that Russia wished and intended to make a Russian province of Bulgaria, but this is very unlikely; the geographical configuration of the Balkan peninsula would not lend itself to its incorporation in the Russian Empire, the existence between the two of the compact and vigorous national block of Rumania, a Latin race and then already an independent state, was an insurmountable obstacle, and, finally, it is quite possible for Russia to obtain possession or control of Constantinople without owning all the intervening littoral.

That Russia should wish to have a controlling voice in the destinies of Bulgaria and in those of the whole peninsula was natural, and it was just as natural that Bulgaria should resent its pretensions. The eventual result of this, however, was that Bulgaria inevitably entered the sphere of Austrian and ultimately of German influence or rather calculation, a contingency probably not foreseen by its statesmen at the time, and whose full meaning, even if it had, would not have been grasped by them.

The Bulgarians, whatever the origin and the ingredients of their nationality, are by language a purely Slavonic people; their ancestors were the pioneers of Slavonic civilization as expressed in its monuments of theological literature. Nevertheless, they have never been enthusiastic Pan-Slavists, any more than the Dutch have ever been ardent Pan-Germans; it is as unreasonable to expect such a thing of the one people as it is of the other. The Bulgarians indeed think themselves superior to the Slavs by reason of the warlike and glorious traditions of the Tartar tribe that gave them their name and infused the Asiatic element into their race, thus endowing them with greater stability, energy, and consistency than is possessed by purely Slav peoples. These latter, on the other hand, and notably the Serbians, for the same reason affect contempt for the mixture of blood and for what they consider the Mongol characteristics of the Bulgarians. What is certain is that between Bulgarians and Germans (including German Austrians and Magyars) there has never existed that elemental, ineradicable, and insurmountable antipathy which exists between German (and Magyar) and Slav wherever the two races are contiguous, from the Baltic to the Adriatic; nothing is more remarkable than the way in which the Bulgarian people has been flattered, studied, and courted in Austria-Hungary and Germany, during the last decade, to the detriment of the purely Slav Serb race with whom it is always compared. The reason is that with the growth of the Serb national movement, from 1903 onwards, Austria-Hungary and Germany felt an instinctive and perfectly well-justified fear of the Serb race, and sought to neutralize the possible effect of its growing power by any possible means.

It is not too much to say, in summing up, that Russian influence, which had been growing stronger in Bulgaria up till 1877-8, has since been steadily on the decline; Germany and Austria-Hungary, who reduced Bulgaria to half the size that Count Ignatiyev had made it by the Treaty of San Stefano, reaped the benefit, especially the commercial benefit, of the war which Russia had waged. Intellectually, and especially as regards the replenishment and renovation of the Bulgarian language, which, in spite of numerous Turkish words introduced during the Ottoman rule, is essentially Slavonic both in substance and form, Russian influence was especially powerful, and has to a certain extent maintained itself. Economically, owing partly to geographical conditions, both the Danube and the main oriental railway linking Bulgaria directly with Budapest and Vienna, partly to the fact that Bulgaria's best customers for its cereals are in central and western Europe, the connexion between Bulgaria and Russia is infinitesimal. Politically, both Russia and Bulgaria aiming at the same thing, the possession of Constantinople and the hegemony of the Balkan peninsula, their relations were bound to be difficult.

The first Bulgarian Parliament met in 1879 under trying conditions. Both Russian and Bulgarian hopes had been dashed by the Treaty of Berlin. Russian influence was still paramount, however, and the viceroy controlled the organization of the administration. An ultra-democratic constitution was arranged for, a fact obviously not conducive to the successful government of their country by the quite inexperienced Bulgarians. For a ruler recourse had inevitably to be had to the rabbit-warren of Germanic princes, who were still ingenuously considered neutral both in religion and in politics. The choice fell on Prince Alexander of Battenberg, nephew of the Empress of Russia, who had taken part in the campaign of the Russian army. Prince Alexander was conscientious, energetic, and enthusiastic, but he was no diplomat, and from the outset his honesty precluded his success. From the very first he failed to keep on good terms with Russia or its representatives, who at that time were still numerous in Bulgaria, while he was helpless to stem the ravages of parliamentary government. The Emperor Alexander III, who succeeded his father Alexander II in 1881, recommended him to insist on being made dictator, which he successfully did. But when he found that this only meant an increase of Russian influence he reverted to parliamentary government (in September 1883); this procedure discomfited the representatives of Russia, discredited him with the Emperor, and threw him back into the vortex of party warfare, from which he never extricated himself.

Meanwhile the question of eastern Rumelia, or rather southern Bulgaria, still a Turkish province, began to loom. A vigorous agitation for the reunion of the two parts of the country had been going on for some time, and on September 18, 1885, the inhabitants of Philippopolis suddenly proclaimed the union under Prince Alexander, who solemnly announced his approval at Tirnovo and triumphantly entered their city on September 21. Russia frowned on this independence of spirit. Serbia, under King Milan, and instigated by Austria, inaugurated the policy which has so often been followed since, and claimed territorial compensation for Bulgaria's aggrandisement; it must be remembered that it was Bismarck who, by the Treaty of Berlin, had arbitrarily confined Serbia to its inadequate limits of those day.

On November 13 King Milan declared war, and began to march on Sofia, which is not far from the Serbo-Bulgarian frontier. Prince Alexander, the bulk of whose army was on the Turkish frontier, boldly took up the challenge. On November 18 took place the battle of Slivnitsa, a small town about twenty miles north-west of Sofia, in which the Bulgarians were completely victorious. Prince Alexander, after hard fighting, took Pirot in Serbia on November 27, having refused King Milan's request for an armistice, and was marching on Nish, when Austria intervened, and threatened to send troops into Serbia unless fighting ceased. Bulgaria had to obey, and on March 3, 1886, a barren treaty of peace was imposed on the belligerents at Bucarest. Prince Alexander's position did not improve after this, indeed it would have needed a much more skilful navigator to steer through the many currents which eddied round him. A strong Russophile party formed itself in the army; on the night of August 21, 1886, some officers of this party, who were the most capable in the Bulgarian army, appeared at Sofia, forced Alexander to resign, and abducted him; they put him on board his yacht on the Danube and escorted him to the Russian town of Reni, in Bessarabia; telegraphic orders came from St. Petersburg, in answer to inquiries, that he could proceed with haste to western Europe, and on August 26 he found himself at Lemberg. But those who had carried out this *coup d'etat* found that it was not at all popular in the country. A counter-revolution, headed by the statesman Stambulov, was immediately initiated, and on September 3 Prince Alexander reappeared in Sofia amidst tumultuous applause. Nevertheless his position was hopeless; the Emperor Alexander III forced him to abdicate, and on September 7, 1886, he left Bulgaria for good, to the regret of the majority of the people. He died in Austria, in 1893, in his thirty-seventh year. At his departure a regency was constituted, at the head of which was Stambulov.

12.

The Regeneration under Prince Ferdinand of Saxe-Coburg, 1886-1908

Stambulov was born at Tirnovo in 1854 and was of humble origin. He took part in the insurrection of 1876 and in the war of liberation, and in 1884 became president of the Sobraniye (Parliament). From 1886 till 1894 he was virtually dictator of Bulgaria. He was intensely patriotic and also personally ambitious, determined, energetic, ruthlessly cruel and unscrupulous, but incapable of deceit; these qualities were apparent in his powerful and grim expression of face, while his manner inspired the weak with terror and the strongest with respect. His policy in general was directed against Russia. At the general election held in October 1886 he had all his important opponents imprisoned beforehand, while armed sentries discouraged ill-disposed voters from approaching the ballot-boxes. Out of 522 elected deputies, there were 470 supporters of Stambulov. This implied the complete suppression of the Russophile party and led to a rupture with St. Petersburg.

Whatever were Stambulov's methods, and few would deny that they were harsh, there is no doubt that something of the sort was necessary to restore order in the country. But once having started on this path he found it difficult to stop, and his tyrannical bearing, combined with the delay in finding a prince, soon made him unpopular. There were several revolutionary outbreaks directed against him, but these were all crushed. At length the, at that time not particularly alluring, throne of Bulgaria was filled by Prince Ferdinand of Saxe-Coburg, who was born in 1861 and was the son of the gifted Princess Clementine of Bourbon-Orleans, daughter of Louis-Philippe. This young man combined great ambition and tenacity of purpose with extreme prudence, astuteness, and patience; he was a consummate diplomat. The election of this prince was viewed with great disfavour by Russia, and for fear of offending the Emperor Alexander III none of the European powers recognized him.

Ferdinand, unabashed, cheerfully installed himself in Sofia with his mother in July 1886, and took care to make the peace with his suzerain, the Sultan Abdul Hamid. He wisely left all power in the hands of the unattractive and to him, unsympathetic prime minister, Stambulov, till he himself felt secure in his position, and till the dictator should have made himself thoroughly hated. Ferdinand's clever and wealthy mother cast a beneficent and civilizing glow around him, smoothing away many difficulties by her womanly tact and philanthropic activity, and, thanks to his influential connexions in the courts of Europe and his attitude of calm expectancy, his prestige in his own country rapidly increased. In 1893 he married Princess Marie-Louise of Bourbon-Parma. In May 1894, as a result of a social misadventure in which he became involved, Stambulov sent in his resignation, confidently expecting a refusal. To his mortification it was accepted; thereupon he initiated a violent press campaign, but his halo had faded, and on July 15 he was savagely attacked in the street by unknown men, who afterwards escaped, and he died three days later. So intense were the emotions of the people that his grave had to be guarded by the military for two months. In November 1894 followed the death of the Emperor Alexander III, and as a result of this double event the road to a reconciliation with Russia was opened. Meanwhile the German Emperor, who was on good terms with Princess Clementine, had paved the way for Ferdinand at Vienna, and when, in March 1896, the Sultan recognized him as Prince of Bulgaria and Governor-General of eastern Rumelia, his international position was assured. Relations with Russia were still further improved by the rebaptism of the infant Crown Prince Boris according to the rites of the eastern Church, in February 1896, and a couple of years later Ferdinand and his wife and child paid a highly successful state visit to Peterhof. In September 1902 a memorial church was erected by the Emperor Nicholas II at the Shipka Pass, and later an equestrian statue of the Tsar-Liberator Alexander II was placed opposite the House of Parliament in Sofia.

Bulgaria meanwhile had been making rapid and astonishing material progress. Railways were built, exports increased, and the general condition of the country greatly improved. It is the fashion to compare the wonderful advance made by Bulgaria during the thirty-five years of its new existence with the very much slower progress made by Serbia during a much longer period. This is insisted on especially by publicists in Austria-Hungary and Germany, but it is forgotten that even before the last Balkan war the geographical position of Bulgaria with its seaboard was much more favourable to its economic development than that of Serbia, which the Treaty of Berlin had hemmed in by Turkish and Austro-Hungarian territory; moreover, Bulgaria being double the size of the Serbia of those days, had far greater resources upon which to draw.

From 1894 onwards Ferdinand's power in his own country and his influence abroad had been steadily growing. He always appreciated the value of railways, and became almost as great a traveller as the German Emperor. His estates in the south of Hungary constantly required his attention, and he was a frequent visitor in Vienna. The German Emperor, though he could not help admiring Ferdinand's success, was always a little afraid of him; he felt that Ferdinand's gifts were so similar to his own that he would be unable to count on him in an emergency. Moreover, it was difficult to reconcile Ferdinand's ambitions in extreme south-eastern Europe with his own. Ferdinand's relations with Vienna, on the other hand, and especially with the late Archduke Francis Ferdinand, were both cordial and intimate.

The gradual aggravation of the condition of the Turkish Empire, notably in Macedonia, the unredeemed Bulgaria, where since the insurrection of 1902-3 anarchy, always endemic, had deteriorated into a reign of terror, and, also the unmistakably growing power and spirit of Serbia since the accession of the Karageorgevich dynasty in 1903, caused uneasiness in Sofia, no less than in Vienna and Budapest. The Young

Turkish revolution of July 1908, and the triumph of the Committee of Union and Progress, disarmed the critics of Turkey who wished to make the forcible introduction of reforms a pretext for their interference; but the potential rejuvenation of the Ottoman Empire which it foreshadowed indicated the desirability of rapid and decisive action. In September, after fomenting a strike on the Oriental Railway in eastern Roumelia (which railway was Turkish property), the Sofia Cabinet seized the line with a military force on the plea of political necessity. At the same time Ferdinand, with his second wife, the Protestant Princess Eleonora of Reuss, whom he had married in March of that year, was received with regal honours by the Emperor of Austria at Budapest. On October 5, 1908, at Tirnovo, the ancient capital, Ferdinand proclaimed the complete independence of Bulgaria and eastern Rumelia under himself as King *(Tsar* in Bulgarian), and on October 7 Austria-Hungary announced the annexation of Bosnia and Hercegovina, the two Turkish provinces administered by it since 1879, nominally under Turkish suzerainty.

13.
The Kingdom, 1908-13
(cf. Chaps. 14, 20)

The events which have taken place in Bulgaria since 1908 hinge on the Macedonian question, which has not till now been mentioned. The Macedonian question was extremely complicated; it started on the assumption that the disintegration of Turkey, which had been proceeding throughout the nineteenth century, would eventually be completed, and the question was how in this eventuality to satisfy the territorial claims of the three neighbouring countries, Bulgaria, Serbia, and Greece, claims both historical and ethnological, based on the numbers and distribution of their 'unredeemed' compatriots in Macedonia, and at the same time avoid causing the armed interference of Europe.

The beginnings of the Macedonian question in its modern form do not go farther back than 1885, when the ease with which eastern Rumelia (i.e. southern Bulgaria) threw off the Turkish yoke and was spontaneously united with the semi-independent principality of northern Bulgaria affected the imagination of the Balkan statesmen. From that time Sofia began to cast longing eyes on Macedonia, the whole of which was claimed as 'unredeemed Bulgaria', and Stambulov's last success in 1894 was to obtain from Turkey the consent to the establishment of two bishops of the Bulgarian (Exarchist) Church in Macedonia, which was a heavy blow for the Greek Patriarchate at Constantinople.

Macedonia had been envisaged by the Treaty of Berlin, article 23 of which stipulated for reforms in that province; but in those days the Balkan States were too young and weak to worry themselves or the European powers over the troubles of their co-religionists in Turkey; their hands were more than full setting their own houses in some sort of order, and it was in nobody's interest to reform Macedonia, so article 23 remained the expression of a philanthropic sentiment. This indifference on the part of Europe left the door open for the Balkan States, as soon as they had energy to spare, to initiate their campaign for extending their spheres of influence in Macedonia.

From 1894 onwards Bulgarian propaganda in Macedonia increased, and the Bulgarians were soon followed by Greeks and Serbians. The reason for this passionate pegging out of claims and the bitter rivalry of the three nations which it engendered was the following: The population of Macedonia was nowhere, except in the immediate vicinity of the borders of these three countries, either purely Bulgar or purely Greek or purely Serb; most of the towns contained a percentage of at least two of these nationalities, not to mention the Turks (who after all were still the owners of the country by right of conquest), Albanians, Tartars, Rumanians (Vlakhs), and others; the city of Salonika was and is almost purely Jewish, while in the country districts Turkish, Albanian, Greek, Bulgar, and Serb villages were inextricably confused. Generally speaking, the coastal strip was mainly Greek (the coast itself purely so), the interior mainly Slav. The problem was for each country to peg out as large a claim as possible, and so effectively, by any means in their power, to make the majority of the population contained in that claim acknowledge itself to be Bulgar, or Serb, or Greek, that when the agony of the Ottoman Empire was over, each part of Macedonia would automatically fall into the arms of its respective deliverers. The game was played through the appropriate media of churches and schools, for the unfortunate Macedonian peasants had first of all to be enlightened as to who they were, or rather as to who they were told they had got to consider themselves, while the Church, as always, conveniently covered a multitude of political aims; when those methods flagged, a bomb would be thrown at, let us say, a Turkish official by an *agent provocateur* of one of the three players, inevitably resulting in the necessary massacre of innocent Christians by the ostensibly brutal but really equally innocent Turks, and an outcry in the European press.

Bulgaria was first in the field and had a considerable start of the other two rivals. The Bulgars claimed the whole of Macedonia, including Salonika and all the Aegean coast (except Chalcidice), Okhrida, and Monastir; Greece claimed all southern Macedonia, and Serbia parts of northern and central Macedonia known as Old Serbia. The crux of the whole problem was, and is, that the claims of Serbia and Greece do not clash, while that of Bulgaria, driving a thick wedge between Greece and Serbia, and thus giving Bulgaria the undoubted hegemony of the peninsula, came into irreconcilable conflict with those of its rivals. The importance of this point was greatly emphasized by the existence of the Nish-Salonika railway, which is Serbia's only direct outlet to the sea, and runs through Macedonia from north to south, following the right or western bank of the river Vardar. Should Bulgaria straddle that, Serbia would be economically at its mercy, just as in the north it was already, to its bitter cost, at the mercy of Austria-Hungary. Nevertheless, Bulgarian propaganda had been so effectual that Serbia and Greece never expected they would eventually be able to join hands so easily and successfully as they afterwards did.

The then unknown quantity of Albania was also a factor. This people, though small in numbers, was formidable in character, and had never been effectually subdued by the Turks. They would have been glad to have a boundary contiguous with that of Bulgaria (with whom they had no quarrel) as a support against their hereditary enemies, Serbs in the north and Greeks in the south, who were more than inclined to encroach on their territory. The population of Macedonia, being still under Turkish rule, was uneducated and ignorant; needless to say it had no national consciousness, though this was less true of the Greeks than of the Slavs. It is the Slav population of Macedonia that has engendered so much heat and caused so much blood to be spilt. The dispute as to whether it is rather Serb or Bulgar has caused interminable and most bitter controversy. The truth is that it *was* neither the one nor the other, but that, the ethnological and linguistic missionaries of Bulgaria having been first in the field, a majority of the Macedonian Slavs had been so long and so persistently told that they were Bulgars, that after a few years Bulgaria could, with some truth, claim that this fact was so.

Macedonia had been successively under Greek, Bulgar, and Serb, before Turkish, rule, but the Macedonian Slavs had, under the last, been so cut off both from Bulgars and Serbs, that ethnologically and linguistically they did not develop the characteristics of either of these two races, which originally belonged to the same southern Slav stock, but remained a primitive neutral Slav type. If the Serbs had been first in the field instead of the Bulgars, the Macedonian Slavs could just as easily have been made into Serbs, sufficiently plausibly to convince the most knowing expert. The well-known recipe for making a Macedonian Slav village Bulgar is to add-*ov* or-*ev* (pronounced-*off,-yeff*) on to the names of all the male inhabitants, and to make it Serb it is only necessary to add further the syllable-*ich,-ov* and-*ovich* being respectively the equivalent in

Bulgarian and Serbian of our termination-*son*, e. g. *Ivanov* in Bulgarian, and *Jovanovit* in Serbian = *Johnson*.

In addition to these three nations Rumania also entered the lists, suddenly horrified at discovering the sad plight of the Vlakh shepherds, who had probably wandered with unconcern about Macedonia with their herds since Roman times. As their vague pastures could not possibly ever be annexed to Rumania, their case was merely used in order to justify Rumania in claiming eventual territorial compensation elsewhere at the final day of reckoning. Meanwhile, their existence as a separate and authentic nationality in Turkey was officially recognized by the Porte in 1906.

The stages of the Macedonian question up to 1908 must at this point be quite briefly enumerated. Russia and Austria-Hungary, the two 'most interested powers', who as far back as the eighteenth century had divided the Balkans into their respective spheres of interest, east and west, came to an agreement in 1897 regarding the final settlement of affairs in Turkey; but it never reached a conclusive stage and consequently was never applied. The Macedonian chaos meanwhile grew steadily worse, and the serious insurrections of 1902-3, followed by the customary reprisals, thoroughly alarmed the powers. Hilmi Pasha had been appointed Inspector-General of Macedonia in December 1902, but was not successful in restoring order. In October 1903 the Emperor Nicholas II and the Emperor of Austria, with their foreign ministers, met at Muerzsteg, in Styria, and elaborated a more definite plan of reform known as the Muerzsteg programme, the drastic terms of which had been largely inspired by Lord Lansdowne, then British Secretary of State for Foreign Affairs; the principal feature was the institution of an international gendarmerie, the whole of Macedonia being divided up into five districts to be apportioned among the several great powers. Owing to the procrastination of the Porte and to the extreme complexity of the financial measures which had to be elaborated in connexion with this scheme of reforms, the last of the negotiations was not completed, nor the whole series ratified, until

April 1907, though the gendarmerie officers had arrived in Macedonia in February 1904.

At this point again it is necessary to recall the position in regard to this question of the various nations concerned. Great Britain and France had no territorial stake in Turkey proper, and did their utmost to secure reform not only in the *vilayets* of Macedonia, but also in the realm of Ottoman finance. Italy's interest centred in Albania, whose eventual fate, for geographical and strategic reasons, could not leave it indifferent. Austria-Hungary's only care was by any means to prevent the aggrandizement of the Serb nationality and of Serbia and Montenegro, so as to secure the control, if not the possession, of the routes to Salonika, if necessary over the prostrate bodies of those two countries which defiantly barred Germanic progress towards the East. Russia was already fatally absorbed in the Far Eastern adventure, and, moreover, had, ever since the war of 1878, been losing influence at Constantinople, where before its word had been law; the Treaty of Berlin had dealt a blow at Russian prestige, and Russia had ever since that date been singularly badly served by its ambassadors to the Porte, who were always either too old or too easy-going. Germany, on the other hand, had been exceptionally fortunate or prudent in the choice of its representatives. The general trend of German diplomacy in Turkey was not grasped until very much later, a fact which redounds to the credit of the German ambassadors at Constantinople. Ever since the triumphal journey of William II to the Bosphorus in 1889, German influence, under the able guidance of Baron von Radowitz, steadily increased. This culminated in the regime of the late Baron Marschall von Bieberstein, who was ambassador from 1897 to 1912. It was German policy to flatter, support, and encourage Turkey in every possible way, to refrain from taking part with the other powers in the invidious and perennial occupation of pressing reforms on Abdul Hamid, and, above all, to give as much pocket-money to Turkey and its extravagant ruler as they asked for. Germany, for instance, refused to send officers or to have a district assigned it in Macedonia in 1904, and declined to take part in the naval demonstration off Mitylene in 1905. This attitude of Germany naturally encouraged the Porte in its policy of delay and subterfuge, and Turkey soon came to look on Germany as its only strong, sincere, and disinterested friend in Europe. For the indefinite continuance of chaos and bloodshed in Macedonia, after the other powers had really braced themselves to the thankless task of putting the reforms into practice, Germany alone was responsible.

The blow which King Ferdinand had inflicted on the prestige of the Young Turks in October 1908, by proclaiming his independence, naturally lent lustre to the Bulgarian cause in Macedonia. Serbia, baffled by the simultaneous Austrian annexation of Bosnia and Hercegovina, and maddened by the elevation of Bulgaria to the rank of a kingdom (its material progress had hitherto been discounted in Serbian eyes by the fact that it was a mere vassal principality), seemed about to be crushed by the two iron pots jostling it on either side. Its international position was at that time such that it could expect no help or encouragement from western Europe, while the events of 1909 (cf. p. 144) showed that Russia was not then in a position to render active assistance. Greece, also screaming aloud for compensation, was told by its friends amongst the great powers that if it made a noise it would get nothing, but that if it behaved like a good child it might some day be given Krete. Meanwhile Russia, rudely awakened by the events of 1908 to the real state of affairs in the Near East, beginning to realize the growth of German influence at Constantinople, and seeing the unmistakable resuscitation of Austria-Hungary as a great power, made manifest by the annexation of Bosnia and Hercegovina, temporarily reasserted its influence in Bulgaria. From the moment when Baron Aehrenthal announced his chimerical scheme of an Austrian railway through the *Sandjak* of Novi Pazar in January 1908—everybody knows that the railway already built through Serbia along the Morava valley is the only commercially remunerative and strategically practicable road from Berlin, Vienna, and Budapest to Salonika and Constantinople—Russia realized that the days of the

Muerzsteg programme were over, that henceforward it was to be a struggle between Slav and Teuton for the ownership of Constantinople and the dominion of the Near East, and that something must be done to retrieve the position in the Balkans which it was losing. After Baron Aehrenthal, in January 1909, had mollified the Young Turks by an indemnity, and thus put an end to the boycott, Russia in February of the same year liquidated the remains of the old Turkish war indemnity of 1878 still due to itself by skilfully arranging that Bulgaria should pay off its capitalized tribute, owed to its ex-suzerain the Sultan, by very easy instalments to Russia instead.

The immediate effects of the Young Turk revolution amongst the Balkan States, and the events, watched benevolently by Russia, which led to the formation of the Balkan League, when it was joyfully realized that neither the setting-up of parliamentary government, nor even the overthrow of Abdul Hamid, implied the commencement of the millennium in Macedonia and Thrace, have been described elsewhere (pp. 141, 148). King Ferdinand and M. Venezelos are generally credited with the inception and realisation of the League, though it was so secretly and skilfully concerted that it is not yet possible correctly to apportion praise for the remarkable achievement. Bulgaria is a very democratic country, but King Ferdinand, owing to his sagacity, patience, and experience, and also thanks to his influential dynastic connexions and propensity for travel, has always been virtually his own foreign minister; in spite of the fact that he is a large feudal Hungarian landlord, and has temperamental leanings towards the Central European Empires, it is quite credible that King Ferdinand devoted all his undeniable talents and great energy to the formation of the League when he saw that the moment had come for Bulgaria to realize its destiny at Turkey's expense, and that, if the other three Balkan States could be induced to come to the same wise decision, it would be so much the better for all of them. That Russia could do anything else than whole-heartedly welcome the formation of the Balkan League was absolutely impossible. Pan-Slavism had long since ceased to be the force it was, and nobody in Russia dreamed of or desired the incorporation of any Balkan territory in the Russian Empire. It is possible to control Constantinople without possessing the Balkans, and Russia could only rejoice if a Greco-Slavonic league should destroy the power of the Turks and thereby make impossible the further advance of the Germanic powers eastward.

That Russia was ever in the least jealous of the military successes of the league, which caused such gnashing of teeth in Berlin, Vienna, and Budapest, is a mischievous fiction, the emptiness of which was evident to any one who happened to be in Russia during the winter of 1912-13.

The years 1908 to 1912 were outwardly uneventful in Bulgaria, though a great deal of quiet work was done in increasing the efficiency of the army, and the material prosperity of the country showed no falling off. Relations with the other Balkan States, especially with Serbia and Montenegro, improved considerably, and there was ample room for such improvement. This was outwardly marked by frequent visits paid to each other by members of the several royal families of the three Slavonic kingdoms of the Balkans. In May 1912 agreements for the eventual delimitation of the provinces to be conquered from Turkey in the event of war were signed between Bulgaria and Serbia, and Bulgaria and Greece. The most controversial district was, of course, Macedonia. Bulgaria claimed central Macedonia, with Monastir and Okhrida, which was the lion's share, on ethnical grounds which have been already discussed, and it was expected that Greece and Serbia, by obtaining other acquisitions elsewhere, would consent to have their territories separated by the large Bulgarian wedge which was to be driven between them. The exact future line of demarcation between Serbian and Bulgarian territory was to be left to arbitration. The possible creation of an independent Albania was not contemplated.

In August 1912 the twenty-fifth anniversary of King Ferdinand's arrival in Bulgaria was celebrated with much rejoicing at the ancient capital of Tirnovo, and was marred only by the news of the terrible massacre of Bulgars by Turks at Kochana in Macedonia; this event, however, opportune though mournful, tended considerably to increase the volume of the wave of patriotism which swept through the country. Later in the same month Count Berchtold startled Europe with his 'progressive decentralization' scheme of reform for Macedonia. The manner in which this event led to the final arrangements for the declaration of war on Turkey by the four Balkan States is given in full elsewhere (cf. p. 151).

The Bulgarian army was fully prepared for the fray, and the autumn manoeuvres had permitted the concentration unobserved of a considerable portion of it, ready to strike when the time came. Mobilisation was ordered on September 30, 1912. On October 8 Montenegro declared war on Turkey. On October 13 Bulgaria, with the other Balkan States, replied to the remonstrances of Russia and Austria by declaring that its patience was at length exhausted, and that the sword alone was able to enforce proper treatment of the Christian populations in European Turkey. On October 17 Turkey, encouraged by the sudden and unexpected conclusion of peace with Italy after the Libyan war, declared war on Bulgaria and Serbia, and on October 18 King Ferdinand addressed a sentimental exhortation to his people to liberate their fellow-countrymen, who were still groaning under the Crescent.

The number of Turkish troops opposing the Bulgarians in Thrace was about 180,000, and they had almost exactly the same number wherewith to oppose the Serbians in Macedonia; for, although Macedonia was considered by the Turks to be the most important theatre of war, yet the proximity of the Bulgarian frontier to Constantinople made it necessary to retain a large number of troops in Thrace. On October 19 the Bulgarians took the frontier town of Mustafa Pasha. On October 24 they defeated the Turks at Kirk-Kilisse (or Lozengrad), further east. From October 28 to November 2 raged the terrific battle of Lule-Burgas, which resulted in a complete and brilliant victory of the Bulgarians over the Turks. The defeat and humiliation of the Turks was as rapid and thorough in Thrace as it had been in Macedonia, and by the middle of November the remains of the Turkish army were entrenched behind the impregnable lines of Chataldja, while a large garrison was shut up in Adrianople, which had been invested by the end of October. The Bulgarian army, somewhat exhausted by this brilliant and lightning campaign, refrained from storming the lines of Chataldja, an operation which could not fail to involve losses such as the Bulgarian nation was scarcely in a position to bear, and on December 3 the armistice was signed. The negotiations conducted in London for two months led, however, to no result, and on February 3, 1913, hostilities were resumed. These, for the Bulgarians, resolved themselves into the more energetic prosecution of the siege of Adrianople, which had not been raised during the armistice. To their assistance Serbia, being able to spare troops from Macedonia, sent 50,000 men and a quantity of heavy siege artillery, an arm which the Bulgarians lacked. On March 26, 1913, the fortress surrendered to the allied armies.

The Conference of London, which took place during the spring of that year, fixed the new Turco-Bulgarian boundary by drawing the famous Enos-Midia line, running between these two places situated on the shores respectively of the Aegean and the Black Sea. This delimitation would have given Bulgaria possession of Adrianople. But meanwhile Greece and especially Serbia, which latter country had been compelled to withdraw from the Adriatic coast by Austria, and was further precluded from ever returning there by the creation of the independent state of Albania, determined to retain possession of all that part of Macedonia, including the whole valley of the Vardar with its important railway, which they had conquered, and thus secure their common frontier. In May 1913 a military convention was concluded between them, and the Balkan League, the relations between the members of which had been becoming more strained ever since January, finally dissolved. Bulgaria, outraged by this callous disregard of the agreements as to the partition of Macedonia signed a year previously by itself and its ex-allies, did not wait for the result of the arbitration which was actually proceeding in Russia, but in an access of indignation rushed to arms.

This second Balkan war, begun by Bulgaria during the night of June 30, 1913, by a sudden attack on the Serbian army in Macedonia, resulted in its undoing. In order to defeat the Serbs and Greeks the south-eastern and northern frontiers were denuded of troops. But the totally unforeseen happened. The Serbs were victorious, defeating the Bulgars in Macedonia, the Turks, seeing Thrace empty of Bulgarian troops, re-occupied Adrianople, and the Rumanian army, determined to see fair play before it was too late, invaded Bulgaria from the north and marched on Sofia. By the end of July the campaign was over and Bulgaria had to submit to fate.

By the terms of the Treaty of Bucarest, which was concluded on August 10, 1913, Bulgaria obtained a considerable part of Thrace and eastern Macedonia, including a portion of the Aegean coast with the seaport of Dedeagach, but it was forced to 'compensate' Rumania with a slice of its richest province (the districts of Dobrich and Silistria in north-eastern Bulgaria), and it lost central Macedonia, a great part of which it would certainly have been awarded by Russia's arbitration. On September 22, 1913, the Treaty of Constantinople was signed by Bulgaria and Turkey; by its terms Turkey retained possession of Adrianople and of a far larger part of Thrace than its series of ignominious defeats in the autumn of 1912 entitled it to.

In the fatal quarrel between Bulgaria and Serbia which caused the disruption of the Balkan League, led to the tragic second Balkan war of July 1913, and naturally left behind the bitterest feelings, it is difficult to apportion the blame. Both Serbia and Bulgaria were undoubtedly at fault in the choice of the methods by which they sought to adjust their difference, but the real guilt is to be found neither in Sofia nor in Belgrade, but in Vicuna and Budapest. The Balkan League barred the way of the Germanic Powers to the East; its disruption weakened Bulgaria and again placed Serbia at the mercy of the Dual Monarchy. After these trying and unremunerative experiences it is not astonishing that the Bulgarian people and its ambitious ruler should have retired to the remote interior of their shell.

* * * * *

Explanation of Serbian orthography

c = ts
[)c] = ch (as in *church*)
['c] = " " " but softer
[)s] = sh
[)z] = zh (as z in *azure*)
gj = g (as in *George*)
j = y

SERBIA.

14.

The Serbs under Foreign Supremacy, 650-1168

The manner of the arrival of the Slavs in the Balkan peninsula, of that of the Bulgars, and of the formation of the Bulgarian nationality has already been described (cf. p. 26). The installation of the Slavs in the lands between the Danube, the Aegean, and the Adriatic was completed by about A.D. 650. In the second half of the seventh century the Bulgars settled themselves in the eastern half of the peninsula and became absorbed by the Slavs there, and from that time the nationality of the Slavs in the western half began to be more clearly defined. These latter, split up into a number of tribes, gradually grouped themselves into three main divisions: Serbs (or Serbians), Croats (or Croatians), and Slovenes. The Serbs, much the most numerous of the three, occupied roughly the modern kingdom of Serbia (including Old Serbia and northern Macedonia), Montenegro, and most of Bosnia, Hercegovina, and Dalmatia; the Croats occupied the more western parts of these last three territories and Croatia; the Slovenes occupied the modern Carniola and southern Carinthia. Needless to say, none of these geographical designations existed in those days except Dalmatia, on the coast of which the Latin influence and nomenclature maintained itself. The Slovenes, whose language is closely akin to but not identical with Serbian (or Croatian), even to-day only number one and a half million, and do not enter into this narrative, as they have never played any political role in the Balkan peninsula.

The Serbs and the Croats were, as regards race and language, originally one people, the two names having merely geographical signification. In course of time, for various reasons connected with religion and politics, the distinction was emphasized, and from a historical point of view the Serbo-Croatian race has always been divided into two. It is only within the last few years that a movement has taken place, the object of which is to reunite Serbs and Croats into one nation and eventually into one state. The movement originated in Serbia, the Serbs maintaining that they and the Croats are one people because they speak the same language, and that racial and linguistic unity outweighs religious divergence. A very large number of Croats agree with the Serbs in this and support their views, but a minority for long obstinately insisted that there was a racial as well as a religious difference, and that fusion was impossible. The former based their argument on facts, the latter theirs on prejudice, which is notoriously difficult to overcome. Latterly the movement in favour of fusion grew very much stronger among the Croats, and together with that in Serbia resulted in the Pan-Serb agitation which, gave the pretext for the opening of hostilities in July 1914.

The designation Southern Slav (or Jugo-Slav, *jug*, pronounced yug, = *south* in Serbian) covers Serbs and Croats, and also includes Slovenes; it is only used with reference to the Bulgarians from the point of view of philology (the group of South Slavonic languages including Bulgarian, Serbo-Croatian and Slovene; the East Slavonic, Russian; and the West Slavonic, Polish and Bohemian).

In the history of the Serbs and Croats, or of the Serbo-Croatian race, several factors of a general nature have first to be considered, which have influenced its whole development. Of these, the physical nature of the country in which they settled, between the Danube and Save and the Adriatic, is one of the most important. It is almost everywhere mountainous, and though the mountains themselves never attain as much as 10,000 feet in height, yet they cover the whole country with an intricate network and have always formed an obstacle to easy communication between the various parts of it. The result of this has been twofold. In the first place it has, generally speaking, been a protection against foreign penetration and conquest, and in so far was beneficial. Bulgaria, further east, is, on the whole, less mountainous, in spite of the Balkan range which stretches the whole length of it; for this reason, and also on account of its geographical position, any invaders coming from the north or north-east, especially if aiming at Constantinople or Salonika, were bound to sweep over it. The great immemorial highway from the north-west to the Balkan peninsula crosses the Danube at Belgrade and follows the valley of the Morava to Nish; thence it branches off eastwards, going through Sofia and again crossing all Bulgaria to reach Constantinople, while the route to Salonika follows the Morava southwards from Nish and crosses the watershed into the valley of the Vardar, which flows into the Aegean. But even this road, following the course of the rivers Morava and Vardar, only went through the fringe of Serb territory, and left untouched the vast mountain region between the Morava and the Adriatic, which is really the home of the Serb race.

In the second place, while it has undoubtedly been a protection to the Serb race, it has also been a source of weakness. It has prevented a welding together of the people into one whole, has facilitated the rise of numerous political units at various times, and generally favoured the dissipation of the national strength, and militated against national organization and cohesion. In the course of history this process has been emphasized rather than diminished, and to-day the Serb race is split up into six political divisions, while Bulgaria, except for those Bulgars claimed as 'unredeemed' beyond the frontier, presents a united whole. It is only within the last thirty years, with the gradual improvement of communications (obstructed to an incredible extent by the Austro-Hungarian government) and the spread of education, that the Serbs in the different countries which they inhabit have become fully conscious of their essential identity and racial unity.

No less important than the physical aspect of their country on the development of the Serbs has been the fact that right through the middle of it from south to north there had been drawn a line of division more than two centuries before their arrival. Artificial boundaries are proverbially ephemeral, but this one has lasted throughout the centuries, and it has been baneful to the Serbs. This dividing line, drawn first by the Emperor Diocletian, has been described on p. 14; at the division of the Roman Empire into East and West it was again followed, and it formed the boundary between the dioceses of Italy and Dacia; the line is roughly the same as the present political boundary between Montenegro and Hercegovina, between the kingdom of Serbia and Bosnia; it stretched from the Adriatic to the river Save right across the Serb territory. The Serbo-Croatian race unwittingly occupied a country that was cut in two by the line that divides East from West, and separates Constantinople and the Eastern Church from Rome and the Western. This curious accident has had consequences fatal to the unity of the race, since it has played into the hands of ambitious and unscrupulous neighbours. As to the extent of the country occupied by the Serbs at the beginning of their history it is difficult to be accurate.

The boundary between the Serbs in the west of the peninsula and the Bulgars in the east has always been a matter of dispute. The present political frontier between Serbia and Bulgaria, starting in the north from the mouth of the river Timok on the southern bank of the Danube and going southwards slightly east of Pirot, is ethnographically approximately correct till it reaches the newly acquired and much-disputed territories in Macedonia, and represents fairly accurately the line that has divided the two nationalities ever since they were first differentiated in the seventh century. In the confused state of Balkan politics in the Middle Ages the political influence of Bulgaria often extended west of this line and included Nish and the Morava valley, while at other times that of

Serbia extended east of it. The dialects spoken in these frontier districts represent a transitional stage between the two languages; each of the two peoples naturally considers them more akin to its own, and resents the fact that any of them should be included in the territory of the other. Further south, in Macedonia, conditions are similar. Before the Turkish conquest Macedonia had been sometimes under Bulgarian rule, as in the times of Simeon, Samuel, and John Asen II, sometimes under Serbian, especially during the height of Serbian power in the fourteenth century, while intermittently it had been a province of the Greek Empire, which always claimed it as its own. On historical grounds, therefore, each of the three nations can claim possession of Macedonia. From an ethnographic point of view the Slav population of Macedonia (there were always and are still many non-Slav elements) was originally the same as that in the other parts of the peninsula, and probably more akin to the Serbs, who are pure Slavs, than to the Slavs of Bulgaria, who coalesced with their Asiatic conquerors. In course of time, however, Bulgarian influences, owing to the several periods when the Bulgars ruled the country, began to make headway. The Albanians also (an Indo-European or Aryan race, but not of the Greek, Latin, or Slav families), who, as a result of all the invasions of the Balkan peninsula, had been driven southwards into the inaccessible mountainous country now known as Albania, began to spread northwards and eastwards again during the Turkish dominion, pushing back the Serbs from the territory where they had long been settled. During the Turkish dominion neither Serb nor Bulgar had any influence in Macedonia, and the Macedonian Slavs, who had first of all been pure Slavs, like the Serbs, then been several times under Bulgar, and finally, under Serb influence, were left to themselves, and the process of differentiation between Serb and Bulgar in Macedonia, by which in time the Macedonian Slavs would have become either Serbs or Bulgars, ceased. The further development of the Macedonian question is treated elsewhere (cf. chap. 13).

The Serbs, who had no permanent or well-defined frontier in the east, where their neighbours were the Bulgars, or in the south, where they were the Greeks and Albanians, were protected on the north by the river Save and on the west by the Adriatic. They were split up into a number of tribes, each of which was headed by a chief called in Serbian *[)z]upan* and in Greek *arch[=o]n*. Whenever any one of these managed, either by skill or by good fortune, to extend his power over a few of the neighbouring districts he was termed *veliki* (=great) *[)z]upan*. From the beginning of their history, which is roughly put at A.D. 650, until A.D. 1196, the Serbs were under foreign domination. Their suzerains were nominally always the Greek emperors, who had 'granted' them the land they had taken, and whenever the emperor happened to be energetic and powerful, as were Basil I (the Macedonian, 867-86), John Tzimisces (969-76), Basil II (976-1025), and Manuel Comnenus (1143-80), the Greek supremacy was very real. At those times again when Bulgaria was very powerful, under Simeon (893-927), Samuel (977-1014), and John Asen II (1218-41), many of the more easterly and southerly Serbs came under Bulgarian rule, though it is instructive to notice that the Serbs themselves do not recognize the West Bulgarian or Macedonian kingdom of Samuel to have been a Bulgarian state. The Bulgars, however, at no time brought all the Serb lands under their sway.

Intermittently, whenever the power of Byzantium or of Bulgaria waned, some Serb princeling would try to form a political state on a more ambitious scale, but the fabric always collapsed at his death, and the Serbs reverted to their favourite occupation of quarrelling amongst themselves. Such wore the attempts of [)C]aslav, who had been made captive by Simeon of Bulgaria, escaped after his death, and ruled over a large part of central Serbia till 960, and later of Bodin, whose father, Michael, was even recognized as king by Pope Gregory VII; Bodin formed a state near the coast, in the Zeta river district (now Montenegro), and ruled there from 1081 to 1101. But as a rule the whole of the country peopled by the Serbs was split into a number of tiny principalities always at war with one another. Generally speaking, this country gradually became divided into two main geographical divisions: (1) the *Pomorje*, or country *by the sea*, which included most of the modern Montenegro and the southern halves of Hercegovina and Dalmatia, and (2) the *Zagorje*, or country *behind the hills*, which included most of the modern Bosnia, the western half of the modern kingdom of Serbia, and the northern portions of Montenegro and Hercegovina, covering all the country between the *Pomorje* and the Save; to the north of the *Pomorje* and *Zagorje* lay Croatia. Besides their neighbours in the east and south, those in the north and west played an important part in Serbian history even in those early days.

Towards the end of the eighth century, after the decline of the power of the Avars, Charlemagne extended his conquests eastwards (he made a great impression on the minds of the Slavs, whose word for king, *kral* or *korol*, is derived directly from his name), and his son Louis conquered the Serbs settled in the country between the rivers Save and Drave. This is commemorated in the name of the mass of hill which lies between the Danube and the Save, in eastern Slavonia, and is to this day known as *Fru[)s]ka Gora*, or French Hill. The Serbs and Bulgars fought against the Franks, and while the Bulgars held their own, the Serbs were beaten, and those who did not like the rule of the new-comers had to migrate southwards across the Save; at the same time the Serbs between the rivers Morava and Timok (eastern Serbia) were subjected by the Bulgars. With the arrival of the Magyars, in the ninth century, a wall was raised between the Serbs and central and western Europe on land. Croatia and Slavonia (between the Save and the Drave) were gradually drawn into the orbit of the Hungarian state, and in 1102, on the death of its own ruler, Croatia was absorbed by Hungary and has formed part of that country ever since. Hungary, aiming at an outlet on the Adriatic, at the same time subjected most of Dalmatia and parts of Bosnia. In the west Venice had been steadily growing in power throughout the tenth century, and by the end of it had secured control of all the islands off Dalmatia and of a considerable part of the coast. All the cities on the mainland acknowledged the supremacy of Venice and she was mistress of the Adriatic.

In the interior of the Serb territory, during the eleventh and twelfth centuries, three political centres came into prominence and shaped themselves into larger territorial units. These were: (1) Raska, which had been Caslav's centre and is considered the birth-place of the Serbian state (this district, with the town of Ras as its centre, included the south-western part of the modern kingdom of Serbia and what was the Turkish *sandjak* or province of Novi-Pazar); (2) Zeta, on the coast (the modern Montenegro); and (3) Bosnia, so called after the river Bosna, which runs through it. Bosnia, which roughly corresponded to the modern province of that name, became independent in the second half of the tenth century, and was never after that incorporated in the Serbian state. At times it fell under Hungarian influence; in the twelfth century, during the reign of Manuel Comnenus, who was victorious over the Magyars, Bosnia, like all other Serb territories, had to acknowledge the supremacy of Constantinople.

It has already been indicated that the Serbs and Croats occupied territory which, while the Church was still one, was divided between two dioceses, Italy and Dacia, and when the Church itself was divided, in the eleventh century, was torn apart between the two beliefs. The dividing line between the jurisdictions of Rome and Constantinople ran from north to south through Bosnia, but naturally there has always been a certain vagueness about the extent of their respective jurisdictions. In later years the terms Croat and Roman Catholic on the one hand, and Serb and Orthodox on the other, became interchangeable. Hercegovina and eastern Bosnia have always been predominantly Orthodox, Dalmatia and western Bosnia predominantly Roman Catholic. The loyalty of the Croatians to Austria-Hungary has been largely owing to the influence of Roman Catholicism.

During the first centuries of Serbian history Christianity made slow progress in the western half of the Balkan peninsula. The Dalmatian coast was always under the influence of Rome, but the interior was long pagan. It is doubtful whether the brothers Cyril and Methodius (cf. chap. 5) actually passed through Serb territory, but in the tenth century their teachings and writings were certainly current there. At the time of the division of the Churches all the Serb lands except the Dalmatian coast, Croatia, and western Bosnia, were faithful to Constantinople, and the Greek hierarchy obtained complete control of the ecclesiastical administration. The elaborate organisation and opulent character of the Eastern Church was, however, especially in the hands of the Greeks, not congenial to the Serbs, and during the eleventh and twelfth centuries the Bogomil heresy (cf. chap, 6), a much more primitive and democratic form of Christianity, already familiar in the East as the Manichaean heresy, took hold of the Serbs' imagination and made as rapid and disquieting progress in their country as it had already done in the neighbouring Bulgaria; inasmuch as the Greek hierarchy considered this teaching to be socialistic, subversive, and highly dangerous to the ecclesiastical supremacy of Constantinople, all of which indeed it was, adherence to it became amongst the Serbs a direct expression of patriotism.

15.

The Rise and Fall of the Serbian Empire and the Extinction of Serbian Independence, 1168-1496

From 1168 the power of the Serbs, or rather of the central Serb state of Raska, and the extent of its territory gradually but steadily increased. This was outwardly expressed in the firm establishment on the throne of the national Nemanja dynasty, which can claim the credit of having by its energy, skill, and good fortune fashioned the most imposing and formidable state the Serb race has ever known. This dynasty ruled the country uninterruptedly, but not without many quarrels, feuds, and rivalries amongst its various members, from 1168 until 1371, when it became extinct.

There were several external factors which at this time favoured the rise of the Serbian state. Byzantium and the Greek Empire, to which the Emperor Manuel Comnenus had by 1168 restored some measure of its former greatness and splendour, regaining temporary control, after a long war with Hungary, even over Dalmatia, Croatia, and Bosnia, after this date began definitively to decline, and after the troublous times of the fourth crusade (1204), when for sixty years a Latin empire was established on the Bosphorus, never again recovered as a Christian state the position in the Balkan peninsula which it had so long enjoyed. Bulgaria, too, after the meteoric glory of its second empire under the Asen dynasty (1186-1258), quite went to pieces, the eastern and northern parts falling under Tartar, the southern under Greek influence, while the western districts fell to Serbia. In the north, on the other hand, Hungary was becoming a dangerous and ambitious neighbour. During the thirteenth century, it is true, the attention of the Magyars was diverted by the irruption into and devastation of their country by their unwelcome kinsmen from Asia, the Tartars, who wrought great havoc and even penetrated as far as the Adriatic coast. Nevertheless Hungary was always a menace to Serbia; Croatia, Slavonia, and the interior of Dalmatia, all purely Serb territories, belonged to the Hungarian crown, and Bosnia was under the supremacy of the Magyars, though nominally independent.

The objects of the Magyars were twofold—to attain the hegemony of the Balkan peninsula by conquering all the still independent Serb territories, and to bring the peninsula within the pale of Rome. They were not successful in either of these objects, partly because their wars with the Serbian rulers always failed to reach a decision, partly because their plans conflicted with those of the powerful Venetian republic. The relations between Venice and Serbia were always most cordial, as their ambitions did not clash; those of Venice were not continental, while those of Serbia were never maritime. The semi-independent Slavonic city-republic of Ragusa (called Dubrovnik in Serbian) played a very important part throughout this period. It was under Venetian supremacy, but was self-governing and had a large fleet of its own. It was the great place of exchange between Serbia and western Europe, and was really the meeting-place of East and West. Its relations with Serbia were by no means always peaceful; it was a Naboth's vineyard for the rulers and people of the inland kingdom, and it was never incorporated within their dominions. Ragusa and the other cities of the Dalmatian coast were the home during the Middle Ages of a flourishing school of Serbian literature, which was inspired by that of Italy. The influence of Italian civilization and of the Italian Church was naturally strong in the Serb province, much of which was under Venetian rule; the reason for this was that communication by sea with Italy was easier and safer than that by land with Serbia. The long, formidable ranges of limestone mountains which divide the Serbian interior from the Adriatic in almost unbroken and parallel lines have always been a barrier to the extension of Serb power to the coast, and an obstacle to free commercial intercourse. Nevertheless Ragusa was a great trade centre, and one of the factors which most contributed to the economic strength of the Serbian Empire.

The first of the Nemanja dynasty was Stephen, whose title was still only *Veliki ['Z]upan*; he extended Serb territory southwards at the expense of the Greeks, especially after the death of Manuel Comnenus in 1180. He also persecuted the Bogomils, who took refuge in large numbers in the adjacent Serb state of Bosnia. Like many other Serbian rulers, he abdicated in later life in favour of his younger son, Stephen, called Nemanjie (= Nemanya's son), and himself became a monk (1196), travelling for this purpose to Mount Athos, the great monastic centre and home of theological learning of the Eastern Church. There he saw his youngest son, who some years previously had also journeyed thither and entered a monastery, taking the name of Sava.

It was the custom for every Serbian ruler to found a sort of memorial church, for the welfare of his own soul, before his death, and to decorate and endow it lavishly. Stephen and his son together superintended the erection in this sense of the church and monastery of Hilandar on Mount Athos, which became a famous centre of Serbian church life. Stephen died shortly after the completion of the building in 1199, and was buried in it, but in 1207 he was reinterred in the monastery of Studenica, in Serbia, also founded by him.

The reign of Stephen Nernanji['c] (1196-1223) opened with a quarrel between him and his elder brother, who not unnaturally felt he ought to have succeeded his father; the Bulgarians profited by this and seized a large part of eastern Serbia, including Belgrade, Nish, Prizren, and Skoplje. This, together with the fall of Constantinople and the establishment of the Latin Empire in 1204, alarmed the Serbs and brought about a reconciliation between the brothers, and in 1207 Sava returned to Serbia to organise the Church on national lines. In 1219 he journeyed to Nicaea and extracted from the Emperor Theodore Lascaris, who had fallen on evil days, the concession for the establishment of an autonomous national Serbian Church, independent of the Patriarch of Constantinople. Sava himself was at the head of the new institution. In 1220 he solemnly crowned his brother King *(Kralj)* of Serbia, the natural consequence of his activities in the previous year. For this reason Stephen Nemanji['c] is called 'The First-Crowned'. He was succeeded in 1223 by his son Stephen Radoslav, and he in turn was deposed by his brother Stephen Vladislav in 1233. Both these were crowned by Sava, and Vladislav married the daughter of Tsar John Asen II, under whom Bulgaria was then at the height of her power. Sava journeyed to Palestine, and on his return paid a visit to the Bulgarian court at Tirnovo, where he died in 1236. His body was brought to Serbia and buried in the monastery of Mile[)s]evo, built by Vladislav. This extremely able churchman and politician, who did a great deal for the peaceful development of his country, was canonized and is regarded as the patron saint of Serbia.

The reign of Vladislav's son and successor, Stephen Uro[)s] I (1242-76), was characterized by economic development and the strengthening of the internal administration. In external affairs he made no conquests, but defeated a combination of the Bulgarians with Ragusa against him, and after the war the Bulgarian ruler married his daughter. In his wars against Hungary he was unsuccessful, and the Magyars remained in possession of a large part of northern Serbia. In 1276 he was deposed by his son, Stephen Dragutin, who in his turn, after an unsuccessful war against the Greeks, again masters of Constantinople since 1261, was deposed and succeeded by his brother, Stephen Uro[)s] II, named Milutin, in 1282. This king ruled from 1282 till 1321, and during his reign the country made very great material progress; its mineral wealth especially, which included gold and silver mines, began to be exploited. He extended the boundaries of his kingdom in the north, making the Danube and the Save the frontier. The usual revolt against paternal authority was made by his son Stephen, but was unsuccessful, and the rebel was banished to Constantinople.

It was the custom of the Serbian kings to give appanages to their sons, and the inevitable consequence of this system was the series of provincial rebellions which occurred in almost every reign. When the revolt succeeded, the father (or brother) was granted in his turn a small appanage. In this case it was the son who was exiled, but he was recalled in 1319 and a reconciliation took place. Milutin died in 1321 and was succeeded by his son, Stephen Uro[)s] III, who reigned till 1331. He is known as Stephen De[)c]anski, after the memorial church which he built at De[)c]ani in western Serbia. His reign was signalized by a great defeat of the combined Bulgarians and Greeks at Kustendil in Macedonia in 1330. The following year his son, Stephen Du[)s]an, rebelled against him and deposed him. Stephen Du[)s]an, who reigned from 1331 till 1355, was Serbia's greatest ruler, and under him the country reached its utmost limits. Provincial and family revolts and petty local disputes with such places as Ragusa became a thing of the past, and he undertook conquest on a grand scale. Between 1331 and 1344 he subjected all Macedonia, Albania, Thessaly, and Epirus. He was careful to keep on good terms with Ragusa and with Hungary, then under Charles Robert. He married the sister of the Bulgarian ruler, and during his reign Bulgaria was completely under Serbian supremacy. The anarchy and civil war which had become perennial at Constantinople, and the weakening of the Greek Empire in face of the growing power of the Turks, no doubt to some extent explain the facility and rapidity of his conquests; nevertheless his power was very formidable, and his success inspired considerable alarm in western Europe. This was increased when, in 1345, he proclaimed his country an empire. He first called together a special Church council, at which the Serbian Church, an archbishopric, whose centre was then at Pe['c] (in Montenegro, Ipek in Turkish), was proclaimed a Patriarchate, with Archbishop Joannice as Patriarch; then this prelate, together with the Bulgarian Patriarch, Simeon, and Nicholas, Archbishop of Okhrida, crowned Stephen Tsar of the Serbs, Bulgars, and Greeks. Upon this the Patriarch of Constantinople gave himself the vain satisfaction of anathematizing the whole of Serbia, as a punishment for this insubordination.

In 1353 the Pope, Innocent VI, persuaded King Louis of Hungary to undertake a crusade against Serbia in the name of Catholicism, but Stephen defeated him and re-established his frontier along the Save and Danube. Later he conquered the southern half of Dalmatia, and extended his empire as far north as the river Cetina. In 1354 Stephen Du[)s]an himself approached the Pope, offering to acknowledge his spiritual supremacy, if he would support him against the Hungarians and the Turks. The Pope sent him an embassy, but eventually Stephen could not agree to the papal conditions, and concluded an alliance, of greater practical utility, with the Venetians. In 1355, however, he suddenly died, at the age of forty-six, and thus the further development and aggrandisement of his country was prematurely arrested.

Stephen Du[)s]an made a great impression on his contemporaries, both by his imposing personal appearance and by his undoubted wisdom and ability. He was especially a great legislator, and his remarkable code of laws, compiled in 1349 and enlarged in 1354, is, outside his own country, his greatest title to fame. During Stephen Du[)s]an's reign the political centre of Serbia, which had for many years gradually tended to shift southwards towards Macedonia, was at Skoplje (Ueskueb in Turkish), which he made his capital. Stephen Du[)s]an's empire extended from the Adriatic in the west to the river Maritsa in the east, from the Save and Danube in the north to the Aegean; it included all the modern kingdoms of Serbia, Montenegro, Albania, and most of Greece, Dalmatia as far north as the river Cetina, as well as the fertile Morava valley, with Nish and Belgrade—the whole eastern part of Serbia, which had for long been under either Bulgar or Magyar control. It did not include the cities of Salonika or Ragusa, nor any considerable part of the modern kingdom of Bulgaria, nor Bosnia, Croatia, North Dalmatia, nor Slavonia (between the Save and Drave), ethnologically all purely Serb lands. From the point of view of nationality, therefore, its boundaries were far from ideal.

Stephen Du[)s]an was succeeded by his son, known as Tsar Uro[)s], but he was as weak as his father had been strong. Almost as soon as he succeeded to the throne, disorders, rebellions, and dissensions broke out and the empire rapidly fell to pieces. With Serbia, as with Bulgaria, the empire entirely hinged on the personality of one man, and when he was gone chaos returned. Such an event for Serbia at this juncture was fatal, as a far more formidable foe than the ruler's rebellious relations was advancing against it. The Turkish conquests were proceeding apace; they had taken Gallipoli in 1354 and Demotika and Adrianople in 1361. The Serbs, who had already had an unsuccessful brush with the advance guard of the new invaders near Demotika in 1351, met them again on the Maritsa river in 1371, and were completely defeated. Several of the upstart princes who had been pulling Stephen Du[)s]an's empire to pieces perished, and Tsar Uro[)s] only survived the battle of the Maritsa two months; he was unmarried, and with him died the Nemanja dynasty and the Serbian Empire.

After this disaster the unity of the Serbian state was completely destroyed, and it has never since been restored in the same measure.

That part of the country to the south of Skoplje fell completely under Turkish control; it was here that the famous national hero, Marko Kraljevi['c] (or King's son), renowned for his prowess, ruled as a vassal prince and mercenary soldier of the Turks; his father was one of the rebel princes who fell at the battle of the river Maritsa in 1371. North of Skoplje, Serbia, with Kru[)s]evac as a new political centre, continued to lead an independent but precarious existence, much reduced in size and glory, under a native ruler, Prince Lazar; all the conquests of Stephen Du[)s]an were lost, and the important coastal province of Zeta, which later developed into Montenegro, had broken away and proclaimed its autonomy directly after the death of Tsar Uro[)s].

In 1375 a formal reconciliation was effected with the Patriarch of Constantinople; the ban placed on the Serbian Church in 1352 was removed and the independence of the Serbian Patriarchate of Pe['c] (Ipek) recognised. Meanwhile neither Greeks, Bulgars, nor Serbs were allowed any peace by the Turks.

In 1389 was fought the great battle of Kosovo Polje, or the Field of Blackbirds, a large plain in Old Serbia, at the southern end of which is Skoplje. At this battle Serbian armies from all the Serb lands, including Bosnia, joined together in defence of their country for the last time. The issue of the battle was for some time in doubt, but was decided by the treachery and flight at the critical moment of one of the Serb leaders, Vuk Brankovi['c], son-in-law of Prince Lazar, with a large number of troops. Another dramatic incident was the murder of Sultan Murad in his tent by another Serbian leader, Milo[)s] Obili['c], who, accused of treachery by his own countrymen, vowed he would prove his good faith, went over to the Turks and, pretending to be a traitor, gained admission to the Sultan's presence and proved his patriotism by killing him. The momentary dismay was put an end to by the energetic conduct of Bayezid, son of Murad, who rallied the Turkish troops and ultimately inflicted total defeat on the Serbians. From the effects of this battle Serbia never recovered; Prince Lazar was captured and executed; his wife, Princess

Milica, had to give her daughter to Bayezid in marriage, whose son thus ultimately claimed possession of Serbia by right of inheritance. Princess Milica and her son Stephen continued to live at Kru[)s]evac, but Serbia was already a tributary of Turkey. In the north, Hungary profited by the course of events and occupied Belgrade and all northern Serbia, but in 1396 the Turks defeated the Magyars severely at the battle of Nikopolis, on the Danube, making the Serbs under Stephen fight on the Turkish side. Stephen also had to help Sultan Bajazet against the Tartars, and fought at the battle of Angora, in 1402, when Tamerlane captured Bayezid.

After Stephen returned to Serbia he made an alliance with Hungary, which gave him back Belgrade and northern Serbia; it was at this time (1403) that Belgrade first became the capital, the political centre having in the course of fifty years moved from the Vardar to the Danube. The disorders which followed the defeat of Bayezid gave some respite to the Serbs, but Sultan Murad II (1421-51) again took up arms against him, and invaded Serbia as far as Kru[)s]evac.

At the death of Stephen (Lazarevi['c]), in 1427, he was succeeded as *Despot* by his nephew, George Brankovi['c]; but the Sultan, claiming Serbia as his own, immediately declared war on him. The Serbian ruler had to abandon Belgrade to the Magyars, and Nish and Kru[)s]evac to the Turks. He then built and fortified the town of Smederevo (or Semendria) lower down on the Danube, in 1428, and made this his capital. He gave his daughter in marriage to the Sultan, but in spite of this war soon broke out again, and in 1441 the Turks were masters of nearly the whole of Serbia. Later George Brankovi['c] made another alliance with Hungary, and in 1444, with the help of John Hunyadi, defeated the Turks and liberated the whole of Serbia as far as the Adriatic, though he remained a tributary of the Sultan. The same year, however, the Magyars broke the treaty of peace just concluded with the Turks, and marched against them under their Polish king, Ladislas; this ended in the disastrous battle of Varna, on the Black Sea, where the king lost his life. In 1451 Sultan Murad II died and was succeeded by the Sultan Mohammed. In 1453 this sultan captured Constantinople (Adrianople had until then been the Turkish capital); in 1456 his armies were besieging Belgrade, but were defeated by John Hunyadi, who, unfortunately for the Serbs, died of the plague shortly afterwards. George Brankovi['c] died the same year, and at his death general disorder spread over the country. The Turks profited by this, overran the whole of Serbia, and in 1459 captured Smederevo, the last Serbian stronghold.

Meanwhile Bosnia had been for nearly a hundred years enjoying a false security as an independent Serb kingdom. Its rulers had hitherto been known by the title of *Ban*, and were all vassals of the King of Hungary; but in 1377 Ban Tvrtko profited by the embarrassments of his suzerain in Poland and proclaimed himself king, the neighbouring kingdom of Serbia having, after 1371, ceased to exist, and was duly crowned in Saint Sava's monastery of Mile[)s]evo. The internal history of the kingdom was even more turbulent than had been that of Serbia. To the endemic troubles of succession and alternating alliances and wars with foreign powers were added those of confession. Bosnia was always a no man's land as regards religion; it was where the Eastern and Western Churches met, and consequently the rivalry between them there was always, as it is now, intense and bitter. The Bogomil heresy, too, early took root in Bosnia and became extremely popular; it was the obvious refuge for those who did not care to become involved in the strife of the Churches. One of the kings of Bosnia, Stephen Thomas, who reigned from 1444 till 1461, was himself a Bogomil, and when at the insistence of the Pope and of the King of Hungary, whose friendship he was anxious to retain, he renounced his heresy, became ostensibly a Roman Catholic, and began to persecute the Bogomils, he brought about a revolution. The rebels fled to the south of Bosnia, to the lands of one Stephen, who sheltered them, proclaimed his independence of Bosnia, and on the strength of the fact that Saint Sava's monastery of Mile[)s]evo was in his territory, announced himself Herzog, or Duke (in Serbian Herceg, though the real Serb equivalent is *Vojvoda*) of Saint Sava, ever since when (1448) that territory has been

88

called Hercegovina. In spite of many promises, neither the Pope nor the King of Hungary did anything to help Bosnia when the Turks began to invade the country after their final subjection of Serbia in 1459. In 1463 they invaded Bosnia and pursued, captured, and slew the last king; their conquest of the country was complete and rapid. A great exodus of the Serb population took place to the south, west, and north; but large numbers, especially of the landowning class, embraced the faith of their conquerors in order to retain possession of their property. In 1482 a similar fate befell Hercegovina. Albania had already been conquered after stubborn resistance in 1478. There remained only the mountainous coastal province of Zeta, which had been an independent principality ever since 1371. Just as inland Serbia had perished between the Turkish hammer and the Hungarian anvil, so maritime Serbia was crushed between Turkey and Venice, only its insignificance and inaccessibility giving it a longer lease of independent life. Ivan Crnojevi['c], one of the last independent rulers of Zeta, who had to fly to Italy in 1480, abandoning his capital, [)Z]abljak, to the Turks, returned in 1481, when the death of Sultan Mohammed temporarily raised the hopes of the mountaineers, and founded Cetinje and made it his capital. His son George, who succeeded him and ruled from 1490 till 1496, is famous as having set up the first Serbian printing-press there. Its activities were naturally not encouraged by the Turkish conquest, but it was of great importance to the national Serbian Church, for which books were printed with it.

In 1496, Venice having wisely made peace with the Sultan some years previously, this last independent scrap of Serb territory was finally incorporated in the Turkish dominions. At the end of the fifteenth century the Turks were masters of all the Serb lands except Croatia, Slavonia, and parts of Dalmatia, which belonged to Hungary, and the Dalmatian coast and islands, which were Venetian. The Turkish conquest of Serbia, which began in 1371 at the battle of the Maritsa, and was rendered inevitable by the battle of Kosovo Polje, in 1389, thus took a hundred and twenty-five years to complete.

16.

The Turkish Dominion, 1496-1796

The lot of the Serbs under Turkish rule was different from that of their neighbours the Bulgars; and though it was certainly not enviable, it was undoubtedly better. The Turks for various reasons never succeeded in subduing Serbia and the various Serb lands as completely as they had subdued, or rather annihilated, Bulgaria. The Serbs were spread over a far larger extent of territory than were the Bulgars, they were further removed from the Turkish centre, and the wooded and mountainous nature of their country facilitated even more than in the case of Bulgaria the formation of bands of brigands and rebels and militated against its systematic policing by the Turks. The number of centres of national life, Serbia proper, Bosnia, Hercogovina, and Montenegro, to take them in the chronological order of their conquest by the Turks, had been notoriously a source of weakness to the Serbian state, as is still the case to-day, but at the same time made it more difficult for the Turks to stamp out the national consciousness. What still further contributed to this difficulty was the fact that many Serbs escaped the oppression of Turkish rule by emigrating to the neighbouring provinces, where they found people of their own race and language, even though of a different faith. The tide of emigration flowed in two directions, westwards into Dalmatia and northwards into Slavonia and Hungary. It had begun already after the final subjection of Serbia proper and Bosnia by the Turks in 1459 and 1463, but after the fall of Belgrade, which was the outpost of Hungary against the Turks, in 1521, and the battle of Mohacs, in 1526, when the Turks completely defeated the Magyars, it assumed great proportions. As the Turks pushed their conquests further north, the Serbs migrated before them; later on, as the Turks receded, large Serb colonies sprang up all over southern Hungary, in the Banat (the country north of the Danube and east of the Theiss), in Syrmia (or Srem, in Serbian, the extreme eastern part of Slavonia, between the Save and the Danube), in Ba[)c]ka (the country between the Theiss and Danube), and in Baranya (between the Danube and the Drave). All this part of southern Hungary and Croatia was formed by the Austrians into a military borderland against Turkey, and the Croats and immigrant Serbs were organized as military colonists with special privileges, on the analogy of the Cossacks in southern Russia and Poland. In Dalmatia the Serbs played a similar role in the service of Venice, which, like Austria-Hungary, was frequently at war with the Turks. During the sixteenth century Ragusa enjoyed its greatest prosperity; it paid tribute to the Sultan, was under his protection, and never rebelled. It had a quasi monopoly of the trade of the entire Balkan peninsula. It was a sanctuary both for Roman Catholic Croats and for Orthodox Serbs, and sometimes acted as intermediary on behalf of its co-religionists with the Turkish authorities, with whom it wielded great influence. Intellectually also it was a sort of Serb oasis, and the only place during the Middle Ages where Serbian literature was able to flourish.

Montenegro during the sixteenth century formed part of the Turkish province of Scutari. Here, as well as in Serbia proper, northern Macedonia (known after the removal northwards of the political centre, in the fourteenth century, as Old Serbia), Bosnia, and Hercegovina, the Turkish rule was firmest, but not harshest, during the first half of the sixteenth century, when the power of the Ottoman Empire was at its height. Soon after the fall of Smederevo, in 1459, the Patriarchate of Pe['c] (Ipek) was abolished, the Serbian Church lost its independence, was merged in the Greco-Bulgar Archbishopric of Okhrida (in southern Macedonia), and fell completely under the control of the Greeks. In 1557, however, through the influence of a Grand Vizier of Serb nationality, the Patriarchate of Pe['c] was revived. The revival of this centre of national life was momentous; through its agency the Serbian monasteries were restored, ecclesiastical books printed, and priests educated, and more fortunate than the Bulgarian national Church, which remained under Greek management, it was able to focus the national enthusiasms and aspirations and keep alive with hope the flame of nationality amongst those Serbs who had not emigrated.

Already, in the second half of the sixteenth century, people began to think that Turkey's days in Europe were numbered, and they were encouraged in this illusion by the battle of Lepanto (1571). But the seventeenth century saw a revival of Turkish power; Krete was added to their empire, and in 1683 they very nearly captured Vienna. In the war which followed their repulse, and in which the victorious Austrians penetrated as far south as Skoplje, the Serbs took part against the Turks; but when later the Austrians were obliged to retire, the Serbs, who had risen against the Turks at the bidding of their Patriarch Arsen III, had to suffer terrible reprisals at their hands, with the result that another wholesale emigration, with the Patriarch at its head, took place into the Austro-Hungarian military borderland. This time it was the very heart of Serbia which was abandoned, namely, Old Serbia and northern Macedonia, including Pe['c] and Prizren. The vacant Patriarchate was for a time filled by a Greek, and the Albanians, many of whom were Mohammedans and therefore Turcophil, spread northwards and eastwards into lands that had been Serb since the seventh century. From the end of the seventeenth century, however, the Turkish power began unmistakably to wane. The Treaty of Carlowitz (1699) left the Turks still in possession of Syrmia (between the Danube and Save) and the Banat (north of the Danube), but during the reign of the Emperor Charles VI their retreat was accelerated. In 1717 Prince Eugen of Savoy captured Belgrade, then, as now, a bulwark of the Balkan peninsula against invasion from the north, and by the Treaty of Passarowitz (Po[)]z]arevac, on the Danube), in 1718, Turkey not only retreated definitively south of the Danube and the Save, but left a large part of northern Serbia in Austrian hands. By the same treaty Venice secured possession of the whole of Dalmatia, where it had already gained territory by the Treaty of Curlowitz in 1699.

But the Serbs soon found out that alien populations fare little better under Christian rule, when they are not of the same confession as their rulers, than under Mohammedan. The Orthodox Serbs in Dalmatia suffered thenceforward from relentless persecution at the hands of the Roman Catholics. In Austria-Hungary too, and in that part of Serbia occupied by the Austrians after 1718, the Serbs discovered that the Austrians, when they had beaten the Turks largely by the help of Serbian levies, were very different from the Austrians who had encouraged the Serbs to settle in their country and form military colonies on their frontiers to protect them from Turkish invasion. The privileges promised them when their help had been necessary were disregarded as soon as their services could be dispensed with. Austrian rule soon became more oppressive than Turkish, and to the Serbs' other woes was now added religious persecution. The result of all this was that a counter-emigration set in and the Serbs actually began to return to their old homes in Turkey. Another war between Austria-Hungary and Turkey broke out in 1737, in which the Austrians were unsuccessful. Prince Eugen no longer led them, and though the Serbs were again persuaded by their Patriarch, Arsen IV, to rise against the Turks, they only did so half-heartedly. By the Treaty of Belgrade, in 1739, Austria had to withdraw north of the Save and Danube, evacuating all northern Serbia in favour of the Turks. From this time onwards the lot of the Serbs, both in Austria-Hungary and in Turkey, went rapidly from bad to worse. The Turks, as the power of their empire declined, and in return for the numerous Serb revolts, had recourse to measures of severe repression; amongst others was that of the final abolition of the Patriarchate of Pee in 1766, whereupon the control of the Serbian Church in Turkey passed entirely into the hands of the Greek Patriarchate of Constantinople.

The Austrian Government similarly, perceiving now for the first time the elements of danger which the resuscitation of the Serbian nationality would contain for the rule of the Hapsburgs, embarked on a systematic persecution of the Orthodox Serbs in southern Hungary and Slavonia. During the reign of Maria Theresa (1740-80), whose policy was to conciliate the Magyars, the military frontier zone was abolished, a series of repressive measures was passed against those Serbs who refused to become Roman Catholics, and the Serbian nationality was refused official recognition. The consequence of this persecution was a series of revolts which were all quelled with due severity, and finally the emigration of a hundred thousand Serbs to southern Russia, where they founded New Serbia in 1752-3.

During the reigns of Joseph II (1780-90) and Leopold II (1790-2) their treatment at the hands of the Magyars somewhat improved. From the beginning of the eighteenth century Montenegro began to assume greater importance in the extremely gradual revival of the national spirit of the Serbs. During the sixteenth and seventeenth centuries it had formed part of the Turkish dominions, though, thanks to the inaccessible nature of its mountain fastnesses, Turkish authority was never very forcibly asserted. It was ruled by a prince-bishop, and its religious independence thus connoted a certain secular freedom of thought if not of action. In the seventeenth century warlike encounters between the Turks and the Montenegrins increased in frequency, and the latter tried to enlist the help of Venice on their side but with indifferent success. The fighting in Montenegro was often rather civil in character, being caused by the ill-feeling which existed between the numerous Montenegrins who had become Mohammedans and those who remained faithful to their national Church. In the course of the eighteenth century the role which fell to Montenegro became more important. In all the other Serb countries the families which naturally took a leading part in affairs were either extinct or in exile, as in Serbia, or had become Mohammedan, and therefore to all intents and purposes Turkish, as in Bosnia and Hercegovina. Ragusa, since the great earthquake in 1667, had greatly declined in power and was no longer of international importance. In Montenegro, on the other hand, there had survived both a greater independence of spirit (Montenegro was, after all, the ancient Zeta, and had always been a centre of national life) and a number of at any rate eugenic if not exactly aristocratic Serb families; these families naturally looked on themselves and on their bishop as destined to play an important part in the resistance to and the eventual overthrow of the Turkish dominion. The prince-bishop had to be consecrated by the Patriarch of Pe['c], and in 1700 Patriarch Arsen III consecrated one Daniel, of the house (which has been ever since then and is now still the reigning dynasty of Montenegro) of Petrovi['c]-Njego[)s], to this office, after he had been elected to it by the council of notables at Cetinje. Montenegro, isolated from the Serbs in the north, and precluded from participating with them in the wars between Austria and Turkey by the intervening block of Bosnia, which though Serb by nationality was solidly Mohammedan and therefore pro-Turkish, carried on its feuds with the Turks independently of the other Serbs. But when Peter the Great initiated his anti-Turkish policy, and, in combination with the expansion of Russia to the south and west, began to champion the cause of the Balkan Christians, he developed intercourse with Montenegro and laid the foundation of that friendship between the vast Russian Empire and the tiny Serb principality on the Adriatic which has been a quaint and persistent feature of eastern European politics ever since. This intimacy did not prevent the Turks giving Montenegro many hard blows whenever they had the time or energy to do so, and did not ensure any special protective clauses in favour of the mountain state whenever the various treaties between Russia and Turkey were concluded. Its effect was rather psychological and financial. From the time when the *Vladika* (= Bishop) Daniel first visited Peter the Great, in 1714, the rulers of Montenegro often made pilgrimages to the Russian capital, and were always sure of finding sympathy as well as pecuniary if not armed support. Bishops in the Orthodox Church are compulsorily celibate, and the succession in Montenegro always descended from uncle to nephew. When Peter I Petrovi['c]-Njego[)s] succeeded, in 1782, the Patriarchate of Pe['c] was no more, so he had to get permission from the Austrian Emperor Joseph II to be consecrated by the Metropolitan of Karlovci (Carlowitz), who was then head of the Serbian national Church.

95

About the same time (1787) an alliance was made between Russia and Austria-Hungary to make war together on Turkey and divide the spoils between them. Although a great rising against Turkey was organised at the same time (1788) in the district of [)S]umadija, in Serbia, by a number of Serb patriots, of whom Kara-George was one and a certain Captain Ko[)c]a, after whom the whole war is called Ko[)c]ina Krajina (=Ko[)c]a's country), another, yet the Austrians were on the whole unsuccessful, and on the death of Joseph II, in 1790, a peace was concluded between Austria and Turkey at Svishtov, in Bulgaria, by which Turkey retained the whole of Bosnia and Serbia, and the Save and Danube remained the frontier between the two countries. Meanwhile the Serbs of Montenegro had joined in the fray and had fared better, inflicting some unpleasant defeats on the Turks under their bishop, Peter I. These culminated in two battles in 1796 (the Montenegrins, not being mentioned in the treaty of peace, had continued fighting), in which the Turks were driven back to Scutari. With this triumph, which the Emperor Paul of Russia signalized by decorating the Prince-Bishop Peter, the independence of the modern state of Montenegro, the first Serb people to recover its liberty, was *de facto* established.

17.
The Liberation of Serbia under Kara-George (1804-13) *and Milo[)s] Obrenovi['c]* (1815-30): 1796-1830

The liberation of Serbia from the Turkish dominion and its establishment as an independent state were matters of much slower and more arduous accomplishment than were the same processes in the other Balkan countries. One reason for this was that Serbia by its peculiar geographical position was cut off from outside help. It was easy for the western powers to help Greece with their fleets, and for Russia to help

96

Rumania and, later, Bulgaria directly with its army, because communication between them was easy. But Serbia on the one hand was separated from the sea, first by Dalmatia, which was always in foreign possession, and then by Bosnia, Hercegovina, and the *sandjak* (or province) of Novi-Pazar, all of which territories, though ethnically Serb, were strongholds of Turkish influence owing to their large Mohammedan population. The energies of Montenegro, also cut off from the sea by Dalmatia and Turkey, were absorbed in self-defence, though it gave Serbia all the support which its size permitted. Communication, on the other hand, between Russia and Serbia was too difficult to permit of military help being rapidly and effectively brought to bear upon the Turks from that quarter. Bessarabia, Wallachia, and Moldavia were then still under Turkish control, and either they had to be traversed or the Danube had to be navigated from its mouth upwards through Turkish territory. The only country which could have helped Serbia was Austria, but as it was against their best interests to do so, the Austrians naturally did all they could not to advance, but to retard the Serbian cause. As a result of all this Serbia, in her long struggle against the Turks, had to rely principally on its own resources, though Russian diplomacy several times saved the renascent country from disaster.

Another reason for the slowness of the emancipation and development of modern Serbia has been the proneness of its people to internal dissension. There was no national dynasty on whom the leadership of the country would naturally devolve after the first successful revolution against Turkish rule, there was not even any aristocracy left, and no foreign ruler was ever asked for by the Serbs or was ever imposed on them by the other nations as in the case of Greece, Rumania, and Bulgaria. On the other hand the rising against Turkey was a rising of the whole people, and it was almost inevitable that as soon as some measure of independence was gained the unity the Serbs had shown when fighting against their oppressors should dissolve and be replaced by bitter rivalries and disputes amongst the various local leaders who had become prominent during the rebellion.

These rivalries early in the nineteenth century resolved themselves into a blood-feud between two families, the Karagjorgjevi['c] and the Obrenovi['c], a quarrel that filled Serbian history and militated against the progress of the Serb people throughout the nineteenth century.

The same reasons which restricted the growth of the political independence of Serbia have also impeded, or rather made impossible, its economic development and material prosperity. Until recent years Austria-Hungary and Turkey between them held Serbia territorially in such a position that whenever Serbia either demurred at its neighbours' tariffs or wished to retaliate by means of its own, the screw was immediately applied and economic strangulation threatened. Rumania and Bulgaria economically could never be of help to Serbia, because the products and the requirements of all three are identical, and Rumania and Bulgaria cannot be expected to facilitate the sale of their neighbours' live stock and cereals, when their first business is to sell their own, while the cost of transit of imports from western Europe through those countries is prohibitive.

After the unsuccessful rebellion of 1788, already mentioned, Serbia remained in a state of pseudo-quiescence for some years. Meanwhile the authority of the Sultan in Serbia was growing ever weaker and the real power was wielded by local Turkish officials, who exploited the country, looked on it as their own property, and enjoyed semi-independence. Their exactions and cruelties were worse than had been those of the Turks in the old days, and it was against them and their troops, not against those of the Sultan, that the first battles in the Serbian war of independence were fought. It was during the year 1803 that the Serbian leaders first made definite plans for the rising which eventually took place in the following year. The ringleader was George Petrovi['c], known as Black George, or Kara-George, and amongst his confederates was Milo[)s] Obrenovi['c]. The centre of the conspiracy was at Topola, in the district of [)S]umadija in central Serbia (between the Morava and the Drina rivers), the native place of Kara-George. The first two years of fighting between the Serbians and, first, the provincial janissaries, and, later, the Sultan's forces, fully rewarded the bravery and energy of the insurgents. By the beginning of 1807 they had virtually freed all northern Serbia by their own unaided efforts and captured the towns of Po[)z]arevac, Smederevo, Belgrade, and [)S]abac. The year 1804 is also notable as the date of the formal opening of diplomatic relations directly between Serbia and Russia. At this time the Emperor Alexander I was too preoccupied with Napoleon to be able to threaten the Sultan (Austerlitz took place in November 1805), but he gave the Serbs financial assistance and commended their cause to the especial care of his ambassador at Constantinople.

In 1807 war again broke out between Russia and Turkey, but after the Peace of Tilsit (June 1807) fighting ceased also between the Turks and the Russians and the Serbs, not before the Russians had won several successes against the Turks on the Lower Danube. It was during the two following years of peace that dissensions first broke out amongst the Serbian leaders; fighting the Turks was the sole condition of existence which prevented them fighting each other. In 1809-10 Russia and the Serbs again fought the Turks, at first without success, but later with better fortune. In 1811 Kara-George was elected *Gospodar*, or sovereign, by a popular assembly, but Serbia still remained a Turkish province. At the end of that year the Russians completely defeated the Turks at Rustchuk in Bulgaria, and, if all had gone well, Serbia might there and then have achieved complete independence.

But Napoleon was already preparing his invasion and Russia had to conclude peace with Turkey in a hurry, which necessarily implied that the Sultan obtained unduly favourable terms. In the Treaty of Bucarest between the two countries signed in May 1812, the Serbs were indeed mentioned, and promised vague internal autonomy and a general amnesty, but all the fortified towns they had captured were to be returned to the Turks, and the few Russian troops who had been helping the Serbs in

Serbia had to withdraw. Negotiations between the Turks and the Serbs for the regulation of their position were continued throughout 1812, but finally the Turks refused all their claims and conditions and, seeing the European powers preoccupied with their own affairs, invaded the country from Bosnia in the west, and also from the east and south, in August 1813. The Serbs, left entirely to their own resources, succumbed before the superior forces of the Turks, and by the beginning of October the latter were again masters of the whole country and in possession of Belgrade. Meanwhile Kara-George, broken in health and unable to cope with the difficulties of the situation, which demanded successful strategy both against the overwhelming forces of the Turks in the field and against the intrigues of his enemies at home, somewhat ignominiously fled across the river to Semlin in Hungary, and was duly incarcerated by the Austrian authorities.

The news of Napoleon's defeat at Leipsic (October 1813) arrived just after that of the re-occupation of Belgrade by the Turks, damped *feu-de-joie* which they were firing at Constantinople, and made them rather more conciliatory and lenient to the Serbian rebels. But this attitude did not last long, and the Serbs soon had reason to make fresh efforts to regain their short-lived liberty. The Congress of Vienna met in the autumn of 1814, and during its whole course Serbian emissaries gave the Russian envoys no peace. But with the return of Napoleon to France in the spring of 1815 and the break-up of the Congress, all that Russia could do was, through its ambassador at Constantinople, to threaten invasion unless the Turks left the Serbs alone. Nevertheless, conditions in Serbia became so intolerable that another rebellion soon took shape, this time under Milo[]s] Obrenovi['c]. This leader was no less patriotic than his rival, Kara-George, but he was far more able and a consummate diplomat. Kara-George had possessed indomitable courage, energy, and will-power, but he could not temporize, and his arbitrary methods of enforcing discipline and his ungovernable temper had made him many enemies. While the credit for the first Serbian revolt (1804-13) undoubtedly belongs chiefly to him, the second revolt owed its more lasting success to the skill of Milo[)s] Obrenovi['c]. The fighting started at Takovo, the home of the Obrenovi['c] family, in April 1815, and after many astonishing successes against the Turks, including the capture of the towns of Rudnik, [)C]a[)c]ak, Po[)z]arevac, and Kraljevo, was all over by July of the same year. The Turks were ready with large armies in the west in Bosnia, and also south of the Morava river, to continue the campaign and crush the rebellion, but the news of the final defeat of Napoleon, and the knowledge that Russia would soon have time again to devote attention to the Balkans, withheld their appetites for revenge, and negotiations with the successful rebels were initiated. During the whole of this period, from 1813 onwards, Milo[)s] Obrenovi['c], as head of a district, was an official of the Sultan in Serbia, and it was one of his principles never to break irreparably with the Turks, who were still suzerains of the country. At the same time, owing to his skill and initiative he was recognized as the only real leader of the movement for independence. From the cessation of the rebellion in 1815 onwards he himself personally conducted negotiations in the name of his people with the various pashas who were deputed to deal with him. While these negotiations went on and the armistice was in force, he was confronted, or rather harassed from behind, by a series of revolts against his growing authority on the part of his jealous compatriots.

In June 1817 Kara-George, who had been in Russia after being released by the Austrians in 1814, returned surreptitiously to Serbia, encouraged by the brighter aspect which affairs in his country seemed to be assuming. But the return of his most dangerous rival was as unwelcome to Milo[)s] as it was to the Turkish authorities at Belgrade, and, measures having been concerted between them, Kara-George was murdered on July 26,1817, and the first act in the blood-feud between the two families thus committed. In November of the same year a *skup[)s]tina*, or national assembly, was held at Belgrade, and Milo[)s] Obrenovi['c], whose position was already thoroughly assured, was elected hereditary prince *(knez)* of the country.

Meanwhile events of considerable importance for the future of the Serb race had been happening elsewhere. Dalmatia, the whole of which had been in the possession of Venice since the Treaty of Carlowitz in 1699, passed into the hands of Austria by the Treaty of Campo Formio in 1797, when the Venetian republic was extinguished by Napoleon. The Bocche di Cuttaro, a harbour both strategically and commercially of immense value, which had in the old days belonged to the Serb principality of Zeta or Montenegro, and is its only natural outlet on the Adriatic, likewise became Venetian in 1699 and Austrian in 1797, one year after the successful rebellion of the Montenegrins against the Turks.

By the Treaty of Pressburg between France and Austria Dalmatia became French in 1805. But the Montenegrins, supported by the Russians, resisted the new owners and occupied the Bocche; at the Peace of Tilsit in 1807, however, this important place was assigned to France by Russia, and Montenegro had to submit to its loss. In 1806 the French occupied Ragusa, and in 1808 abolished the independence of the ancient Serb city-republic. In 1812 the Montenegrins, helped by the Russians and British, again expelled the French and reoccupied Cattaro; but Austria was by now fully alive to the meaning this harbour would have once it was in the possession of Montenegro, and after the Congress of Vienna in 1815 took definitive possession of it as well as of all the rest of Dalmatia, thus effecting the complete exclusion of the Serb race for all political and commercial purposes from the Adriatic, its most natural and obvious means of communication with western Europe.

Though Milo[)s] had been elected prince by his own people, it was long before he was recognized as such by the Porte. His efforts for the regularization of his position entailed endless negotiations in Constantinople; these were enlivened by frequent anti-Obrenovi['c] revolts in Serbia, all of which Milo[)s] successfully quelled. The revolution in Greece in 1821 threw the Serbian question from the international point of view into the shade, but the Emperor Nicholas I, who succeeded his brother Alexander I on the Russian throne in 1825, soon showed that he took a lively and active interest in Balkan affairs. Pan-Slavism had scarcely become fashionable in those days, and it was still rather as the protector of its co-religionists under the Crescent that Russia intervened. In 1826 Russian and Turkish delegates met at Akerman in Bessarabia, and in September of that year signed a convention by which the Russian protectorate over the Serbs was recognized, the Serbs were granted internal autonomy, the right to trade and erect churches, schools, and printing-presses, and the Turks were forbidden to live in Serbia except in eight garrison towns; the garrisons were to be Turkish, and tribute was still to be paid to the Sultan as suzerain. These concessions, announced by Prince Milo[)s] to his people at a special *skup[)s]tina* held at Kragujevac in 1827, evoked great enthusiasm, but the urgency of the Greek question again delayed their fulfilment. After the battle of Navarino on October 20, 1827, in which the British, French, and Russian fleets defeated the Turkish, the Turks became obstinate and refused to carry out the stipulations of the Convention of Akerman in favour of Serbia. Thereupon Russia declared war on Turkey in April 1828, and the Russian armies crossed the Danube and the Balkans and marched on Constantinople.

Peace was concluded at Adrianople in 1829, and Turkey agreed to carry out immediately all the stipulations of the Treaty of Bucarest (1812) and the Convention of Akerman (1826). The details took some time to settle, but in November 1830 the *hatti-sherif* of the Sultan, acknowledging Milo[)s] as hereditary prince of Serbia, was publicly read in Belgrade. All the concessions already promised were duly granted, and Serbia became virtually independent, but still tributary to the Sultan. Its territory included most of the northern part of the modern kingdom of Serbia, between the rivers Drina, Save, Danube, and Timok, but not the districts of Nish, Vranja, and Pirot. Turkey still retained Bosnia and Hercegovina, Macedonia, the *sandjak* of Novi-Pazar, which separated Serbia from Montenegro, and Old Serbia (northern Macedonia).

18.

The Throes of Regeneration: Independent Serbia,
1830-1903

During his rule of Serbia, which lasted virtually from 1817 till 1839, Prince Milo[)s] did a very great deal for the welfare of his country. He emancipated the Serbian Church from the trammels of the Greek Patriarchate of Constantinople in 1831, from which date onwards it was ruled by a Metropolitan of Serb nationality, resident at Belgrade. He encouraged the trade of the country, a great deal of which he held in his own hands; he was in fact a sort of prototype of those modern Balkan business-kings of whom King George of Greece and King Carol of Rumania were the most notable examples. He raised an army and put it on a permanent footing, and organized the construction of roads, schools, and churches. He was, however, an autocratic ruler of the old school, and he had no inclination to share the power for the attainment of which he had laboured so many years and gone through so much. From his definite installation as hereditary prince discontent at his arbitrary methods of government amongst his ex-equals increased, and after several revolts he was forced eventually to grant a constitution in 1835. This, however, remained a dead letter, and things went on as before. Later in the same year he paid a prolonged visit to his suzerain at Constantinople, and while he was there the situation in Serbia became still more serious. After his return he was, after several years of delay and of growing unpopularity, compelled to agree to another constitution which was forced on him, paradoxically enough, by the joint efforts of the Tsar and of the Sultan, who seemed to take an unnatural pleasure in supporting the democratic Serbians against their successful colleague in autocracy, who had done so much for his turbulent subjects. Serbia even in those days was essentially and uncompromisingly democratic, but even so Milo[)s] obstinately refused to carry out the provisions of the constitution or in any way to submit to a curtailment of his power, and in 1839 he left his ungrateful principality and took refuge in Rumania, where he possessed an estate, abdicating in favour of his elder son Milan. This Prince Milan, known as Obrenovi['c] II, was seriously ill at the time of his accession, and died within a month of it. He was succeeded by his younger brother Michael, known as Obrenovi['c] III, who was then only sixteen years of age. This prince, though young, had a good head on his shoulders, and eventually proved the most gifted ruler modern Serbia has ever had. His first reign (1840-2), however, did not open well. He inaugurated it by paying a state visit to Constantinople, but the Sultan only recognized him as elective prince and insisted on his having two advisers approved and appointed by the Porte. Michael on his return showed his determination to have nothing to do with them, but this led to a rebellion headed by one of them, Vu[)c]i['c], and, though Michael's rule was not as arbitrary as his father's, he had to bow to the popular will which supported Vu[)c]i['c] and cross the river to Semlin. After a stormy interval, during which the Emperor Nicholas I tried to intervene in favour of Michael, Alexander Karagjorgjevi['c], son of Kara-George, was elected prince (1843). No sooner was this representative of the rival dynasty installed, however, than rebellions in favour of Michael occurred. These were thrown into the shade by the events of 1848, In that memorable year of revolutions the Magyars rose against Austria and the Serbs in southern Hungary rose against the Magyars. Prince Alexander resolved to send military help to his oppressed countrymen north of the Save and Danube, and, though the insurgents were unsuccessful, Prince Alexander gained in popularity amongst the Serbs by the line of action he had taken. During the Crimean War, on the other hand, Serbia remained strictly neutral, to the annoyance of the Tsar; at the Congress of Paris (1856) the exclusive protectorate of Russia was replaced by one of all the powers, and Russian influence in the western Balkans was thereby weakened. Prince Alexander's prudence, moreover, cost him his popularity, and in 1858 he in his turn had to bid farewell to his difficult countrymen.

In December of the same year the veteran Prince Milo['s] Obrenovi['c] I was recalled to power as hereditary prince. His activities during his second reign were directed against Turkish influence, which was still strong, and he made efforts to have the Turkish populations removed from the eight garrison towns, including Belgrade, where they still lived in spite of the fact that their emigration had been stipulated for in 1830. Unfortunately he did not live long enough to carry out his plans, for he fell ill at Topchider, the summer palace near Belgrade, in the autumn of 1860, and died a few days afterwards. He was again succeeded by his son Michael Obrenovi['c] III, who was already thirty-six years of age. This able prince's second reign was brilliantly successful, and it was a disaster for which his foolish countrymen had to pay dearly, when, by their fault, it was prematurely cut short in 1868. His first act was with the consent of a specially summoned *skup[)s]tina* to abolish the law by which he could only appoint and remove his counsellors with the approval of the Porte. Next he set about the organization and establishment of a regular army of 30,000 men. In 1862 an anti-Turkish rebellion broke out amongst the Serbs in Hercegovina (still, with Bosnia, a Turkish province), and the Porte, accusing Prince Michael of complicity, made warlike preparations against him.

Events, however, were precipitated in such a way that, without waiting for the opening of hostilities, the Turkish general in command of the fortress of Belgrade turned his guns on the city; this provoked the intervention of the powers at Constantinople, and the entire civilian Turkish population had to quit the country (in accordance with the stipulations of 1830), only Turkish garrisons remaining in the fortresses of [)S]abac, Belgrade, Smederevo, and Kladovo, along the northern river frontier, still theoretically the boundary of the Sultan's dominions. After this success Prince Michael continued his military preparations in order to obtain final possession of the fortresses when a suitable occasion should arise. This occurred in 1866, when Austria was engaged in the struggle with Prussia, and the policy of Great Britain became less Turcophil than it had hitherto been. On April 6, 1867, the four fortresses, which had been in Serbian possession from 1804 to 1813, but had since then been garrisoned by the Turks, were delivered over to Serbia and the last Turkish soldier left Serbian soil without a shot having been fired. Though Serbia after this was still a vassal state, being tributary to the Sultan, these further steps on the road to complete independence were a great triumph, especially for Prince Michael personally. But this very triumph actuated his political opponents amongst his own countrymen, amongst whom were undoubtedly adherents of the rival dynasty, to revenge, and blind to the interests of their people they foolishly and most brutally murdered this extremely capable and conscientious prince in the deer park near Topchider on June 10, 1868. The opponents of the Obrenovi['c] dynasty were, however, baulked in their plans, and a cousin of the late prince was elected to the vacant and difficult position. This ruler, known as Milan Obrenovi['c] IV, who was only fourteen years of age at the time of his accession (1868), was of a very different character from his predecessor. The first thing that happened during his minority was the substitution of the constitution of 1838 by another one which was meant to give the prince and the national assembly much more power, but which, eventually, made the ministers supreme.

The prince came of age in 1872 when he was eighteen, and he soon showed that the potential pleasures to be derived from his position were far more attractive to him than the fulfilment of its obvious duties. He found much to occupy him in Vienna and Paris and but little in Belgrade. At the same time the Serb people had lost, largely by its own faults, much of the respect and sympathy which it had acquired in Europe during Prince Michael's reign. In 1875 a formidable anti-Turkish insurrection (the last of many) broke out amongst the Serbs of Bosnia and Hercegovina, and all the efforts of the Turks to quell it were unavailing. In June 1876 Prince Milan was forced by the pressure of public opinion to declare war on

Turkey in support of the 'unredeemed' Serbs of Bosnia, and Serbia was joined by Montenegro. The country was, however, not materially prepared for war, the expected sympathetic risings in other parts of Turkey either did not take place or failed, and the Turks turned their whole army on to Serbia, with the result that in October the Serbs had to appeal to the Tsar for help and an armistice was arranged, which lasted till February 1877. During the winter a conference was held in Constantinople to devise means for alleviating the lot of the Christians in Turkey, and a peace was arranged between Turkey and Serbia whereby the *status quo ante* was restored. But after the conference the heart of Turkey was again hardened and the stipulations in favour of the Christians were not carried out.

In 1877 Russia declared war on Turkey (cf. chap. 10), and in the autumn of the same year Serbia joined in. This time the armies of Prince Milan were more successful, and conquered and occupied the whole of southern Serbia including the towns and districts of Nish, Pirot, Vranja, and Leskovac, Montenegro, which had not been included in the peace of the previous winter, but had been fighting desperately and continuously against the Turks ever since it had begun actively to help the Serb rebels of Hercegovina in 1875, had a series of successes, as a result of which it obtained possession of the important localities of Nik['s]i['c], Podgorica, Budua, Antivari, and Dulcigno, the last three on the shore of the Adriatic. By the Treaty of San Stefano the future interests of both Serbia and Montenegro were jeopardised by the creation of a Great Bulgaria, but that would not have mattered if in return they had been given control of the purely Serb provinces of Bosnia and Hercegovina, which ethnically they can claim just as legitimately as Bulgaria claims most of Macedonia. The Treaty of San Stefano was, however, soon replaced by that of Berlin. By its terms both Serbia and Montenegro achieved complete independence and the former ceased to be a tributary state of Turkey. The Serbs were given the districts of southern Serbia which they had occupied, and which are all ethnically Serb except Pirot, the population of which is a sort of cross between Serb and Bulgar.

The Serbs also undertook to build a railway through their country to the Turkish and Bulgarian frontiers. Montenegro was nearly doubled in size, receiving the districts of Nik['s]i['c], Podgorica, and others; certain places in the interior the Turks and Albanians absolutely refused to surrender, and to compensate for these Montenegro was given a strip of coast with the townlets of Antivari and Dulcigno. The memory of Gladstone, who specially espoused Montenegro's cause in this matter, is held in the greatest reverence in the brave little mountain country, but unfortunately the ports themselves are economically absolutely useless. Budua, higher up the Dalmatian coast, which would have been of some use, was handed over to Austria, to which country, already possessed of Cattaro and all the rest of Dalmatia, it was quite superfluous. Greatest tragedy of all for the future of the Serb race, the administration of Bosnia and Hercegovina was handed over 'temporarily' to Austria-Hungary, and Austrian garrisons were quartered throughout those two provinces, which they were able to occupy only after the most bitter armed opposition on the part of the inhabitants, and also in the Turkish *sandjak* or province of Novi-Pazar, the ancient Raska and cradle of the Serb state; this strip of mountainous territory under Turkish administrative and Austrian military control was thus converted into a fortified wedge which effectually kept the two independent Serb states of Serbia and Montenegro apart. After all these events the Serbs had to set to work to put their enlarged house in order. But the building of railways and schools and the organization of the services cost a lot of money, and as public economy is not a Serbian virtue the debt grew rapidly. In 1882 Serbia proclaimed itself a kingdom and was duly recognized by the other nations. But King Milan did not learn to manage the affairs of his country any better as time went on. He was too weak to stand alone, and having freed himself from Turkey he threw himself into the arms of Austria, with which country he concluded a secret military convention. In 1885, when Bulgaria and 'Eastern Rumelia' successfully coalesced and Bulgaria thereby received a considerable increase of territory and power, the Serbs, prompted by jealousy, began to grow restless, and King Milan, at the instigation of Austria, foolishly declared war on Prince Alexander of Battenberg. This speedily ended in the disastrous battle of Slivnitsa (cf. chap. II); Austria had to intervene to save its victim, and Serbia got nothing for its trouble but a large increase of debt and a considerable decrease of military reputation. In addition to all this King Milan was unfortunate in his conjugal relations; his wife, the beautiful Queen Natalie, was a Russian, and as he himself had Austrian sympathies, they could scarcely be expected to agree on politics. But the strife between them extended from the sphere of international to that of personal sympathies and antipathies. King Milan was promiscuous in affairs of the heart and Queen Natalie was jealous. Scenes of domestic discord were frequent and violent, and the effect of this atmosphere on the character of their only child Alexander, who was born in 1876, was naturally bad.

The king, who had for some years been very popular with, his subjects with all his failings, lost his hold on the country after the unfortunate war of 1885, and the partisans of the rival dynasty began to be hopeful once more. In 1888 King Milan gave Serbia a very much more liberal constitution, by which the ministers were for the first time made really responsible to the *skup[)s]tina* or national assembly, replacing that of 1869, and the following year, worried by his political and domestic failures, discredited and unpopular both at home and abroad, he resigned in favour of his son Alexander, then aged thirteen. This boy, who had been brought up in what may be called a permanent storm-centre, both domestic and political, was placed under a regency, which included M. Risti['c], with a radical ministry under M. Pa[)s]i['c], an extremely able and patriotic statesman of pro-Russian sympathies, who ever since he first became prominent in 1877 had been growing in power and influence. But trouble did not cease with the abdication of King Milan. He and his wife played Box and Cox at Belgrade for the next four years, quarrelling and being reconciled, intriguing and fighting round the throne and person of their son. At last both parents agreed to leave the country and give the unfortunate youth a chance. King Milan settled in Vienna, Queen Natalie in Biarritz. In 1893 King Alexander suddenly declared himself of age and arrested all his ministers and regents one evening while they were dining with him. The next year he abrogated the constitution of 1888, under which party warfare in the Serbian parliament had been bitter and uninterrupted, obstructing any real progress, and restored that of 1869. Ever since 1889 (the date of the accession of the German Emperor) Berlin had taken more interest in Serbian affairs, and it has been alleged that it was William II who, through the wife of the Rumanian minister at his court, who was sister of Queen Natalie, influenced King Alexander in his abrupt and ill-judged decisions. It was certainly German policy to weaken and discredit Serbia and to further Austrian influence at Belgrade at the expense of that of Russia. King Milan returned for a time to Belgrade in 1897, and the reaction, favourable to Austria, which had begun in 1894, increased during his presence and under the ministry of Dr. Vladan Gjorgjevi['c], which lasted from 1897 till 1900. This state of repression caused unrest throughout the country. All its energies were absorbed in fruitless political party strife, and no material or moral progress was possible. King Alexander, distracted, solitary, and helpless in the midst of this unending welter of political intrigue, committed an extremely imprudent act in the summer of 1900. Having gone for much-needed relaxation to see his mother at Biarritz, he fell violently in love with her lady in waiting, Madame Draga Ma[)s]in, the divorced wife of a Serbian officer. Her somewhat equivocal past was in King Alexander's eyes quite eclipsed by her great beauty and her wit, which had not been impaired by conjugal infelicity. Although she was thirty-two, and he only twenty-four, he determined to marry her, and the desperate opposition of his parents, his army, his ministers, and his people, based principally on the fact that the woman was known to be incapable of child-birth, only precipitated the accomplishment of his intention. This unfortunate and headstrong action on the part of the young king, who, though deficient in tact and intuition, had plenty of energy and was by no means stupid, might have

111

been forgiven him by his people if, as was at first thought possible, it had restored internal peace and prosperity in the country and thereby enabled it to prepare itself to take a part in the solution oL those foreign questions which vitally affected Serb interests and were already looming on the horizon. But it did not. In 1901 King Alexander granted another constitution and for a time attempted to work with a coalition ministry; but this failed, and a term of reaction with pro-Austrian tendencies, which were favoured by the king and queen, set in. This reaction, combined with the growing disorganization of the finances and the general sense of the discredit and failure which the follies of its rulers had during the last thirty years brought on the country; completely undermined the position of the dynasty and made a catastrophe inevitable. This occurred, as is well known, on June 10, 1903, when, as the result of a military conspiracy, King Alexander, the last of the Obrenovi['c] dynasty, his wife, and her male relatives were murdered. This crime was purely political, and it is absurd to gloss it over or to explain it merely as the result of the family feud between the two dynasties. That came to an end in 1868, when the murder of Kara-George in 1817 by the agency of Milo[)]s] Obrenovi['c] was avenged by the lunatic assassination of the brilliant Prince Michael Obrenovi['c] III. It is no exaggeration to say that, from the point of view of the Serbian patriot, the only salvation of his country in 1903 lay in getting rid of the Obrenovi['c] dynasty, which had become pro-Austrian, had no longer the great gifts possessed by its earlier members, and undoubtedly by its vagaries hindered the progress of Serbia both in internal and external politics. The assassination was unfortunately carried out with unnecessary cruelty, and it is this fact that made such a bad impression and for so long militated against Serbia in western Europe; but it must be remembered that civilization in the Balkans, where political murder, far from being a product of the five hundred years of Turkish dominion, has always been endemic, is not on the same level in many respects as it is in the rest of Europe. Life is one of the commodities which are still cheap in backward countries.

Although King Alexander and his wife can in no sense be said to have deserved the awful fate that befell them, it is equally true that had any other course been adopted, such as deposition and exile, the wire-pulling and intriguing from outside, which had already done the country so much harm, would have become infinitely worse. Even so, it was long before things in any sense settled down. As for the alleged complicity of the rival dynasty in the crime, it is well established that that did not exist. It was no secret to anybody interested in Serbian affairs that something catastrophic was about to happen, and when the tragedy occurred it was natural to appeal to the alternative native dynasty to step into the breach. But the head of that dynasty was in no way responsible for the plot, still less for the manner in which it was carried out, and it was only after much natural hesitation and in the face of his strong disinclination that Prince Peter Karagjorgjevi['c] was induced to accept the by no means enviable, easy, or profitable task of guiding Serbia's destiny. The Serbian throne in 1903 was a source neither of glory nor of riches, and it was notoriously no sinecure.

After the tragedy, the democratic constitution of 1888 was first of all restored, and then Prince Peter Karagjorgjevi['c], grandson of Kara-George, the leader of the first Serbian insurrection of 1804-13, who was at that time fifty-nine years of age, was unanimously elected king. He had married in 1883 a daughter of Prince Nicholas of Montenegro and sister of the future Queen of Italy, but she had been dead already some years at the time of his accession, leaving him with a family of two sons and a daughter.

19.

Serbia, Montenegro, and the Serbo-Croats in Austria-Hungary, 1903-8

It was inevitable that, after the sensation which such an event could not fail to cause in twentieth-century Europe, it should take the country where it occurred some time to live down the results. Other powers, especially those of western Europe, looked coldly on Serbia and were in no hurry to resume diplomatic intercourse, still less to offer diplomatic support. The question of the punishment and exile of the conspirators was almost impossible of solution, and only time was able to obliterate the resentment caused by the whole affair. In Serbia itself a great change took place. The new sovereign, though he laboured under the greatest possible disadvantages, by his irreproachable behaviour, modesty, tact, and strictly constitutional rule, was able to withdraw the court of Belgrade from the trying limelight to which it had become used. The public finances began to be reorganized, commerce began to improve in spite of endless tariff wars with Austria-Hungary, and attention was again diverted from home to foreign politics. With the gradual spread of education and increase of communication, and the growth of national self-consciousness amongst the Serbs and Croats of Austria-Hungary and the two independent Serb states, a new movement for the closer intercourse amongst the various branches of the Serb race for south Slav unity, as it was called, gradually began to take shape. At the same time a more definitely political agitation started in Serbia, largely inspired by the humiliating position of economic bondage in which the country was held by Austria-Hungary, and was roughly justified by the indisputable argument: 'Serbia must expand or die.' Expansion at the cost of Turkey seemed hopeless, because even the acquisition of Macedonia would give Serbia a large alien population and no maritime outlet. It was towards the Adriatic that the gaze of the

Serbs was directed, to the coast which was ethnically Serbian and could legitimately be considered a heritage of the Serb race.

Macedonia was also taken into account, schools and armed bands began their educative activity amongst those inhabitants of the unhappy province who were Serb, or who lived in places where Serbs had lived, or who with sufficient persuasion could be induced to call themselves Serb; but the principal stream of propaganda was directed westwards into Bosnia and Hercegovina. The antagonism between Christian and Mohammedan, Serb and Turk, was never so bitter as between Christian and Christian, Serb and German or Magyar, and the Serbs were clever enough to see that Bosnia and Hercegovina, from every point of view, was to them worth ten Macedonias, though it would he ten times more difficult to obtain. Bosnia and Hercegovina, though containing three confessions, were ethnically homogeneous, and it was realised that these two provinces were as important to Serbia and Montenegro as the rest of Italy had been to Piedmont.

It must at this time be recalled in what an extraordinary way the Serb race had fortuitously been broken up into a number of quite arbitrary political divisions. Dalmatia (three per cent. of the population of which is Italian and all the rest Serb or Croat, preponderatingly Serb and Orthodox in the south and preponderating Croat or Roman Catholic in the north) was a province of Austria and sent deputies to the Reichsrath at Vienna; at the same time it was territorially isolated from Austria and had no direct railway connexion with any country except a narrow-gauge line into Bosnia. Croatia and Slavonia, preponderatingly Roman Catholic, were lands of the Hungarian crown, and though they had a provincial pseudo-autonomous diet at Agram, the capital of Croatia, they sent deputies to the Hungarian parliament at Budapest. Thus what had in the Middle Ages been known as the triune kingdom of Croatia, Slavonia, and Dalmatia, with a total Serbo-Croat population of three millions, was divided between Austria and Hungary.

Further, there were about 700,000 Serbs and Croats in the south of Hungary proper, cast and north of the Danube, known as the Banat and Ba[)c]ka, a district which during the eighteenth and early nineteenth centuries was the hearth and home of Serb literature and education, but which later waned in importance in that respect as independent Serbia grew. These Serbs were directly dependent on Budapest, the only autonomy they possessed being ecclesiastical. Bosnia and Hercegovina, still nominally Turkish provinces, with a Slav population of nearly two million (850,000 Orthodox Serbs, 650,000 Mohammedan Serbs, and the rest Roman Catholics), were to all intents and purposes already imperial lands of Austria-Hungary, with a purely military and police administration; the shadow of Turkish sovereignty provided sufficient excuse to the *de facto* owners of these provinces not to grant the inhabitants parliamentary government or even genuine provincial autonomy. The Serbs in Serbia numbered nearly three millions, those in Montenegro about a quarter of a million; while in Turkey, in what was known as Old Serbia (the *sandjak* of Novi-Pasar between Serbia and Montenegro and the vilayet of Korovo), and in parts of northern and central Macedonia, there were scattered another half million. These last, of course, had no voice at all in the management of their own affairs. Those in Montenegro lived under the patriarchal autocracy of Prince Nicholas, who had succeeded his uncle, Prince Danilo, in 1860, at the age of nineteen. Though no other form of government could have turned the barren rocks of Montenegro into fertile pastures, many of the people grew restless with the restricted possibilities of a career which the mountain principality offered them, and in latter years migrated in large numbers to North and South America, whither emigration from Dalmatia and Croatia too had already readied serious proportions. The Serbs in Serbia were the only ones who could claim to be free, but even this was a freedom entirely dependent on the economic malevolence of Austria-Hungary and Turkey. Cut up in this way by the hand of fate into such a number of helpless fragments, it was inevitable that the Serb race, if it possessed

116

any vitality, should attempt, at any cost, to piece some if not all of them together and form an ethnical whole which, economically and politically, should be master of its own destinies. It was equally inevitable that the policy of Austria-Hungary should be to anticipate or definitively render any such attempt impossible, because obviously the formation of a large south Slav state, by cutting off Austria from the Adriatic and eliminating from the dual monarchy all the valuable territory between the Dalmatian coast and the river Drave, would seriously jeopardize its position as a great power; it must be remembered, also, that Austria-Hungary, far from decomposing, as it was commonly assumed was happening, had been enormously increasing in vitality ever since 1878.

The means adopted by the governments of Vienna and Budapest to nullify the plans of Serbian expansion were generally to maintain the political *emiettement* of the Serb race, the isolation of one group from another, the virtually enforced emigration of Slavs on a large scale and their substitution by German colonists, and the encouragement of rivalry and discord between Roman Catholic Croat and Orthodox Serb. No railways were allowed to be built in Dalmatia, communication between Agram and any other parts of the monarchy except Fiume or Budapest was rendered almost impossible; Bosnia and Hercegovina were shut off into a watertight compartment and endowed with a national flag composed of the inspiring colours of brown and buff; it was made impossible for Serbs to visit Montenegro or for Montenegrins to visit Serbia except via Fiume, entailing the bestowal of several pounds on the Hungarian state steamers and railways. As for the *sandjak* of Novi-Pazar, it was turned into a veritable Tibet, and a legend was spread abroad that if any foreigner ventured there he would be surely murdered by Turkish brigands; meanwhile it was full of Viennese ladies giving picnics and dances and tennis parties to the wasp-waisted officers of the Austrian garrison. Bosnia and Hercegovina, on the other hand, became the model touring provinces of Austria-Hungary, and no one can deny that their great natural beauties were made more enjoyable by the construction of railways, roads, and hotels. At the same time this was not a work of pure philanthropy, and the emigration statistics are a good indication of the joy with which the Bosnian peasants paid for an annual influx of admiring tourists. In spite of all these disadvantages, however, the Serbo-Croat provinces of Austria-Hungary could not be deprived of all the benefits of living within a large and prosperous customs union, while being made to pay for all the expenses of the elaborate imperial administration and services; and the spread of education, even under the Hapsburg regime, began to tell in time. Simultaneously with the agitation which emanated from Serbia and was directed towards the advancement, by means of schools and religious and literary propaganda, of Serbian influence in Bosnia and Hercegovina, a movement started in Dalmatia and Croatia for the closer union of those two provinces. About 1906 the two movements found expression in the formation of the Serbo-Croat or Croato-Serb coalition party, composed of those elements in Dalmatia, Croatia, and Slavonia which favoured closer union between the various groups of the Serb race scattered throughout those provinces, as well as in Serbia, Montenegro, Bosnia, Hercegovina, and Turkey. Owing to the circumstances already described, it was impossible for the representatives of the Serb race to voice their aspirations unanimously in any one parliament, and the work of the coalition, except in the provincial diet at Agram, consisted mostly of conducting press campaigns and spreading propaganda throughout those provinces. The most important thing about the coalition was that it buried religious antagonism and put unity of race above difference of belief. In this way it came into conflict with the ultramontane Croat party at Agram, which wished to incorporate Bosnia, Hercegovina, and Dalmatia with Croatia and create a third purely Roman Catholic Slav state in the empire, on a level with Austria and Hungary; also to a lesser extent with the intransigent Serbs of Belgrade, who affected to ignore Croatia and Roman Catholicism, and only dreamed of bringing Bosnia, Hercegovina, and as much of Dalmatia as they could under their own rule; and finally it had to overcome the hostility of the Mohammedan

Serbs of Bosnia, who disliked all Christians equally, could only with the greatest difficulty be persuaded that they were really Serbs and not Turks, and honestly cared for nothing but Islam and Turkish coffee, thus considerably facilitating the germanization of the two provinces. The coalition was wisely inclined to postpone the programme of final political settlement, and aimed immediately at the removal of the material and moral barriers placed between the Serbs of the various provinces of Austria-Hungary, including Bosnia and Hercegovina. If they had been sure of adequate guarantees they would probably have agreed to the inclusion of *all* Serbs and Croats within the monarchy, because the constitution of all Serbs and Croats in an independent state (not necessarily a kingdom) without it implied the then problematic contingencies of a European war and the disruption of Austria-Hungary. Considering the manifold handicaps under which Serbia and its cause suffered, the considerable success which its propaganda met with in Bosnia and Hercegovina and other parts of Austria-Hungary, from 1903 till 1908, is a proof, not only of the energy and earnestness of its promoters and of the vitality of the Serbian people, but also, if any were needed, of the extreme unpopularity of the Hapsburg regime in the southern Slav provinces of the dual monarchy. Serbia had no help from outside. Russia was entangled in the Far East and then in the revolution, and though the new dynasty was approved in St. Petersburg Russian sympathy with Serbia was at that time only lukewarm. Relations with Austria-Hungary were of course always strained; only one single line of railway connected the two countries, and as Austria-Hungary was the only profitable market, for geographical reasons, for Serbian products, Serbia could be brought to its knees at any moment by the commercial closing of the frontier. It was a symbol of the economic vassalage of Serbia and Montenegro that the postage between both of these countries and any part of Austria-Hungary was ten centimes, that for letters between Serbia and Montenegro, which had to make the long detour through Austrian territory, was twenty-five. But though this opened the Serbian markets to Austria, it also incidentally opened Bosnia, when the censor could be circumvented to propaganda by pamphlet and correspondence. Intercourse with western Europe was restricted by distance, and, owing to dynastic reasons, diplomatic relations were altogether suspended for several years between this country and Serbia. The Balkan States Exhibition held in London during the summer of 1907, to encourage trade between Great Britain and the Balkans, was hardly a success. Italy and Serbia had nothing in common. With Montenegro even, despite the fact that King Peter was Prince Nicholas's son-in-law, relations were bad. It was felt in Serbia that Prince Nicholas's autocratic rule acted as a brake on the legitimate development of the national consciousness, and Montenegrin students who visited Belgrade returned to their homes full of wild and unsuitable ideas. However, the revolutionary tendencies, which some of them undoubtedly developed, had no fatal results to the reigning dynasty, which continued as before to enjoy the special favour as well as the financial support of the Russian court, and which, looked on throughout Europe as a picturesque and harmless institution, it would have been dangerous, as it was quite unnecessary, to touch.

Serbia was thus left entirely to its own resources in the great propagandist activity which filled the years 1903 to 1908. The financial means at its disposal were exiguous in the extreme, especially when compared with the enormous sums lavished annually by the Austrian and German governments on their secret political services, so that the efforts of its agents cannot be ascribed to cupidity. Also it must be admitted that the kingdom of Serbia, with its capital Belgrade, thanks to the internal chaos and dynastic scandals of the previous forty years, resulting in superficial dilapidation, intellectual stagnation, and general poverty, lacked the material as well as the moral glamour which a successful Piedmont should possess. Nobody could deny, for instance, that, with all its natural advantages, Belgrade was at first sight not nearly such an attractive centre as Agram or Sarajevo, or that the qualities which the Serbs of Serbia had displayed since their emancipation were hardly such as to command the unstinted confidence and admiration of their as yet unredeemed compatriots. Nevertheless the Serbian propaganda in favour of what was really a Pan-Serb movement met with great success, especially in Bosnia, Hercegovina, and Old Serbia (northern Macedonia).

Simultaneously the work of the Serbo-Croat coalition in Dalmatia, Croatia, and Slavonia made considerable progress in spite of clerical opposition and desperate conflicts with the government at Budapest. Both the one movement and the other naturally evoked great alarm and emotion in the Austrian and Hungarian capitals, as they were seen to be genuinely popular and also potentially, if not actually, separatist in character. In October 1906 Baron Achrenthal succeeded Count Goluchowski as Minister for Foreign Affairs at Vienna, and very soon initiated a more vigorous and incidentally anti-Slav foreign policy than his predecessor. What was now looked on as the Serbian danger had in the eyes of Vienna assumed such proportions that the time for decisive action was considered to have arrived. In January 1908 Baron Achrenthal announced his scheme for a continuation of the Bosnian railway system through the *sandjak* of Novi-Pazar to link up with the Turkish railways in Macedonia. This plan was particularly foolish in conception, because, the Bosnian railways being narrow and the Turkish normal gauge, the line would have been useless for international commerce, while the engineering difficulties were such that the cost of construction would have been prohibitive. But the possibilities which this move indicated, the palpable evidence it contained of the notorious *Drang nach Osten* of the Germanic powers towards Salonika and Constantinople, were quite sufficient to fill the ministries of Europe, and especially those of Russia, with extreme uneasiness. The immediate result of this was that concerted action between Russia and Austria-Hungary in the Balkans was thenceforward impossible, and the Muerzsteg programme, after a short and precarious existence, came to an untimely end (cf. chap. 12). Serbia and Montenegro, face to face with this new danger which threatened permanently to separate their territories, were beside themselves, and immediately parried with the project, hardly more practicable in view of their international credit, of a Danube-Adriatic railway. In July 1908 the nerves of Europe were still further tried by the Young Turk revolution in Constantinople. The imminence of this movement was known to Austro-German diplomacy, and doubtless this knowledge, as well as the fear of the Pan-Serb movement, prompted the Austrian foreign minister to take steps towards the definitive regularization of his country's position in Bosnia and Hercegovina—provinces whose suzerain was still the Sultan of Turkey. The effect of the Young Turk coup in the Balkan States was as any one who visited them at that time can testify, both pathetic and intensely humorous. The permanent chaos of the Turkish empire, and the process of watching for years its gradual but inevitable decomposition, had created amongst the neighbouring states an atmosphere of excited anticipation, which was really the breath of their nostrils; it had stimulated them during the endless Macedonian insurrections to commit the most awful outrages against each other's nationals and then lay the blame at the door of the unfortunate Turk; and if the Turk should really regenerate himself, not only would their occupation be gone, but the heavily-discounted legacies would assuredly elude their grasp. At the same time, since the whole policy of exhibiting and exploiting the horrors of Macedonia, and of organizing guerilla bands and provoking intervention, was based on the refusal of the Turks to grant reforms, as soon as the ultra-liberal constitution of Midhat Pasha, which, had been withdrawn after a brief and unsuccessful run in 1876, was restored by the Young Turks, there was nothing left for the Balkan States to do but to applaud with as much enthusiasm as they could simulate. The emotions experienced by the Balkan peoples during that summer, beneath the smiles which they had to assume, were exhausting even for southern temperaments. Bulgaria, with its characteristic matter-of-factness, was the first to adjust itself to the new and trying situation in which the only certainty was that something decisive had got to be done with all possible celerity. On October 5, 1908, Prince Ferdinand sprang on an astonished continent the news that he renounced the Turkish suzerainty (ever since 1878 the Bulgarian principality had been a tributary and vassal state of the Ottoman Empire, and therefore, with all its astonishingly rapid progress and material prosperity, a subject for commiseration in the kingdoms of Serbia and Greece) and proclaimed the independence of Bulgaria, with himself, as Tsar of the Bulgars, at its head. Europe had not recovered from this shock, still less Belgrade and Athens, when, two days later. Baron Aehrenthal announced the formal annexation of Bosnia and Hercegovina by the Emperor Francis Joseph. Whereas most people had virtually forgotten the Treaty of Berlin and had come to look on Austria as just as permanently settled in these two provinces as was Great Britain in Egypt and Cyprus, yet the formal breach of the stipulations of that treaty on Austria's part, by annexing the provinces without notice to or consultation with the other parties concerned, gave the excuse for a somewhat ridiculous hue and cry on the part of the other powers, and especially on that of Russia. The effect of these blows from right and left on Serbia was literally paralysing. When Belgrade recovered the use of its organs, it started to scream for war and revenue, and initiated an international crisis from which Europe did not recover till the following year. Meanwhile, almost unobserved by the peoples of Serbia and Montenegro, Austria had, in order to reconcile the Turks with the loss of their provinces, good-naturedly, but from the Austrian point of view short-sightedly, withdrawn its garrisons from the *sandjak* of Novi-Pazar, thus evacuating the long-coveted corridor which was the one thing above all else necessary to Serbia and Montenegro for the realization of their plans.

20.

Serbia and Montenegro, and the two Balkan Wars, 1908-13 (cf. Chap, 13)

The winter of 1908-9 marked the lowest ebb of Serbia's fortunes. The successive *coups* and *faits accomplis* carried out by Austria, Turkey, and Bulgaria during 1908 seemed destined to destroy for good the Serbian plans for expansion in any direction whatever, and if these could not be realized then Serbia must die of suffocation. It was also well understood that for all the martial ardour displayed in Belgrade the army was in no condition to take the field any more than was the treasury to bear the cost of a campaign; Russia had not yet recovered from the Japanese War followed by the revolution, and indeed everything pointed to the certainty that if Serbia indulged in hostilities against Austria-Hungary it would perish ignominiously and alone. The worst of it was that neither Serbia nor Montenegro had any legal claim to Bosnia and Hercegovina: they had been deluding themselves with the hope that their ethnical identity with the people of these provinces, supported by the effects of their propaganda, would induce a compassionate and generous Europe at least to insist on their being given a part of the coveted territory, and thus give Serbia access to the coast, when the ambiguous position of these two valuable provinces, still nominally Turkish but already virtually Austrian, came to be finally regularized. As a matter of fact, ever since Bismarck, Gorchakov, and Beaconsfield had put Austria-Hungary in their possession in 1878, no one had seriously thought that the Dual Monarchy would ever voluntarily retire from one inch of the territory which had been conquered and occupied at such cost, and those who noticed it were astonished at the evacuation by it of the *sandjak* of Novi-Pazar. At the same time Baron Achrenthal little foresaw what a hornet's nest he would bring about his ears by the tactless method in which the annexation was carried out. The first effect was to provoke a complete boycott of Austro-Hungarian goods and trading vessels throughout the Ottoman Empire, which was so harmful to the Austrian export trade that in January 1909 Count Achrenthal had to indemnify Turkey with the sum of L2,500,000 for his technically stolen property. Further, the attitude of Russia and Serbia throughout the whole winter remained so provocative and threatening that, although war was generally considered improbable, the Austrian army had to be kept on a war footing, which involved great expense and much popular discontent. The grave external crisis was only solved at the end of March 1909; Germany had had to deliver a veiled ultimatum at St. Petersburg, the result of which was the rescue of Austria-Hungary from an awkward situation by the much-advertised appearance of its faithful ally in shining armour. Simultaneously Serbia had to eat humble pie and declare, with complete absence of truth, that the annexation of Bosnia and Hercegovina had not affected its interests.

Meanwhile the internal complications in the southern Slav provinces of Austria-Hungary were growing formidable. Ever since the summer of 1908 arrests had been going on among the members of the Croato-Serb coalition, who were accused of favouring the subversive Pan-Serb movement. The press of Austria-Hungary magnified the importance of this agitation in order to justify abroad the pressing need for the formal annexation of Bosnia and Hercegovina. The fact was that, though immediate danger to the monarchy as a result of the Pan-Serb agitation was known not to exist, yet in the interests of Austrian foreign policy, the Serbs had to be compromised in the eyes of Europe, the Croato-Serb coalition within the Dual Monarchy had to be destroyed to gratify Budapest in particular, and the religious and political discord between Croat and Serb, on which the foundation of the power of Austria-Hungary, and especially that of Hungary, in the south rested, and which was in a fair way of being eliminated through the efforts of the coalition, had to be revived by some means or other. It is not possible here to go into the details of the notorious Agram high treason trial, which was the outcome

125

of all this. It suffices to say that it was a monstrous travesty of justice which lasted from March till October 1909, and though it resulted in the ostensible destruction of the coalition and the imprisonment of many of its members, it defeated its own ends, as it merely fanned the flame of nationalistic feeling against Vienna and Budapest, and Croatia has ever since had to be governed virtually by martial law. This was followed in December 1909 by the even more famous Friedjung trial. In March 1909 Count Achrenthal had begun in Vienna a violent press campaign against Serbia, accusing the Serbian Government and dynasty of complicity in the concoction of nefarious designs and conspiracies against the integrity of Austria-Hungary. This campaign was thought to be the means of foreshadowing and justifying the immediate military occupation of Serbia. Unfortunately its instigator had not been sufficiently particular as to the choice of his tools and his methods of using them. Among the contributors of the highly tendencious articles was the well-known historian Dr. Friedjung, who made extensive use of documents supplied him by the Vienna Foreign Office. His accusations immediately provoked an action for libel on the part of three leaders of the Croato-Serb coalition who were implicated, in December 1909. The trial, which was highly sensational, resulted in the complete vindication and rehabilitation both of those three Austrian subjects in the eyes of the whole of Austria-Hungary and of the Belgrade Foreign Office in those of Europe; the documents on which the charges were based were proven to be partly forgeries, partly falsified, and partly stolen by various disreputable secret political agents of the Austrian Foreign Office, and one of the principal Serbian 'conspirators', a professor of Belgrade University, proved that he was in Berlin at the time when he had been accused of presiding over a revolutionary meeting at Belgrade. But it also resulted in the latter discrediting of Count Achrenthal as a diplomat and of the methods by which he conducted the business of the Austrian Foreign Office, and involved his country in the expenditure of countless millions which it could ill afford.

There never was any doubt that a subversive agitation had been going on, and that it emanated in part from Serbia, but the Serbian Foreign Office, under the able management of Dr. Milovanovi['c] and Dr. Spalajkovi['c] (one of the principal witnesses at the Friedjung trial), was far too clever to allow any of its members, or indeed any responsible person in Serbia, to be concerned in it, and the brilliant way in which the clumsy and foolish charges were refuted redounded greatly to the credit of the Serbian Government. Count Achrenthal had overreached himself, and moreover the wind had already been taken out of his sails by the public recantation on Serbia's part of its pretensions to Bosnia, which, as already mentioned, took place at the end of March 1909, and by the simultaneous termination of the international crisis marked by Russia's acquiescence in the *fait accompli* of the annexation. At the same time the Serbian Crown Prince George, King Peter's elder son, who had been the leader of the chauvinist war-party in Serbia, and was somewhat theatrical in demeanour and irresponsible in character, renounced his rights of succession in favour of his younger brother Prince Alexander, a much steadier and more talented young man. It is certain that when he realized how things were going to develop Count Achrenthal tried to hush up the whole incident, but it was too late, and Dr. Friedjung insisted on doing what he could to save his reputation as a historian. In the end he was made the principal scapegoat, though the press of Vienna voiced its opinion of the Austrian Foreign Office in no measured tones, saying, amongst other things, that if the conductors of its diplomacy must use forgeries, they might at any rate secure good ones. Eventually a compromise was arranged, after the defendant had clearly lost his case, owing to pressure being brought to bear from outside, and the Serbian Government refrained from carrying out its threat of having the whole question threshed out before the Hague Tribunal.

The cumulative effect of all these exciting and trying experiences was the growth of a distinctly more sympathetic feeling towards Serbia in Europe at large, and especially a rallying of all the elements throughout the Serb and Croat provinces of Austria-Hungary, except the extreme clericals of Agram, to the Serbian cause; briefly, the effect was the exact opposite of that desired by Vienna and Budapest. Meanwhile events had been happening elsewhere which revived the drooping interest and flagging hopes of Serbia in the development of foreign affairs. The attainment of power by the Young Turks and the introduction of parliamentary government had brought no improvement to the internal condition of the Ottoman Empire, and the Balkan peoples made no effort to conceal their satisfaction at the failure of the revolution to bring about reform by magic. The counter-revolution of April 1909 and the accession of the Sultan Mohammed V made things no better. In Macedonia, and especially in Albania, they had been going from bad to worse. The introduction of universal military service and obligatory payment of taxes caused a revolution in Albania, where such innovations were not at all appreciated. From 1909 till 1911 there was a state of perpetual warfare in Albania, with which the Young Turks, in spite of cruel reprisals, were unable to cope, until, in the summer of that year, Austria threatened to intervene unless order were restored; some sort of settlement was patched up, and an amnesty was granted to the rebels by the new Sultan. This unfortunate man, after being rendered almost half-witted by having been for the greater part of his life kept a prisoner by his brother the tyrant Abdul Hamid, was now the captive of the Young Turks, and had been compelled by them to make as triumphal a progress as fears for his personal safety would allow through the provinces of European Turkey. But it was obvious to Balkan statesmen that Turkey was only changed in name, and that, if its threatened regeneration had slightly postponed their plans for its partition amongst themselves, the ultimate consummation of these plans must be pursued with, if possible, even greater energy and expedition than before. It was also seen by the more perspicacious of them that the methods hitherto adopted must in future be radically altered. A rejuvenated though unreformed Turkey, bent on self-preservation, could not be despised, and it was understood that if the revolutionary bands of the three Christian nations (Greece, Serbia, and Bulgaria) were to continue indefinitely to cut each others' throats in Macedonia the tables might conceivably be turned on them.

From 1909 onwards a series of phenomena occurred in the Balkans which ought to have given warning to the Turks, whose survival in Europe had been due solely to the fact that the Balkan States had never been able to unite. In the autumn of 1909 King Ferdinand of Bulgaria met Crown Prince Alexander of Serbia and made an expedition in his company to Mount Kopaonik in Serbia, renowned for the beauty of its flora. This must have struck those who remembered the bitter feelings which had existed between the two countries for years and had been intensified by the events of 1908. Bulgaria had looked on Serbia's failures with persistent contempt, while Serbia had watched Bulgaria's successful progress with speechless jealousy, and the memory of Slivnitsa was not yet obliterated. In the summer of 1910 Prince Nicholas of Montenegro celebrated the fiftieth anniversary of his reign and his golden wedding. The festivities were attended by King Ferdinand of Bulgaria and the Crown Prince Boris, by the Crown Prince Alexander of Serbia and his sister, grandchildren of Prince Nicholas, by his two daughters the Queen of Italy and the Grand Duchess Anastasia of Russia, and by their husbands, King Victor Emmanuel and the Grand Duke Nicholas. The happiness of the venerable ruler, who was as respected throughout Europe as he was feared throughout his principality, was at the same time completed by his recognition as king by all the governments and sovereigns of the continent. The hopes that he would simultaneously introduce a more liberal form of government amongst his own people were unfortunately disappointed.

The year 1911, it need scarcely be recalled, was extremely fateful for the whole of Europe. The growing restlessness and irritability manifested by the German Empire began to make all the other governments feel exceedingly uneasy. The French expedition to Fez in April was followed by the Anglo-Franco-German crisis of July; war was avoided, and France was recognized as virtually master of Morocco, but the soreness of the diplomatic defeat rendered Germany a still more trying neighbour than it had been before. The first repercussion was the war which broke out in September 1911 between Italy and Turkey for the possession of Tripoli and Cyrenaica, which Italy, with its usual insight, saw was vital to its position as a Mediterranean power and therefore determined to acquire before any other power had time or courage to do so. In the Balkans this was a year of observation and preparation. Serbia, taught by the bitter lesson of 1908 not to be caught again unprepared, had spent much money and care on its army during the last few years and had brought it to a much higher state of efficiency. In Austria-Hungary careful observers were aware that something was afoot and that the gaze of Serbia, which from 1903 till 1908 had been directed westwards to Bosnia and the Adriatic, had since 1908 been fixed on Macedonia and the Aegean. The actual formation of the Balkan League by King Ferdinand and M. Venezelos may not have been known, but it was realized that action of some sort on the part of the Balkan States was imminent, and that something must be done to forestall it. In February 1912 Count Aehrenthal died, and was succeeded by Count Berchtold as Austro-Hungarian Minister for Foreign Affairs. In August of the same year this minister unexpectedly announced his new and startling proposals for the introduction of reforms in Macedonia, which nobody in the Balkans who had any material interest in the fate of that province genuinely desired at that moment; the motto of the new scheme was 'progressive decentralization', blessed words which soothed the great powers as much as they alarmed the Balkan Governments. But already in May 1912 agreements between Bulgaria and Greece and between Bulgaria and Serbia had been concluded, limiting their respective zones of influence in the territory which they hoped to conquer. It was, to any one who has any knowledge of Balkan history, incredible that the various Governments had been able to come to any agreement at all. That arrived at by Bulgaria and Serbia divided Macedonia between them in such a way that Bulgaria should obtain central Macedonia with

Monastir and Okhrida, and Serbia northern Macedonia or Old Serbia; there was an indeterminate zone between the two spheres, including Skoplje (Ueskueb, in Turkish), the exact division of which it was agreed to leave to arbitration at a subsequent date.

The Macedonian theatre of war was by common consent regarded as the most important, and Bulgaria here promised Serbia the assistance of 100,000 men. The Turks meanwhile were aware that all was not what it seemed beyond the frontiers, and in August 1912 began collecting troops in Thrace, ostensibly for manoeuvres. During the month of September the patience of the four Governments of Greece, Bulgaria, Serbia, and Montenegro, which had for years with the utmost self-control been passively watching the awful sufferings of their compatriots under Turkish misrule, gradually became exhausted. On September 28 the four Balkan Governments informed Russia that the Balkan League was an accomplished fact, and on the 30th the representatives of all four signed the alliance, and mobilization was ordered in Greece, Bulgaria, and Serbia. The population of Montenegro was habitually on a war footing, and it was left to the mountain kingdom from its geographically favourable position to open hostilities. On October 8 Montenegro declared war on Turkey, and after a series of brilliant successes along the frontier its forces settled down to the wearisome and arduous siege of Scutari with its impregnable sentinel, Mount Tarabo[)s], converted into a modern fortress; the unaccustomed nature of these tasks, to which the Montenegrin troops, used to the adventures of irregular warfare, were little suited, tried the valour and patience of the intrepid mountaineers to the utmost. By that time Europe was in a ferment, and both Russia and Austria, amazed at having the initiative in the regulation of Balkan affairs wrested from them, showered on the Balkan capitals threats and protests, which for once in a way were neglected.

On October 13 Greece, Bulgaria, and Serbia replied that the offer of outside assistance and advice had come too late, and that they had decided themselves to redress the intolerable and secular wrongs of their long-suffering compatriots in Macedonia by force of arms. To their dismay a treaty of peace was signed at Lausanne about the same time between Turkey and Italy, which power, it had been hoped, would have distracted Turkey's attention by a continuance of hostilities in northern Africa, and at any rate immobilized the Turkish fleet. Encouraged by this success Turkey boldly declared war on Bulgaria and Serbia on October 17, hoping to frighten Greece and detach it from the league; but on the 18th the Greek Government replied by declaring war on Turkey, thus completing the necessary formalities. The Turks were confident of an early and easy victory, and hoped to reach Sofia, not from Constantinople and Thrace, but pushing up north-eastwards from Macedonia. The rapid offensive of the Serbian army, however, took them by surprise, and they were completely overwhelmed at the battle of Kumanovo in northern Macedonia on October 23-4, 1912. On the 31st King Peter made his triumphal entry into Skoplje (ex-Ueskueb), the ancient capital of Serbia under Tsar Stephen Du[)s]an in the fourteenth century. From there the Serbian army pursued the Turks southward, and at the battles of Prilep (November 5) and Monastir (November 19), after encountering the most stubborn opposition, finally put an end to their resistance in this part of the theatre of war. On November 9 the Greeks entered Salonika.

Meanwhile other divisions of the Serbian army had joined hands with the Montenegrins, and occupied almost without opposition the long-coveted *sandjak* of Novi-Pazar (the ancient Serb Ra[)s]ka), to the inexpressible rage of Austria-Hungary, which had evacuated it in 1908 in favour of its rightful owner, Turkey. At the same time a Serbian expeditionary corps marched right through Albania, braving great hardships on the way, and on November 30 occupied Durazzo, thus securing at last a foothold on the Adriatic. Besides all this, Serbia, in fulfilment of its treaty obligations, dispatched 50,000 splendidly equipped men, together with a quantity of heavy siege artillery, to help the Bulgarians at the siege of Adrianople. On December 3 an armistice was signed between the belligerents, with the condition that the three besieged Turkish fortresses of Adrianople,

Scutari, and Yanina must not be re-victualled, and on December 16, 1912, peace negotiations were opened between representatives of the belligerent countries in London. Meanwhile the Germanic powers, dismayed by the unexpected victories of the Balkan armies and humiliated by the crushing defeats in the field of the German-trained Turkish army, had since the beginning of November been doing everything in their power to support their client Turkey and prevent its final extinction and at the same time the blighting of their ambitions eventually to acquire the Empire of the Near East. During the conference in London between the plenipotentiaries of the belligerents, parallel meetings took place between the representatives of the great powers, whose relations with each other were strained and difficult in the extreme. The Turkish envoys prolonged the negotiations, as was their custom; they naturally were unwilling to concede their European provinces to the despised and hated Greek and Slavonic conquerors, but the delays implied growing hardships for their besieged and starving garrisons in Thrace, Epirus, and Albania. On January 23, 1913, a quasi-revolution occurred in the Turkish army, headed by Enver Bey and other Young Turk partisans, and approved by the Austrian and German embassies, with the object of interrupting the negotiations and staking all on the result of a final battle. As a result of these events, and of the palpable disingenuousness of the Turks in continuing the negotiations in London, the Balkan delegates on January 29 broke them off, and on February 3, 1913, hostilities were resumed. At length, after a siege of nearly five months, Adrianople, supplied with infinitely better artillery than the allies possessed, was taken by the combined Serbian and Bulgarian forces on March 26, 1913. The Serbian troops at Adrianople captured 17,010 Turkish prisoners, 190 guns, and the Turkish commander himself, Shukri Pasha.

At the outbreak of the war in the autumn of 1912 the Balkan States had observed all the conventions, disavowing designs of territorial aggrandizement and proclaiming their resolve merely to obtain guarantees for the better treatment of the Christian inhabitants of Macedonia; the powers, for their part, duly admonished the naughty children of south-eastern Europe to the effect that no alteration of the territorial *status quo ante* would under any circumstances be tolerated. During the negotiations in London, interrupted in January, and resumed in the spring of 1913 after the fall of Adrianople, it was soon made clear that in spite of all these magniloquent declarations nothing would be as it had been before. Throughout the winter Austria-Hungary had been mobilizing troops and massing them along the frontiers of Serbia and Montenegro, any increase in the size of which countries meant a crushing blow to the designs of the Germanic powers and the end to all the dreams embodied in the phrase 'Drang nach Osten' ('pushing eastwards').

In the spring of 1913 Serbia and Montenegro, instead of being defeated by the brave Turks, as had been confidently predicted in Vienna and Berlin would be the case, found themselves in possession of the *sandjak* of Novi-Pazar, of northern and central Macedonia (including Old Serbia), and of the northern half of Albania. The presence of Serbian troops on the shore of the Adriatic was more than Austria could stand, and at the renewed conference of London it was decided that they must retire. In the interests of nationality, in which the Balkan States themselves undertook the war, it was desirable that at any rate an attempt should be made to create an independent state of Albania, though no one who knew the local conditions felt confident as to its ultimate career. Its creation assuaged the consciences of the Liberal Government in Great Britain and at the same time admirably suited the strategic plans of Austria-Hungary. It left that country a loophole for future diplomatic efforts to disturb the peace of south-eastern Europe, and, with its own army in Bosnia and its political agents and irregular troops in Albania, Serbia and Montenegro, even though enlarged as it was generally recognized they must be, would be held in a vice and could be threatened and bullied from the south now as well as from the north whenever it was in the interests of Vienna and Budapest to apply the screw. The independence of Albania was declared at the conference of London on May 30, 1913. Scutari was included in it as being a purely Albanian town, and King Nicholas and his army, after enjoying its coveted flesh-pots for a few halcyon weeks, had, to their mortification, to retire to the barren fastnesses of the Black Mountain. Serbia, frustrated by Austria in its attempts, generally recognized as legitimate, to obtain even a commercial outlet on the Adriatic, naturally again diverted its aims southwards to Salonika. The Greeks were already in possession of this important city and seaport, as well as of the whole of southern Macedonia. The Serbs were in possession of central and northern Macedonia, including Monastir and Okhrida, which they had at great sacrifices conquered from the Turks. It had been agreed that Bulgaria, as its share of the spoils, should have all central Macedonia, with Monastir and Okhrida, although on ethnical grounds the Bulgarians have only very slightly better claim to the country and towns west of the Vardar than any of the other Balkan nationalities. But at the time that the agreement had been concluded it had been calculated in Greece and Serbia that Albania, far from being made independent, would be divided between them, and that Serbia, assured of a strip of coast on the Adriatic, would have no interest in the control of the river Vardar and of the railway which follows its course connecting the interior of Serbia with the port of Salonika. Greece and Serbia had no ground whatever for quarrel and no cause for mutual distrust, and they were determined, for political and commercial reasons, to have a considerable extent of frontier from west to east in common. The creation of an independent Albania completely altered the situation. If Bulgaria should obtain central Macedonia and thus secure a frontier from north to south in common with the newly-formed state of Albania, then Greece would be at the mercy of its hereditary enemies the Bulgars and Arnauts (Albanians) as it had previously been at the mercy of the Turks, while Serbia would have two frontiers between itself and the sea instead of one, as before, and its complete economic strangulation would be rendered inevitable and rapid. Bulgaria for its own part naturally refused to waive its claim to central Macedonia, well knowing that the master of the Vardar valley is master of the Balkan peninsula. The first repercussion of the ephemeral treaty of London of May 30, 1913, which created Albania and shut out Serbia from the Adriatic, was, therefore, as the diplomacy of the Germanic powers had all along intended it should be, the beginning of a feud between Greece and Serbia on the one hand, and Bulgaria on the other, the disruption of the Balkan League and the salvation, for the ultimate benefit of Germany, of what was left of Turkey in Europe.

The dispute as to the exact division of the conquered territory in Macedonia between Serbia and Bulgaria had, as arranged, been referred to arbitration, and, the Tsar of Russia having been chosen as judge, the matter was being threshed out in St. Petersburg during June 1913. Meanwhile Bulgaria, determined to make good its claim to the chestnuts which Greece and Serbia had pulled out of the Turkish fire, was secretly collecting troops along its temporary south-western frontier* with the object, in approved Germanic fashion, of suddenly invading and occupying all Macedonia, and, by the presentation of an irrevocable *fait accompli*, of relieving the arbitrator of his invidious duties or at any rate assisting him in the task.

On the other hand, the relations between Bulgaria and its two allies had been noticeably growing worse ever since January 1913; Bulgaria felt aggrieved that, in spite of its great sacrifices, it had not been able to occupy so much territory as Greece and Serbia, and the fact that Adrianople was taken with Serbian help did not improve the feeling between the two Slav nations. The growth of Bulgarian animosity put Greece and Serbia on their guard, and, well knowing the direction which an eventual attack would take, these two countries on June 2, 1913, signed a military convention and made all the necessary dispositions for resisting any aggression on Bulgaria's part. At one o'clock in the morning of June

---

*   This was formed by the stream Zletovska, a tributary of the river Bregalnica, which in its turn falls into the Vardar on its left or eastern bank about 40 miles south of Skoplje (Ueskueb).

30 the Bulgarians, without provocation, without declaration of war, and without warning, crossed the Bregalnica (a tributary of the Vardar) and attacked the Serbs. A most violent battle ensued which lasted for several days; at some points the Bulgarians, thanks to the suddenness of their offensive, were temporarily successful, but gradually the Serbs regained the upper hand and by July 1 the Bulgarians were beaten. The losses were very heavy on both sides, but the final issue was a complete triumph for the Serbian army. Slivnitsa was avenged by the battle of the Bregalnica, just as Kosovo was by that of Kumanovo. After a triumphant campaign of one month, in which the Serbs were joined by the Greeks, Bulgaria had to bow to the inevitable. The Rumanian army had invaded northern Bulgaria, bent on maintaining the Balkan equilibrium and on securing compensation for having observed neutrality during the war of 1912-13, and famine reigned at Sofia. A conference was arranged at Bucarest, and the treaty of that name was signed there on August 10, 1913. By the terms of this treaty Serbia retained the whole of northern and central Macedonia, including Monastir and Okhrida, and the famous *sandjak* of Novi-Pazar was divided between Serbia and Montenegro. Some districts of east-central Macedonia, which were genuinely Bulgarian, were included in Serbian territory, as Serbia naturally did not wish, after the disquieting and costly experience of June and July 1913, to give the Bulgarians another chance of separating Greek from Serbian territory by a fresh surprise attack, and the further the Bulgarians could be kept from the Vardar river and railway the less likelihood there was of this. The state of feeling in the Germanic capitals and in Budapest after this ignominious defeat of their protege Bulgaria and after this fresh triumph of the despised and hated Serbians can be imagined. Bitterly disappointed first at seeing the Turks vanquished by the Balkan League—their greatest admirers could not even claim that the Turks had had any 'moral' victories—their chagrin, when they saw the Bulgarians trounced by the Serbians, knew no bounds. That the secretly prepared attack on Serbia by Bulgaria was planned in Vienna and Budapest there is no doubt. That Bulgaria was justified in feeling

disappointment and resentment at the result of the first Balkan War no one denies, but the method chosen to redress its wrongs could only have been suggested by the Germanic school of diplomacy.

In Serbia and Montenegro the result of the two successive Balkan Wars, though these had exhausted the material resources of the two countries, was a justifiable return of national self-confidence and rejoicing such as the people, humiliated and impoverished as it had habitually been by its internal and external troubles, had not known for very many years. At last Serbia and Montenegro had joined hands. At last Old Serbia was restored to the free kingdom. At last Skoplje, the mediaeval capital of Tsar Stephen Du[)s]an, was again in Serbian territory. At last one of the most important portions of unredeemed Serbia had been reclaimed. Amongst the Serbs and Croats of Bosnia, Hercegovina, Dalmatia, Croatia, Slavonia, and southern Hungary the effect of the Serbian victories was electrifying. Military prowess had been the one quality with which they, and indeed everybody else, had refused to credit the Serbians of the kingdom, and the triumphs of the valiant Serbian peasant soldiers immediately imparted a heroic glow to the country whose very name, at any rate in central Europe, had become a byword, and a synonym for failure; Belgrade became the cynosure and the rallying-centre of the whole Serbo-Croatian race. But Vienna and Budapest could only lose courage and presence of mind for the moment, and the undeniable success of the Serbian arms merely sharpened their appetite for revenge. In August 1913 Austria-Hungary, as is now known, secretly prepared an aggression on Serbia, but was restrained, partly by the refusal of Italy to grant its approval of such action, partly because the preparations of Germany at that time were not complete. The fortunate Albanian question provided, for the time being, a more convenient rod with which to beat Serbia. Some Serbian troops had remained in possession of certain frontier towns and districts which were included in the territory of the infant state of Albania pending the final settlement of the frontiers by a commission. On October 18, 1913, Austria addressed an ultimatum to Serbia to evacuate these, as its continued occupation of them caused offence and disquiet to the Dual Monarchy. Serbia meekly obeyed. Thus passed away the last rumble of the storms which had filled the years 1912-13 in south-eastern Europe.

The credulous believed that the Treaty of Bucarest had at last brought peace to that distracted part of the world. Those who knew their central Europe realized that Berlin had only forced Vienna to acquiesce in the Treaty of Bucarest because the time had not yet come. But come what might, Serbia and Montenegro, by having linked up their territory and by forming a mountain barrier from the Danube to the Adriatic, made it far more difficult for the invader to push his way through to the East than it would have been before the battles of Kumanovo and Bregalnica.

GREECE.

1.

From Ancient to Modern Greece

The name of Greece has two entirely different associations in our minds. Sometimes it calls up a wonderful literature enshrined in a 'dead language', and exquisite works of a vanished art recovered by the spade; at other times it is connected with the currant-trade returns quoted on the financial page of our newspapers or with the 'Balance of Power' discussed in their leading articles. Ancient and Modern Greece both mean much to us, but usually we are content to accept them as independent phenomena, and we seldom pause to wonder whether there is any deeper connexion between them than their name. It is the purpose of these pages to ask and give some answer to this question.

The thought that his own Greece might perish, to be succeeded by another Greece after the lapse of more than two thousand years, would have caused an Ancient Greek surprise. In the middle of the fifth century B.C., Ancient Greek civilization seemed triumphantly vigorous and secure. A generation before, it had flung back the onset of a political power which combined all the momentum of all the other contemporary civilizations in the world; and the victory had proved not merely the superiority of Greek arms—the Spartan spearman and the Athenian galley—but the superior vitality of Greek politics—the self-governing, self-sufficing city-state. In these cities a wonderful culture had burst into flower—an art expressing itself with equal mastery in architecture, sculpture, and drama, a science which ranged from the most practical medicine to the most abstract mathematics, and a philosophy which blended art, science, and religion into an ever-developing and ever more harmonious view of the universe. A civilization so brilliant and so versatile as this seemed to have an infinite future before it, yet even here death lurked in ambush.

When the cities ranged themselves in rival camps, and squandered their strength on the struggle for predominance, the historian of the Peloponnesian war could already picture Athens and Sparta in ruins,[*] and the catastrophe began to warp the soul of Plato before he had carried Greek philosophy to its zenith. This internecine strife of free communities was checked within a century by the imposition of a single military autocracy over them all, and Alexander the Great crowned his father Philip's work by winning new worlds for Hellenism from the Danube to the Ganges and from the Oxus to the Nile. The city-state and its culture were to be propagated under his aegis, but this vision vanished with Alexander's death, and Macedonian militarism proved a disappointment. The feuds of these crowned condottieri harassed the cities more sorely than their own quarrels, and their arms could not even preserve the Hellenic heritage against external foes. The Oriental rallied and expelled Hellenism again from the Asiatic hinterland, while the new cloud of Rome was gathering in the west. In four generations[**] of the most devastating warfare the world had seen, Rome conquered all the coasts of the Mediterranean. Greek city and Greek dynast went down before her, and the political sceptre passed irrevocably from the Hellenic nation.

Yet this political abdication seemed to open for Hellenic culture a future more brilliant and assured than ever. Rome could organize as well

---

[*]   Thucydides, Book I, chap. 10.
[**]   264-146 B.C.

as conquer. She accepted the city-state as the municipal unit of the Roman Empire, thrust back the Oriental behind the Euphrates, and promoted the Hellenization of all the lands between this river-frontier and the Balkans with much greater intensity than the Macedonian imperialists. Her political conquests were still further counterbalanced by her spiritual surrender, and Hellenism was the soul of the new Latin culture which Rome created, and which advanced with Roman government over the vast untutored provinces of the west and north, bringing them, too, within the orbit of Hellenic civilization. Under the shadow of the Roman Empire, Plutarch, the mirror of Hellenism, could dwell in peace in his little city-state of Chaeronea, and reflect in his writings all the achievements of the Hellenic spirit as an ensample to an apparently endless posterity.

Yet the days of Hellenic culture were also numbered. Even Plutarch lived* to look down from the rocky citadel of Chaeronea upon Teutonic raiders wasting the Kephisos vale, and for more than three centuries successive hordes of Goths searched out and ravaged the furthest corners of European Greece. Then the current set westward to sweep away** the Roman administration in the Latin provinces, and Hellenism seemed to have been granted a reprieve. The Greek city-state of Byzantium on the Black Sea Straits had been transformed into the Roman administrative centre of Constantinople, and from this capital the Emperor Justinian in the sixth century A.D. still governed and defended the whole Greek-speaking world. But this political glamour only threw the symptoms of inward dissolution into sharper relief. Within the framework of the Empire the municipal liberty of the city-state had been stifled and extinguished by the waxing jungle of bureaucracy, and the spiritual culture which the city-state fostered, and which was more essential to Hellenism than any political institutions, had been part ejected, part exploited, and wholly compromised by a new gospel from the east.

---

*   About A.D. 100
**   A.D. 404-476

While the Oriental had been compelled by Rome to draw his political frontier at the Euphrates, and had failed so far to cross the river-line, he had maintained his cultural independence within sight of the Mediterranean. In the hill country of Judah, overlooking the high road between Antioch and Alexandria, the two chief foci of Hellenism in the east which the Macedonians had founded, and which had grown to maturity under the aegis of Rome, there dwelt a little Semitic community which had defied all efforts of Greek or Roman to assimilate it, and had finally given birth to a world religion about the time that a Roman punitive expedition razed its holy city of Jerusalem to the ground.* Christianity was charged with an incalculable force, which shot like an electric current from one end of the Roman Empire to the other. The highly-organized society of its adherents measured its strength in several sharp conflicts with the Imperial administration, from which it emerged victorious, and it was proclaimed the official religious organization of the Empire by the very emperor that founded Constantinople.**

The established Christian Church took the best energies of Hellenism into its service. The Greek intellectuals ceased to become lecturers and professors, to find a more human and practical career in the bishop's office. The Nicene Creed, drafted by an 'oecumenical' conference of bishops under the auspices of Constantine himself,*** was the last notable formulation of Ancient Greek philosophy. The cathedral of Aya Sophia, with which Justinian adorned Constantinople, was the last original creation of Ancient Greek art.**** The same Justinian closed the University of Athens, which had educated the world for nine hundred years and more, since Plato founded his college in the Academy. Six recalcitrant professors went into exile for their spiritual freedom, but they found

---

*   A.D. 70.
**   Constantine the Great recognized Christianity in A.D. 313 and founded Constantinople in A.D. 328.
***   A.D. 325.
**** Completed A.D. 538.

the devout Zoroastrianism of the Persian court as unsympathetic as the devout Christianity of the Roman. Their humiliating return and recantation broke the 'Golden Chain' of Hellenic thought for ever.

Hellenism was thus expiring from its own inanition, when the inevitable avalanche overwhelmed it from without. In the seventh century A.D. there was another religious eruption in the Semitic world, this time in the heart of Arabia, where Hellenism had hardly penetrated, and under the impetus of Islam the Oriental burst his bounds again after a thousand years. Syria was reft away from the Empire, and Egypt, and North Africa as far as the Atlantic, and their political severance meant their cultural loss to Greek civilization. Between the Koran and Hellenism no fusion was possible. Christianity had taken Hellenism captive, but Islam gave it no quarter, and the priceless library of Alexandria is said to have been condemned by the caliph's order to feed the furnaces of the public baths.

While Hellenism was thus cut short in the east, a mortal blow was struck at its heart from the north. The Teuton had raided and passed on, but the lands he had depopulated were now invaded by immigrants who had come to stay. As soon as the last Goth and Lombard had gone west of the Isonzo, the Slavs poured in from the north-eastern plains of Europe through the Moravian gap, crossed the Danube somewhere near the site of Vienna, and drifted down along the eastern face of the Alps upon the Adriatic littoral. Rebuffed by the sea-board, the Slavonic migration was next deflected east, and filtered through the Bosnian mountains, scattering the Latin-speaking provincials before it to left and right, until it debouched upon the broad basin of the river Morava. In this concentration-area it gathered momentum during the earlier part of the seventh century A.D., and then burst out with irresistible force in all directions, eastward across the Maritsa basin till it reached the Black Sea, and southward down the Vardar to the shores of the Aegean.

Beneath this Slavonic flood the Greek race in Europe was engulfed. A few fortified cities held out, Adrianople on the Maritsa continued to cover Constantinople; Salonika at the mouth of the Vardar survived a two hundred years siege; while further south Athens, Korinth, and Patras escaped extinction. But the tide of invasion surged around their walls. The Slavs mastered all the open country, and, pressing across the Korinthian Gulf, established themselves in special force throughout the Peloponnesos. The thoroughness of their penetration is witnessed to this day by the Slavonic names which still cling to at least a third of the villages, rivers, and mountains in European Greece, and are found in the most remote as well as in the most accessible quarters of the land.*

With the coming of the Slavs darkness descends like a curtain upon Greek history. We catch glimpses of Arab hosts ranging across Anatolia at will and gazing at Slavonic hordes across the narrow Bosphorus. But always the Imperial fleet patrols the waters between, and always the triple defences of Constantinople defy the assailant. Then after about two centuries the floods subside, the gloom disperses, and the Greek world emerges into view once more. But the spectacle before us is unfamiliar, and most of the old landmarks have been swept away.

By the middle of the ninth century A.D., the Imperial Government had reduced the Peloponnesos to order again, and found itself in the presence of three peoples. The greater part of the land was occupied by 'Romaioi'—normal, loyal, Christian subjects of the empire—but in the hilly country between Eurotas, Taygetos, and the sea, two Slavonic tribes still maintained themselves in defiant savagery and worshipped their Slavonic gods, while beyond them the peninsula of Tainaron, now known as Maina, sheltered communities which still clung to the pagan name of Hellene and knew no other gods but Zeus, Athena, and Apollo. Hellene and Slav need not concern us. They were a vanishing minority,

---

*   For example: Tsimova and Panitsa in the Tainaron peninsula (Maina); Tsoupana and Khrysapha in Lakonia; Dhimitzana, Karytena, and Andhritsena in the centre of Peloponnesos, and Vostitsa on its north coast; Dobrena and Kaprena in Boiotia; Vonitza on the Gulf of Arta; Kardhitsa in the Thessalian plain.

and the Imperial Government was more successful in obliterating their individuality than in making them contribute to its exchequer. The future lay with the Romaioi.

The speech of these Romaioi was not the speech of Rome. 'Romaika,' as it is still called popularly in the country-side, is a development of the 'koine' or 'current' dialect of Ancient Greek, in which the Septuagint and the New Testament are written. The vogue of these books after the triumph of Christianity and the oncoming of the Dark Age, when they were the sole intellectual sustenance of the people, gave the idiom in which they were composed an exclusive prevalence. Except in Tzakonia— the iron-bound coast between Cape Malea and Nauplia Bay—all other dialects of Ancient Greek became extinct, and the varieties of the modern language are all differentiations of the 'koine', along geographical lines which in no way correspond with those which divided Doric from Ionian. Yet though Romaic is descended from the 'koine', it is almost as far removed from it as modern Italian is from the language of St. Augustine or Cicero. Ancient Greek possessed a pitch-accent only, which allowed the quantitative values of syllables to be measured against one another, and even to form the basis of a metrical system. In Romaic the pitch-accent has transformed itself into a stress-accent almost as violent as the English, which has destroyed all quantitative relation between accented and unaccented syllables, often wearing away the latter altogether at the termination of words, and always impoverishing their vowel sounds. In the ninth century A.D. this new enunciation was giving rise to a new poetical technique founded upon accent and rhyme, which first essayed itself in folk-songs and ballads,* and has since experimented in the same variety of forms as English poetry.

---

*   The earliest products of the modern technique were called 'city' verses, because they originated in Constantinople, which has remained 'the city' *par excellence* for the Romaic Greek ever since the Dark Age made it the asylum of his civilization.

These humble beginnings of a new literature were supplemented by the rudiments of a new art. Any visitor at Athens who looks at the three tiny churches* built in this period of first revival, and compares them with the rare pre-Norman churches of England, will find the same promise of vitality in the Greek architecture as in his own. The material—worked blocks of marble pillaged from ancient monuments, alternating with courses of contemporary brick—produces a completely new aesthetic effect upon the eye; and the structure—a grouping of lesser cupolas round a central dome—is the very antithesis of the 'upright-and-horizontal' style which confronts him in ruins upon the Akropolis.

These first achievements of Romaic architecture speak by implication of the characteristic difference between the Romaios and the Hellene. The linguistic and the aesthetic change were as nothing compared to the change in religion, for while the Hellene had been a pagan, the Romaios was essentially a member of the Christian Church. Yet this new and determining characteristic was already fortified by tradition. The Church triumphant had swiftly perfected its organisation on the model of the Imperial bureaucracy. Every Romaios owed ecclesiastical allegiance, through a hierarchy of bishops and metropolitans, to a supreme patriarch at Constantinople, and in the ninth century this administrative segregation of the imperial from the west-European Church had borne its inevitable fruit in a dogmatic divergence, and ripened into a schism between the Orthodox Christianity of the east on the one hand and the Catholicism of the Latin world on the other.

The Orthodox Church exercised an important cultural influence over its Romaic adherents. The official language of its scriptures, creeds, and ritual had never ceased to be the Ancient Greek 'koine' and by keeping the Romaios familiar with this otherwise obsolete tongue it kept him in touch with the unsurpassable literature of his Ancient Greek predecessors. The vast body of Hellenic literature had perished during the Dark Age, when

---

*   The Old Metropolitan, the Kapnikaria, and St. Theodore.

all the energies of the race were absorbed by the momentary struggle for survival; but about a third of the greatest authors' greatest works had been preserved, and now that the stress was relieved, the wreckage of the remainder was sedulously garnered in anthologies, abridgements, and encyclopaedias. The rising monasteries offered a safe harbourage both for these compilations and for such originals as survived unimpaired, and in their libraries they were henceforth studied, cherished, and above all recopied with more or less systematic care.

The Orthodox Church was thus a potent link between past and present, but the most direct link of all was the political survival of the Empire. Here, too, many landmarks had been swept away. The marvellous system of Roman Law had proved too subtle and complex for a world in the throes of dissolution. Within a century of its final codification by Justinian's commissioners) it had begun to fall into disuse, and was now replaced by more summary legislation, which was as deeply imbued with Mosaic principles as the literary language with the Hebraisms of the New Testament, and bristled with barbarous applications of the *Lex Talionis*. The administrative organization instituted by Augustus and elaborated by Diocletian had likewise disappeared, and the army-corps districts were the only territorial units that outlasted the Dark Age. Yet the tradition of order lived on. The army itself preserved Roman discipline and technique to a remarkable degree, and the military districts were already becoming the basis for a reconstituted civil government. The wealth of Latin technicalities incorporated in the Greek style of ninth-century officialdom witnesses to this continuity with the past and to the consequent political superiority of the Romaic Empire over contemporary western Europe.

Within the Imperial frontiers the Romaic race was offered an apparently secure field for its future development. In the Balkan peninsula the Slav had been expelled or assimilated to the south of a line stretching from Avlona to Salonika. East of Salonika the empire still controlled little more in Europe than the ports of the littoral, and a military highway linking them with each other and with Constantinople. But beyond the

Bosphorus the frontier included the whole body of Anatolia as far as Taurus and Euphrates, and here was the centre of gravity both of the Romaic state and of the Romaic nation.

A new Greek nation had in fact come into being, and it found itself in touch with new neighbours, whom the Ancient Greek had never known. Eastward lay the Armenians, reviving, like the Greeks, after the ebb of the Arab flood, and the Arabs themselves, quiescent within their natural bounds and transfusing the wisdom of Aristotle and Hippokrates into their native culture. Both these peoples were sundered from the Orthodox Greek by religion* as well as by language, but a number of nationalities established on his opposite flank had been evangelized from Constantinople and followed the Orthodox patriarch in his schism with Rome. The most important neighbour of the Empire in this quarter was the Bulgarian kingdom, which covered all the Balkan hinterland from the Danube and the Black Sea to the barrier-fortresses of Adrianople and Salonika. It had been founded by a conquering caste of non-Slavonic nomads from the trans-Danubian steppes, but these were completely absorbed in the Slavonic population which they had endowed with their name and had preserved by political consolidation from the fate of their brethren further south. This Bulgarian state included a large 'Vlach' element descended from those Latin-speaking provincials whom the Slavs had pushed before them in their original migration; while the main body of the 'Rumans', whom the same thrust of invasion had driven leftwards across the Danube, had established itself in the mountains of Transylvania, and was just beginning to push down into the Wallachian and Moldavian plains. Like the Bulgars, this Romance population had chosen the Orthodox creed, and so had the purely Slavonic Serbs, who had replaced the Rumans in the basin of the Morava and the Bosnian hills, as far westward as the Adriatic coast. Beyond, the heathen Magyars had

---

* The Armenians split off from the Catholic Church four centuries before the schism between the Roman and Orthodox sections of the latter.

pressed into the Danubian plains like a wedge, and cut off the Orthodox world from the Latin-Teutonic Christendom of the west; but it looked as though the two divisions of Europe were embarked upon the same course of development. Both were evolving a system of strongly-knit nationalities, neither wholly interdependent nor wholly self-sufficient, but linked together in their individual growth by the ties of common culture and religion. In both the darkness was passing. The future of civilization seemed once more assured, and in the Orthodox world the new Greek nation seemed destined to play the leading part.

His cultural and political heritage from his ancient predecessors gave the Romaic Greek in this period of revival an inestimable advantage over his cruder neighbours, and his superiority declared itself in an expansion of the Romaic Empire. In the latter half of the tenth century A.D. the nest of Arab pirates from Spain, which had established itself in Krete and terrorized the Aegean, was exterminated by the Emperor Nikiphoros Phokas, and on the eastern marches Antioch was gathered within the frontier at the Arabs' expense, and advanced posts pushed across Euphrates. In the first half of the eleventh century Basil, 'Slayer of the Bulgars', destroyed the Balkan kingdom after a generation of bitter warfare, and brought the whole interior of the peninsula under the sway of Constantinople. His successors turned their attention to the cast again, and attracted one Armenian principality after another within the Imperial protectorate. Nor was the revival confined to politics. The conversion of the Russians about A.D. 1000 opened a boundless hinterland to the Orthodox Church, and any one who glances at a series of Greek ivory carvings or studies Greek history from the original sources, will here encounter a literary and artistic renaissance remarkable enough to explain the fascination which the barbarous Russian and the outlandish Armenian found in Constantinople. Yet this renaissance had hardly set in before it was paralysed by an unexpected blow, which arrested the development of Modern Greece for seven centuries.

Modern, like Ancient, Greece was assailed in her infancy by a conqueror from the east, and, unlike Ancient Greece, she succumbed. Turkish nomads from the central Asiatic steppes had been drifting into the Moslem world as the vigour of the Arabs waned. First they came as slaves, then as mercenaries, until at last, in the eleventh century, the clan of Seljuk grasped with a strong hand the political dominion of Islam. As champions of the caliph the Turkish sultans disputed the infidels encroachment on the Moslem border. They challenged the Romaic Empire's progress in Armenia, and in A.D. 1071—five years after the Norman founded at Hastings the strong government which has been the making of England—the Seljuk Turk shattered at the battle of Melasgerd that heritage of strong government which had promised so much to Greece.

Melasgerd opened the way to Anatolia. The Arab could make no lodgement there, but in the central steppe of the temperate plateau the Turk found a miniature reproduction of his original environment. Tribe after tribe crossed the Oxus, to make the long pilgrimage to these new marches which their race had won for Islam on the west, and the civilization developed in the country by fifteen centuries of intensive and undisturbed Hellenization was completely blotted out. The cities wore isolated from one another till their commerce fell into decay. The elaborately cultivated lands around them were left fallow till they were good for nothing but the pasturage which was all that the nomad required. The only monuments of architecture that have survived in Anatolia above ground are the imposing khans or fortified rest-houses built by the Seljuk sultans themselves after the consolidation of their rule, and they are the best witnesses of the vigorous barbarism by which Romaic culture was effaced. The vitality of the Turk was indeed unquestionable. He imposed his language and religion upon the native Anatolian peasantry, as the Greek had imposed his before him, and in time adopted their sedentary life, though too late to repair the mischief his own nomadism had wrought. Turk and Anatolian coalesced into one people; every mountain, river, lake, bridge, and village in the country took on a Turkish name, and a new nation was established for ever in the heart of the Romaic world, which nourished itself on the life-blood of the Empire and was to prove the supreme enemy, of the race.

This sequel to Melasgerd sealed the Empire's doom. Robbed of its Anatolian governing class and its Anatolian territorial army, it ceased to be self-sufficient, and the defenders it attracted from the west were at least as destructive as its eastern foes. The brutal regime of the Turks in the pilgrimage places of Syria had roused a storm of indignation in Latin Europe, and a cloud gathered in the west once more. It was heralded by adventurers from Normandy, who had first served the Romaic Government as mercenaries in southern Italy and then expelled their employers, about the time of Melasgerd, from their last foothold in the peninsula. Raids across the straits of Otranto carried the Normans up to the walls of Salonika, their fleets equipped in Sicily scoured the Aegean, and, before the eleventh century was out, they had followed up these reconnoitring expeditions by conducting Latin Christendom on its first crusade. The crusaders assembled at Constantinople, and the Imperial Government was relieved when the flood rolled on and spent itself further east. But one wave was followed by another, and the Empire itself succumbed to the fourth. In A.D. 1204, Constantinople was stormed by a Venetian flotilla and the crusading host it conveyed on board, and more treasures of Ancient Hellenism were destroyed in the sack of its hitherto inviolate citadel than had ever perished by the hand of Arab or Slav.

With the fall of the capital the Empire dissolved in chaos, Venice and Genoa, the Italian trading cities whose fortune had been made by the crusades, now usurped the naval control of the Mediterranean which the Empire had exercised since Nikiphoros pacified Krete. They seized all strategical points of vantage on the Aegean coasts, and founded an 'extra-territorial' community at Pera across the Golden Horn, to monopolize the trade of Constantinople with the Black Sea. The Latins failed to retain their hold on Constantinople itself, for the puppet emperors of their own race whom they enthroned there were evicted within a century by Romaic dynasts, who clung to such fragments of Anatolia as had escaped the Turk. But the Latin dominion was less ephemeral in the southernmost Romaic provinces of Europe. The Latins' castles, more conspicuous than the relics of Hellas, still crown many high hills in Greece, and their French tongue has added another strain, to the varied nomenclature of the country.* Yet there also pandemonium prevailed. Burgundian barons, Catalan condottieri, and Florentine bankers snatched the Duchy of Athens from one another in bewildering succession, while the French princes of Achaia were at feud with their kindred vassals in the west of the Peloponnesos whenever they were not resisting the encroachments of Romaic despots in the south and east. To complete the anarchy, the non-Romaic peoples in the interior of the Balkan peninsula had taken the fall of Constantinople as a signal to throw off the Imperial yoke. In the hinterland of the capital the Bulgars had reconstituted their kingdom. The Romance-speaking Vlachs of Pindus moved down into the Thessalian plains. The aboriginal Albanians, who with their back to the Adriatic had kept the Slavs at bay, asserted their vitality and sent out migratory swarms to the south, which entered the service of the warring princelets and by their prowess won broad lands in every part of continental Greece, where Albanian place-names are to this day only less common than Slavonic. South-eastern Europe was again in the throes of social dissolution, and the convulsions continued till they were stilled impartially by the numbing hand of their ultimate author the Turk.

The Seljuk sultanate in Anatolia, shaken by the crusades, had gone the way of all oriental empires to make room for one of its fractions, which showed a most un-oriental faculty of organic growth. This was the extreme march on the north-western rim of the Anatolian plateau,

---

*   e.g. Klemoutsi, Glarentsa (Clarence) and Gastouni—villages of the currant district in Peloponnesos—and Sant-Omeri, the mountain that overlooks them.

overlooking the Asiatic littoral of the Sea of Marmora. It had been founded by one of those Turkish chiefs who migrated with their clans from beyond the Oxus; and it was consolidated by Othman his son, who extended his kingdom to the cities on the coast and invested his subjects with his own name. In 1355 the Narrows of Gallipoli passed into Ottoman hands, and opened a bridge to unexpected conquests in Europe. Serbia and Bulgaria collapsed at the first attack, and the hosts which marched to liberate them from Hungary and from France only ministered to Ottoman prestige by their disastrous discomfiture. Before the close of the fourteenth century the Ottoman sultan had transferred his capital to Adrianople, and had become immeasurably the strongest power in the Balkan peninsula.

After that the end came quickly. At Constantinople the Romaic dynasty of Palaiologos had upheld a semblance of the Empire for more than a century after the Latin was expelled. But in 1453 the Imperial city fell before the assault of Sultan Mohammed; and before his death the conqueror eliminated all the other Romaic and Latin principalities from Peloponnesos to Trebizond, which had survived as enclaves to mar the uniformity of the Ottoman domain. Under his successors the tide of Ottoman conquest rolled on for half a century more over south-eastern Europe, till it was stayed on land beneath the ramparts of Vienna,* and culminated on sea, after the systematic reduction of the Venetian strongholds, in the capture of Rhodes from the Knights of St. John.** The Romaic race, which had been split into so many fragments during the dissolution of the Empire, was reunited again in the sixteenth century under the common yoke of the Turk.

Even in the Dark Age, Greece had hardly been reduced to so desperate a condition as now. Through the Dark Age the Greek cities had maintained a continuous life, but Mohammed II depopulated Constantinople to

---

*   1526.
**   1522.

repeople it with a Turkish majority from Anatolia. Greek commerce would naturally have benefited by the ejection of the Italians from the Levant, had not the Ottoman Government given asylum simultaneously to the Jews expelled from Spain. These Sephardim established themselves at Constantinople, Salonika, and all the other commercial centres of the Ottoman dominion, and their superiority in numbers and industry made them more formidable urban rivals of the Greeks than the Venetians and Genoese had ever been.

Ousted from the towns, the Greek race depended for its preservation on the peasantry, yet Greece had never suffered worse rural oppression than under the Ottoman regime. The sultan's fiscal demands were the least part of the burden. The paralysing land-tax, collected in kind by irresponsible middlemen, was an inheritance from the Romaic Empire, and though it was now reinforced by the special capitation-tax levied by the sultan on his Christian subjects, the greater efficiency and security of his government probably compensated for the additional charge. The vitality of Greece was chiefly sapped by the ruthless military organization of the Ottoman state. The bulk of the Ottoman army was drawn from a feudal cavalry, bound to service, as in the mediaeval Latin world, in return for fiefs or 'timaria' assigned to them by their sovereign; and many beys and agas have bequeathed their names in perpetuity to the richest villages on the Messenian and Thessalian plains, to remind the modern peasant that his Christian ancestors once tilled the soil as serfs of a Moslem timariot. But the sultan, unlike his western contemporaries, was not content with irregular troops, and the serf-communes of Greece had to deliver up a fifth of their male children every fourth year to be trained at Constantinople as professional soldiers and fanatical Moslems. This corps of 'Janissaries'* was founded in the third generation of the Ottoman dynasty, and was the essential instrument of its military success. One race has never appropriated and exploited the vitality of another in so direct

---

*   Yeni Asker—New soldiery.

or so brutal a fashion, and the institution of 'tribute-children', so long as it lasted, effectually prevented any recovery of the Greek nation from the untimely blows which had stricken it down.

2.

The Awakening of the Nation

During the two centuries that followed the Ottoman conquest of Constantinople, the Greek race was in serious danger of annihilation. Its life-blood was steadily absorbed into the conquering community—quite regularly by the compulsory tribute of children and spasmodically by the voluntary conversion of individual households. The rich apostasized, because too heavy a material sacrifice was imposed upon them by loyalty to their national religion; the destitute, because they could not fail to improve their prospects by adhering to the privileged faith. Even the surviving organization of the Church had only been spared by the Ottoman Government in order to facilitate its own political system—by bringing the peasant, through the hierarchy of priest, bishop, and patriarch, under the moral control of the new Moslem master whom the ecclesiastics henceforth served.

The scale on which wholesale apostasy was possible is shown by the case of Krete, which was conquered by the Turks from Venice just after these two centuries had closed, and was in fact the last permanent addition to the Turkish Empire. No urban or feudal settlers of Turkish blood were imported into the island. To this day the uniform speech of all Kretans is their native Greek. And yet the progressive conversion of whole clans and villages had transferred at least 20 per cent. of the population to the Moslem ranks before the Ottoman connexion was severed again in 1897.

The survival of the Greek nationality did not depend on any efforts of the Greeks themselves. They were indeed no longer capable of effort, but lay passive under the hand of the Turk, like the paralysed quarry of some beast of prey. Their fate was conditional upon the development of the Ottoman state, and, as the two centuries drew to a close, that state entered upon a phase of transformation and of consequent weakness.

The Ottoman organism has always displayed (and never more conspicuously than at the present moment) a much greater stability and vitality than any of its oriental predecessors. There was a vein of genius in its creators, and its youthful expansion permeated it with so much European blood that it became partly Europeanized in its inner tissues— sufficiently to partake, at any rate, in that faculty of indefinite organic growth which has so far revealed itself in European life. This acquired force has carried it on since the time when the impetus of its original institutions became spent—a time when purely oriental monarchies fall to pieces, and when Turkey herself hesitated between reconstruction and dissolution. That critical period began for her with the latter half of the seventeenth century, and incidentally opened new opportunities of life to her subject Greeks.

Substantial relief from their burdens—the primary though negative condition of national revival—accrued to the Greek peasantry from the decay of Ottoman militarism in all its branches. The Turkish feudal aristocracy, which had replaced the landed nobility of the Romaic Empire in Anatolia and established itself on the choicest lands in conquered Europe, was beginning to decline in strength. We have seen that it failed to implant itself in Krete, and its numbers were already stationary elsewhere. The Greek peasant slowly began to regain ground upon his Moslem lord, and he profited further by the degeneration of the janissary corps at the heart of the empire.

The janissaries had started as a militant, almost monastic body, condemned to celibacy, and recruited exclusively from the Christian tribute-children. But in 1566 they extorted the privilege of legal marriage for themselves, and of admittance into the corps for the sons of their wedlock. The next century completed their transformation from a

157

standing army into a hereditary urban militia—an armed and privileged *bourgeoisie*, rapidly increasing in numbers and correspondingly jealous of extraneous candidates for the coveted vacancies in their ranks. They gradually succeeded in abolishing the enrolment of Christian recruits altogether, and the last regular levy of children for that purpose was made in 1676. Vested interests at Constantinople had freed the helpless peasant from the most crushing burden of all.

At the same moment the contemporary tendency in western Europe towards bureaucratic centralization began to extend itself to the Ottoman Empire. Its exponents were the brothers Achmet and Mustapha Koeprili, who held the grand-vizierate in succession. They laid the foundations of a centralized administration, and, since the unadaptable Turk offered no promising material for their policy, they sought their instruments in the subject race. The continental Greeks were too effectively crushed to aspire beyond the preservation of their own existence; but the islands had been less sorely tried, and Khios, which had enjoyed over two centuries* of prosperity under the rule of a Genoese chartered company, and exchanged it for Ottoman sovereignty under peculiarly lenient conditions, could still supply Achmet a century later with officials of the intelligence and education he required, Khiots were the first to fill the new offices of 'Dragoman of the Porte' (secretary of state) and 'Dragoman of the Fleet' (civil complement of the Turkish capitan-pasha); and they took care in their turn to staff the subordinate posts of their administration with a host of pushing friends and dependants. The Dragoman of the Fleet wielded the fiscal, and thereby in effect the political, authority over the Greek islands in the Aegean; but this was not the highest power to which the new Greek bureaucracy attained. Towards the beginning of the eighteenth century Moldavia and Wallachia—the two 'Danubian Provinces' now united in the kingdom of Rumania—were placed in charge of Greek officials with the rank of voivode or prince, and with

---

*   1346-1566.

practically sovereign power within their delegated dominions. A Danubian principality became the reward of a successful dragoman's career, and these high posts were rapidly monopolized by a close ring of official families, who exercised their immense patronage in favour of their race, and congregated round the Greek patriarch in the 'Phanari',* the Constantinopolitan slum assigned him for his residence by Mohammed the Conqueror.

The alliance of this parvenu 'Phanariot' aristocracy with the conservative Orthodox Church was not unnatural, for the Church itself had greatly extended its political power under Ottoman suzerainty. The Ottoman Government hardly regarded its Christian subjects as integral members of the state, and was content to leave their civil government in the hands of their spiritual pastors to an extent the Romaic emperors would never have tolerated. It allowed the Patriarchate at Constantinople to become its official intermediary with the Greek race, and it further extended the Greek patriarch's authority over the other conquered populations of Orthodox faith—Bulgars, Rumans, and Serbs—which had never been incorporated in the ecclesiastical or political organization of the Romaic Empire, but which learnt under Ottoman rule to receive their priests and bishops from the Greek ecclesiastics of the capital, and even to call themselves by the Romaic name. In 1691 Mustapha Koeprili recognized and confirmed the rights of all Christian subjects of the Sultan by a general organic law.

Mustapha's 'New Ordinance' was dictated by the reverses which Christians beyond the frontier were inflicting upon the Ottoman arms, for pressure from without had followed hard upon disintegration within. Achmet's pyrrhic triumph over Candia in 1669 was followed in 1683 by his brother Mustapha's disastrous discomfiture before the walls of Vienna, and these two sieges marked the turn of the Ottoman tide. The

---

* 'Lighthouse-quarter.'

ebb was slow, yet the ascendancy henceforth lay with Turkey's Christian neighbours, and they began to cut short her frontiers on every side.

The Venetians had never lost hold upon the 'Ionian' chain of islands—Corfu, Cefalonia, Zante, and Cerigo—which flank the western coast of Greece, and in 1685 they embarked on an offensive on the mainland, which won them undisputed possession of Peloponnesos for twenty years.[*] Venice was far nearer than Turkey to her dissolution, and spent the last spasm of her energy on this ephemeral conquest. Yet she had maintained the contact of the Greek race with western Europe during the two centuries of despair, and the interlude of her rule in Peloponnesos was a fitting culmination to her work; for, brief though it was, it effectively broke the Ottoman tradition, and left behind it a system of communal self-government among the Peloponnesian Greeks which the returning Turk was too feeble to sweep away. The Turks gained nothing by the rapid downfall of Venice, for Austria as rapidly stepped into her place, and pressed with fresh vigour the attack from the north-west. North-eastward, too, a new enemy had arisen in Russia, which had been reorganized towards the turn of the century by Peter the Great with a radical energy undreamed of by any Turkish Koeprili, and which found its destiny in opposition to the Ottoman Empire. The new Orthodox power regarded itself as the heir of the Romaic Empire from which it had received its first Christianity and culture. It aspired to repay the Romaic race in adversity by championing it against its Moslem oppressors, and sought its own reward in a maritime outlet on the Black Sea. From the beginning of the eighteenth century Russia repeatedly made war on Turkey, either with or without the co-operation of Austria; but the decisive bout in the struggle was the war of 1769-74. A Russian fleet appeared in the Mediterranean, raised an insurrection in Peloponnesos, and destroyed the Turkish squadron in battle. The Russian armies were still more successful on the steppes, and the Treaty of Kutchuk Kainardji

---

[*]   1699-1718.

not only left the whole north coast of the Black Sea in Russia's possession, but contained an international sanction for the rights of the sultan's Orthodox subjects. In 1783 a supplementary commercial treaty extorted for the Ottoman Greeks the right to trade under the Russian flag. The territorial sovereignty of Turkey in the Aegean remained intact, but the Russian guarantee gave the Greek race a more substantial security than the shadowy ordinance of Mustapha Koeprili. The paralysing prestige of the Porte was broken, and Greek eyes were henceforth turned in hope towards Petersburg.

By the end of the eighteenth century the condition of the Greeks had in fact changed remarkably for the better, and the French and English travellers who now began to visit the Ottoman Empire brought away the impression that a critical change in its internal equilibrium was at hand. The Napoleonic wars had just extinguished the Venetian Republic and swept the Ionian Islands into the struggle between England and France for the mastery of the Mediterranean. England had fortified herself in Cefalonia and Zante, France in Corfu, and interest centred on the opposite mainland, where Ali Pasha of Yannina maintained a formidable neutrality towards either power.

The career of Ali marked that phase in the decline of an Oriental empire when the task of strong government becomes too difficult for the central authority and is carried on by independent satraps with greater efficiency in their more limited sphere. Ali governed the Adriatic hinterland with practically sovereign power, and compelled the sultan for some years to invest his sons with the pashaliks of Thessaly and Peloponnesos. The greater part of the Greek race thus came in some degree under his control, and his policy towards it clearly reflected the transition from the old to the new. He waged far more effective war than the distant sultan upon local liberties, and, though the elimination of the feudal Turkish landowner was pure gain to the Greeks, they suffered themselves from the loss of traditional privileges which the original Ottoman conquest had left intact. The Armatoli, a local Christian militia

161

who kept order in the mountainous mainland north of Peloponnesos where Turkish feudatories were rare, were either dispersed by Ali or enrolled in his regular army. And he was ruthless in the extermination of recalcitrant communities, like Agrapha on the Aspropotarno, which had never been inscribed on the taxation-rolls of the Romaic or the Ottoman treasury, or Suli, a robber clan ensconced in the mountains Immediately west of Ali's capital. On the other hand, the administration of these pacified and consolidated dominions became as essentially Greek in character as the Phanariot regime beyond the Danube. Ali was a Moslem and an Albanian, but the Orthodox Greeks were in a majority among his subjects, and he knew how to take advantage of their abilities. His business was conducted by Greek secretaries in the Greek tongue, and Yannina, his capital, was a Greek city. European visitors to Yannina (for every one began the Levantine tour by paying his respects to Ali) were struck by the enterprise and intelligence of its citizens. The doctors were competent, because they had taken their education in Italy or France; the merchants were prosperous, because they had established members of their family at Odessa, Trieste, or even Hamburg, as permanent agents of their firm. A new Greek *bourgeoisie* had arisen, in close contact with the professional life of western Europe, and equally responsive to the new philosophical and political ideas that were being propagated by the French Revolution.

This intellectual ferment was the most striking change of all. Since the sack of Constantinople in 1204, Greek culture had retired into the monasteries—inaccessible fastnesses where the monks lived much the same life as the clansmen of Suli or Agrapha. Megaspelaion, the great cave quarried in the wall of a precipitous Peloponnesian ravine; Meteora, suspended on half a dozen isolated pinnacles of rock in Thessaly, where the only access was by pulley or rope-ladder; 'Ayon Oros', the confederation of monasteries great and small upon the mountain-promontory of Athos—these succeeded in preserving a shadow of the old tradition, at the cost of isolation from all humane influences that might have kept

162

their spiritual inheritance alive. Their spirit was mediaeval, ecclesiastical, and as barren as their sheltering rocks; and the new intellectual disciples of Europe turned to the monasteries in vain. The biggest ruin on Athos is a boys' school planned in the eighteenth century to meet the educational needs of all the Orthodox in the Ottoman Empire, and wrecked on the reefs of monastic obscurantism. But its founder, the Corfiot scholar Evyenios Voulgaris, did not hesitate to break with the past. He put his own educational ideas into practice at Yannina and Constantinople, and contributed to the great achievement of his contemporary, the Khiot Adhamandios Korais, who settled in Paris and there evolved a literary adaptation of the Romaic patois to supersede the lifeless travesty of Attic style traditionally affected by ecclesiastical penmen. But the renaissance was not confined to Greeks abroad. The school on Athos failed, but others established themselves before the close of the eighteenth century in the people's midst, even in the smaller towns and the remoter villages. The still flourishing secondary school of Dhimitzana, in the heart of Peloponnesos, began its existence in this period, and the national revival found expression in a new name. Its prophets repudiated the 'Romaic' name, with its associations of ignorance and oppression, and taught their pupils to think of themselves as 'Hellenes' and to claim in their own right the intellectual and political liberty of the Ancient Greeks.

This spiritual 'Hellenism', however, was only one manifestation of returning vitality, and was ultimately due to the concrete economic development with which it went hand in hand. The Greeks, who had found culture in western Europe, had come there for trade, and their commercial no less than their intellectual activity reacted in a penetrating way upon their countrymen at home. A mountain village like Ambelakia in Thessaly found a regular market for its dyed goods in Germany, and the commercial treaty of 1783 between Turkey and Russia encouraged communities which could make nothing of the land to turn their attention to the sea. Galaxhidi, a village on the northern shore of the Korinthian Gulf, whose only asset was its natural harbour, and Hydhra, Spetza, and Psara, three barren little islands in the Aegean, had begun to lay the foundations of a merchant marine, when Napoleon's boycott and the British blockade, which left no neutral flag but the Ottoman in the Mediterranean, presented the Greek shipmen that sailed under it with an opportunity they exploited to the full. The whitewashed houses of solid stone, rising tier above tier up the naked limestone mountainside, still testify to the prosperity which chance thus suddenly brought to the Hydhriots and their fellow islanders, and did not withdraw again till it had enabled them to play a decisive part in their nation's history.

Their ships were small, but they were home-built, skilfully navigated, and profitably employed in the carrying trade of the Mediterranean ports. Their economic life was based on co-operation, for the sailors, as well as the captain and owner of the ship, who were generally the same person, took shares in the outlay and profit of each voyage; but their political organization was oligarchical—an executive council elected by and from the owners of the shipping. Feud and intrigue were rife between family and family, class and class, and between the native community and the resident aliens, without seriously affecting the vigour and enterprise of the commonwealth as a whole. These seafaring islands on the eve of the modern Greek Revolution were an exact reproduction of the Aigina, Korinth, and Athens which repelled the Persian from Ancient Greece. The germs of a new national life were thus springing up among the Greeks in every direction—in mercantile colonies scattered over the world from Odessa to Alexandria and from Smyrna to Trieste; among Phanariot princes in the Danubian Provinces and their ecclesiastical colleagues at Constantinople; in the islands of the Aegean and the Ionian chain, and upon the mountains of Suli and Agrapha. But the ambitions this national revival aroused were even greater than the reality itself. The leaders of the movement did not merely aspire to liberate the Greek nation from the Turkish yoke. They were conscious of the assimilative power their nationality possessed. The Suliots, for example, were an immigrant Albanian tribe, who had learnt to speak Greek from the

Greek peasants over whom they tyrannized. The Hydhriot and Spetziot islanders were Albanians too, who had even clung to their primitive language during the two generations since they took up their present abode, but had become none the less firmly linked to their Greek-speaking neighbours in Peloponnesos by their common fellowship in the Orthodox Church. The numerous Albanian colonies settled up and down the Greek continent were at least as Greek in feeling as they. And why should not the same prove true of the Bulgarian population, in the Balkans, who had belonged from the beginning to the Orthodox Church, and had latterly been brought by improvident Ottoman policy within the Greek patriarch's fold? Or why should not the Greek administrators beyond the Danube imbue their Ruman subjects with a sound Hellenic sentiment? In fact, the prophets of Hellenism did not so much desire to extricate the Greek nation from the Ottoman Empire as to make it the ruling element in the empire itself by ejecting the Moslem Turks from their privileged position and assimilating all populations of Orthodox faith. These dreams took shape in the foundation of a secret society— the 'Philiki Hetairia' or 'League of Friends'—which established itself at Odessa in 1814 with the connivence of the Russian police, and opened a campaign of propaganda in anticipation of an opportunity to strike.

The initiative came from the Ottoman Government itself. At the weakest moment in its history the empire found in Sultan Mahmud a ruler of peculiar strength, who saw that the only hope of overcoming his dangers lay in meeting them half-way. The national movement of Hellenism was gathering momentum in the background, but it was screened by the personal ambitions of Ali of Yannina, and Mahmud reckoned to forestall both enemies by quickly striking Ali down.

In the winter of 1819-20 Ali was outlawed, and in the spring the invasion of his territories began. Both the Moslem combatants enlisted Christian Armatoli, and all continental Greece was under arms. By the end of the summer Ali's outlying strongholds had fallen, his armies were driven in, and he himself was closely invested in Yannina; but

165

with autumn a deadlock set in, and the sultan's reckoning was thrown out. In November 1820 the veteran soldier Khurshid was appointed to the pashalik of Peloponnesos to hold the Greeks in check and close accounts with Ali. In March 1821, after five months spent in organizing his province, Khurshid felt secure enough to leave it for the Yannina lines. But he was mistaken; for within a month of his departure Peloponnesos was ablaze.

The 'Philiki Hetairia' had decided to act, and the Peloponnesians responded enthusiastically to the signal. In the north Germanos, metropolitan bishop of Patras, rallied the insurgents at the monastery of Megaspelaion, and unfurled the monastic altar-cloth as a national standard. In the south the peninsula of Maina, which had been the latest refuge of ancient Hellenism, was now the first to welcome the new, and to throw off the shadowy allegiance it had paid for a thousand years to Romaic archonts and Ottoman capitan-pashas. Led by Petros Mavromichalis, the chief of the leading clan, the Mainates issued from their mountains. This was in April, and by the middle of May all the open country had been swept clear, and the hosts joined hands before Tripolitza, which was the seat of Ottoman government at the central point of the province. The Turkish garrison attacked, but was heavily defeated at Valtetzi by the tactical skill of Theodore Kolokotronis the 'klepht', who had become experienced in guerrilla warfare through his alternate professions of brigand and gendarme—a career that had increased its possibilities as the Ottoman system decayed. After Kolokotronis's victory, the Greeks kept Tripolitza under a close blockade. Early in October it fell amid frightful scenes of pillage and massacre, and Ottoman dominion in the Peloponnesos fell with it. On January 22, 1822, Korinth, the key to the isthmus, passed into the Greeks' hands, and only four fortresses—Nauplia, Patras, Koron, and Modhon—still held out within it against Greek investment. Not a Turk survived in the Peloponnesos beyond their walls, for the slaughter at Tripolitza was only the most terrible instance of what happened wherever a Moslem colony was found. In Peloponnesos, at any rate, the revolution had been grimly successful.

There had also been successes at sea. The merchant marine of the Greek islands had suffered grievously from the fall of Napoleon and the settlement at Vienna, which, by restoring normal conditions of trade, had destroyed their abnormal monopoly. The revolution offered new opportunities for profitable venture, and in April 1821 Hydhra, Spetza and Psara hastened to send a privateering fleet to sea. As soon as the fleet crossed the Aegean, Samos rid itself of the Turks. At the beginning of June the rickety Ottoman squadron issued from the Dardanelles, but it was chased back by the islanders under the lee of Mitylini. Memories of Russian naval tactics in 1770 led the Psariots to experiment in fire-ships, and one of the two Turkish ships of the line fell a victim to this attack. Within a week of setting sail, the diminished Turkish squadron was back again in the Dardanelles, and the islanders were left with the command of the sea.

The general Christian revolution thus seemed fairly launched, and in the first panic the threatened Moslems began reprisals of an equally general kind. In the larger Turkish cities there were massacres of Christian minorities, and the Government lent countenance to them by murdering its own principal Christian official Gregorios, the Greek patriarch at Constantinople, on April 22, 1821. But Sultan Mahmud quickly recovered himself. He saw that his empire could not survive a racial war, and determined to prevent the present revolt from assuming such a character. His plan was to localize it by stamping out the more distant sparks with all his energy, before concentrating his force at leisure upon the main conflagration.

This policy was justified by the event. On March 6 the 'Philiki Hetairia' at Odessa had opened its own operations in grandiose style by sending a filibustering expedition across the Russo-Turkish frontier under command of Prince Alexander Hypsilantis, a Phanariot in the Russian service. Hypsilantis played for a general revolt of the Ruman population in the Danubian Principalities and a declaration of war against Turkey on the part of Russia. But the Rumans had no desire to assist the Greek bureaucrats who oppressed them, and the Tsar Alexander had been converted by the experiences of 1812-13 to a pacifistic respect for the *status quo*. Prince Hypsilantis was driven ignominiously to internment across the Austrian frontier, little more than a hundred days after his expedition began; and his fiasco assured the Ottoman Government of two encouraging facts—that the revolution would not carry away the whole Orthodox population but would at any rate confine itself to the Greeks; and that the struggle against it would be fought out for the present, at least, without foreign intervention.

In the other direction, however, rebellion was spreading northward from Peloponnesos to continental Greece. Galaxidhi revolted in April, and was followed in June by Mesolonghi—a prosperous town of fishermen, impregnably situated in the midst of the lagoons at the mouth of the Aspropotamo, beyond the narrows of the Korinthian Gulf. By the end of the month, north-western Greece was free as far as the outposts of Khurshid Pasha beyond the Gulf of Arta.

Further eastward, again, in the mountains between the Gulf of Korinth and the river Elladha (Sperkheios), the Armatoli of Ali's faction had held their ground, and gladly joined the revolution on the initiative of their captains Dhiakos and Odhyssevs. But the movement found its limits. The Turkish garrison of Athens obstinately held out during the winter of 1821-2, and the Moslems of Negrepont (Euboia) maintained their mastery in the island. In Agrapha they likewise held their own, and, after one severely punished raid, the Agraphiot Armatoli were induced to re-enter the sultan's service on liberal terms. The Vlachs in the gorges of the Aspropotamo were pacified with equal success; and Dramali, Khurshid's lieutenant, who guarded the communications between the army investing Yannina and its base at Constantinople, was easily able to crush all symptoms of revolt in Thessaly from his head-quarters at Larissa. Still further east, the autonomous Greek villages on

168

the mountainous promontories of Khalkidhiki had revolted in May, in conjunction with the well-supplied and massively fortified monasteries of the 'Ayon Oros'; but the Pasha of Salonika called down the South Slavonic Moslem landowners from the interior, sacked the villages, and amnestied the monastic confederation on condition of establishing a Turkish garrison in their midst and confiscating their arms. The monks' compliance was assisted by the excommunication under which the new patriarch at Constantinople had placed all the insurgents by the sultan's command.

The movement was thus successfully localised on the European continent, and further afield it was still more easily cut short. After the withdrawal of the Turkish squadron, the Greek fleet had to look on at the systematic destruction of Kydhonies,* a flourishing Greek industrial town on the mainland opposite Mitylini which had been founded under the sultan's auspices only forty years before. All that the islanders could do was to take off the survivors in their boats; and when they dispersed to their ports in autumn, the Ottoman ships came out again from the Dardanelles, sailed round Peloponnesos into the Korinthian Gulf, and destroyed Galaxidhi. A still greater catastrophe followed the reopening of naval operations next spring. In March 1822 the Samians landed a force on Khios and besieged the Turkish garrison, which was relieved after three weeks by the arrival of the Ottoman fleet. A month later the Greek fleet likewise appeared on the scene, and on June 18 a Psariot captain, Constantine Kanaris, actually destroyed the Ottoman flag-ship by a daring fire-ship attack. Upon this the Ottoman fleet fled back as usual to the Dardanelles; yet the only consequence was the complete devastation, in revenge, of helpless Khios. The long-shielded prosperity of the island was remorselessly destroyed, the people were either enslaved or massacred, and the victorious fleet had to stand by as passively this time as at the destruction of Kydhonies the season before. In the following

---

*   Turkish Aivali.

summer, again, the same fate befell Trikeri, a maritime community on the Gulf of Volo which had gained its freedom when the rest of Thessaly stirred in vain; and so in 1823 the revolution found itself confined on sea, as well as on land, to the focus where it had originated in April 1821.

This isolation was a practical triumph for Sultan Mahmud. The maintenance of the Ottoman Empire on the basis of Moslem ascendancy was thereby assured; but it remained to be seen whether the isolated area could now be restored to the *status quo* in which the rest of his dominions had been retained.

During the whole season of 1821 the army of Khurshid had been held before Yannina. But in February 1822 Yannina fell, Ali was slain, his treasure seized, and his troops disbanded. The Ottoman forces were liberated for a counterattack on Peloponnesos. Already in April Khurshid broke up his camp at Larissa, and his lieutenant Dramali was given command of the new expedition towards the south. He crossed the Sperkheios at the beginning of July with an army of twenty thousand men.* Athens had capitulated to Odhyssevs ten days before; but it had kept open the road for Dramali, and north-eastern Greece fell without resistance into his hands. The citadel of Korinth surrendered as tamely as the open country, and he was master of the isthmus before the end of the month. Nauplia meanwhile had been treating with its besiegers for terms, and would have surrendered to the Greeks already if they had not driven their bargain so hard. Dramali hurried on southward into the plain to the fortress's relief, raised the siege, occupied the town of Argos, and scattered the Greek forces into the hills. But the citadel of Argos held out against him, and the positions were rapidly reversed. Under the experienced direction of Kolokotronis, the Greeks from their hill-fastnesses ringed round the plain of Argos and scaled up every issue. Dramali's supplies ran out. An attempt of his vanguard to break through

---

*   Including a strong contingent of Moslem Slavs—Bulgarian Pomaks from the Aegean hinterland and Serbian Bosniaks from the Adriatic.

again towards the north was bloodily repulsed, and he barely succeeded two days later in extricating the main body in a demoralized condition, with the loss of all his baggage-train. The Turkish army melted away, Dramali was happy to die at Korinth, and Khurshid was executed by the sultan's command. The invasion of Peloponnesos had broken down, and nothing could avert the fall of Nauplia. The Ottoman fleet hovered for one September week in the offing, but Kanaris's fire-ships took another ship of the line in toll at the roadsteads of Tenedos before it safely regained the Dardanelles. The garrison of Nauplia capitulated in December, on condition of personal security and liberty, and the captain of a British frigate, which arrived on the spot, took measures that the compact should be observed instead of being broken by the customary massacre. But the strongest fortress in Peloponnesos was now in Greek hands.

In the north-west the season had not passed so well. When the Turks invested Ali in Yannina, they repatriated the Suliot exiles in their native mountains. But a strong sultan was just as formidable to the Suliots as a strong pasha, so they swelled their ranks by enfranchising their peasant-serfs, and made common cause with their old enemy in his adversity. Now that Ali was destroyed, the Suliots found themselves in a precarious position, and turned to the Greeks for aid. But on July 16 the Greek advance was checked by a severe defeat at Petta in the plain of Arta. In September the Suliots evacuated their impregnable fortresses in return for a subsidy and a safe-conduct, and Omer Vrioni, the Ottoman commander in the west,* was free to advance in turn towards the south. On November 6 he actually laid siege to Mesolonghi, but here his experiences were as discomfiting as Dramali's. He could not keep open his communications, and after heavy losses retreated again to Arta in January 1823.

In 1823 the struggle seemed to be lapsing into stalemate. The liberated Peloponnesos had failed to propagate the revolution through

---

*   He was a renegade officer of Ali's.

the remainder of the Ottoman Empire; the Ottoman Government had equally failed to reconquer the Peloponnesos by military invasion. This season's operations only seemed to emphasize the deadlock. The Ottoman commander in the west raised an auxiliary force of Moslem and Catholic clansmen from northern Albania, and attempted to reach Mesolonghi once more. But he penetrated no further than Anatolikon—the Mesolonghiots' outpost village at the head of the lagoons—and the campaign was only memorable for the heroic death of Marko Botzaris the Suliot in a night attack upon the Ottoman camp. At sea, the two fleets indulged in desultory cruises without an encounter, for the Turks were still timid and incompetent, while the growing insubordination and dissension on the Greek ships made concerted action there, too, impossible. By the end of the season it was clear that the struggle could only definitively be decided by the intervention of a third party on one side or the other—unless the Greeks brought their own ruin upon themselves.

This indeed was not unlikely to happen; for the new house of Hellenism had hardly arisen before it became desperately divided against itself. The vitality of the national movement resided entirely in the local communes. It was they that had found the fighting men, kept them armed and supplied, and by spontaneous co-operation expelled the Turk from Peloponnesos. But if the co-operation was to be permanent it must have a central organization, and with the erection of this superstructure the troubles began. As early as June 1821 a 'Peloponnesian Senate' was constituted and at once monopolized by the 'Primates', the propertied class that had been responsible for the communal taxes under the Romaic and Ottoman regimes and was allowed to control the communal government in return. About the same time two Phanariot princes threw in their lot with the revolution—Alexander Mavrokordatos and Demetrius, the more estimable brother of the futile Alexander Hypsilantis. Both were saturated with the most recent European political theory, and they committed the peasants and seamen of the liberated districts to an ambitious constitutionalism. In December 1821 a 'National Assembly' met at Epidauros, passed an elaborate organic law, and elected Mavrokordatos first president of the Hellenic Republic.

The struggle for life and death in 1822 had staved off the internal crisis, but the Peloponnesian Senate remained obstinately recalcitrant towards the National Government in defence of its own vested interests; and the insubordination of the fleet in 1823 was of one piece with the political faction which broke out as soon as the immediate danger from without was removed.

Towards the end of 1823 European 'Philhellenes' began to arrive in Greece. In those dark days of reaction that followed Waterloo, self-liberated Hellas seemed the one bright spot on the continent; but the idealists who came to offer her their services were confronted with a sorry spectacle. The people were indifferent to their leaders, and the leaders at variance among themselves. The gentlemanly Phanariots had fallen into the background. Mavrokordatos only retained influence in north-western Greece. In Peloponnesos the Primates were all-powerful, and Kolokotronis the klepht was meditating a popular dictatorship at their expense. In the north-east the adventurer Odhyssevs had won a virtual dictatorship already, and was suspected of intrigue with the Turks; and all this factious dissension rankled into civil war as soon as the contraction of a loan in Great Britain had invested the political control of the Hellenic Republic with a prospective value in cash. The first civil war was fought between Kolokotronis on the one side and the Primates of Hydhra and Peloponnesos on the other; but the issue was decided against Kolokotronis by the adhesion to the coalition of Kolettis the Vlach, once physician to Mukhtar Pasha, the son of Ali, and now political agent for all the northern Armatoli in the national service. The fighting lasted from November 1823 to June 1824, and was followed by another outbreak in November of the latter year, when the victors quarrelled over the spoils, and the Primates were worsted in turn by the islanders and the Armatoli. The nonentity Kondouriottis of Hydhra finally emerged as President of Greece, with the sharp-witted Kolettis as his principal wire-puller, but the disturbances did not cease till the last instalment of the loan had been received and squandered and there was no more spoil to fight for.

Meanwhile, Sultan Mahmud had been better employed. Resolved to avert stalemate by the only possible means, he had applied in the course of 1823 to Mohammed Ali Pasha of Egypt, a more formidable, though more distant, satrap than Ali of Yannina himself. Mohammed Ali had a standing army and navy organized on the European model. He had also a son Ibrahim, who knew how to manoeuvre them, and was ambitious of a kingdom. Mahmud hired the father's troops and the son's generalship for the re-conquest of Peloponnesos, under engagement to invest Ibrahim with the pashalik as soon as he should effectively make it his own. By this stroke of diplomacy a potential rebel was turned into a willing ally, and the preparations for the Egyptian expedition went forward busily through the winter of 1823-4.

The plan of campaign was systematically carried out. During the season of respite the Greek islanders had harried the coasts and commerce of Anatolia and Syria at will. The first task was to deprive them of their outposts in the Aegean, and an advanced squadron of the Egyptian fleet accordingly destroyed the community of Kasos in June 1824, while the Ottoman squadron sallied out of the Dardanelles a month later and dealt out equal measure to Psara. The two main flotillas then effected a junction off Rhodes; and, though the crippled Greek fleet still ventured pluckily to confront them, it could not prevent Ibrahim from casting anchor safely in Soudha Bay and landing his army to winter in Krete. In February 1825 he transferred these troops with equal impunity to the fortress of Modhon, which was still held for the sultan by an Ottoman garrison. The fire-ships of Hydra came to harry his fleet too late, and on land the Greek forces were impotent against his trained soldiers. The Government in vain promoted Kolokotronis from captivity to commandership-in-chief. The whole south-western half of Peloponnesos passed into Ibrahim's hands, and in June 1825 he even penetrated as far as the mills of Lerna on the eastern coast, a few miles south of Argos itself.

174

At the same time the Ottoman army of the west moved south again under a new commander, Rashid Pasha of Yannina, and laid final siege on April 27 to Mesolonghi, just a year after Byron had died of fever within its walls. The Greeks were magnificent in their defence of these frail mud-bastions, and they more than held their own in the amphibious warfare of the lagoons. The struggle was chequered by the continual coming and going of the Greek and Ottoman fleets. They were indeed the decisive factor; for without the supporting squadron Rashid would have found himself in the same straits as his predecessors at the approach of autumn, while the slackness of the islanders in keeping the sea allowed Mesolonghi to be isolated in January 1826. The rest was accomplished by the arrival of Ibrahim on the scene. His heavy batteries opened fire in February; his gunboats secured command of the lagoons, and forced Anatolikon to capitulate in March. In April provisions in Mesolonghi itself gave out, and, scorning surrender, the garrison—men, women, and children together—made a general sortie on the night of April 22. Four thousand fell, three thousand were taken, and two thousand won through. It was a glorious end for Mesolonghi, but it left the enemy in possession of all north-western Greece.

The situation was going from bad to worse. Ibrahim returned to Peloponnesos, and steadily pushed forward his front, ravaging as steadily as he went. Rashid, after pacifying the north-west, moved on to the north-eastern districts, where the national cause had been shaken by the final treachery and speedy assassination of Odhyssevs. Siege was laid to Athens in June, and the Greek Government enlisted in vain the military experience of its Philhellenes. Fabvier held the Akropolis, but Generalissimo Sir Richard Church was heavily defeated in the spring of 1827 in an attempt to relieve him from the Attic coast; Grand Admiral Cochrane saw his fleet sail home for want of payment in advance, when he summoned it for review at Poros; and Karaiskakis, the Greek captain of Armatoli, was killed in a skirmish during his more successful efforts to harass Rashid's communications by land. On June 5, 1827, the Greek garrison of the Akropolis marched out on terms.

It looked as if the Greek effort after independence would be completely crushed, and as if Sultan Mahmud would succeed in getting his empire under control. In September 1826 he had rid it at last of the mischief at its centre by blowing up the janissaries in their barracks at Constantinople. Turkey seemed almost to have weathered the storm when she was suddenly overborne by further intervention on the other side.

Tsar Alexander, the vaccillator, died in November 1825, and was succeeded by his son Nicholas I, as strong a character and as active a will as Sultan Mahmud himself. Nicholas approached the Greek question without any disinclination towards a Turkish war; and both Great Britain and France found an immediate interest in removing a ground of provocation which might lead to such a rude disturbance of the European 'Balance of Power'. On July 6, 1827, a month after Athens surrendered, the three powers concluded a treaty for the pacification of Greece, in which they bound over both belligerent parties to accept an armistice under pain of military coercion. An allied squadron appeared off Navarino Bay to enforce this policy upon the Ottoman and Egyptian fleet which lay united there, and the intrusion of the allied admirals into the bay itself precipitated on October 20 a violent naval battle in which the Moslem flotilla was destroyed. The die was cast; and in April 1828 the Russian and Ottoman Governments drifted into a formal war, which brought Russian armies across the Danube as far as Adrianople, and set the Ottoman Empire at bay for the defence of its capital. Thanks to Mahmud's reorganization, the empire did not succumb to this assault; but it had no more strength to spare for the subjugation of Greece. The Greeks had no longer to reckon with the sultan as a military factor; and in August 1828 they were relieved of Ibrahim's presence as well, by the disembarkation of 14,000 French troops in Peloponnesos to superintend the withdrawal of the Egyptian forces. In March 1829 the three powers delimited the Greek frontier. The line ran east and west from the Gulf of Volo to the Gulf of Arta, and assigned to the new state no more and no less territory than the districts that had effectively asserted their independence against the sultan in 1821. This settlement was the only one possible under the circumstances; but it was essentially transitory, for it neglected the natural line of nationality altogether, and left a numerical majority of the Greek race, as well as the most important centres of its life, under the old regime of servitude.

Even the liberated area was not at the end of its troubles. In the spring of 1827, when they committed themselves into the hands of their foreign patrons, the Greeks had found a new president for the republic in John Kapodistrias, an intimate of Alexander the tsar. Kapodistrias was a Corfiote count, with a Venetian education and a career in the Russian diplomatic service, and no one could have been more fantastically unsuitable for the task of reconstructing the country to which he was called. Kapodistrias' ideal was the *fin-de-siecle* 'police-state'; but 'official circles' did not exist in Greece, and he had no acquaintance with the peasants and sailors whom he hoped to redeem by bureaucracy. He instituted a hierarchically centralized administration which made the abortive constitution of Mavrokordatos seem sober by comparison; he trampled on the liberty of the rising press, which was the most hopeful educational influence in the country; and he created superfluous ministerial portfolios for his untalented brothers. In fact he reglamented Greece from his palace at Aigina like a divinely appointed autocrat, from his arrival in January 1828 till the summer of 1831, when he provoked the Hydhriots to open rebellion, and commissioned the Russian squadron in attendance to quell them by a naval action, with the result that Poros was sacked by the President's regular army and the national fleet was completely destroyed. After that, he attempted to rule as a military dictator, and fell foul of the Mavromichalis of Maina. The Mainates knew better how to deal with the 'police-state' than the Hydhriots; and on October 9, 1831, Kapodistrias was assassinated in Nauplia, at the church door, by two representatives of the Mavromichalis clan.

The country lapsed into utter anarchy. Peloponnesians and Armatoli, Kolokotronists and Kolettists, alternately appointed and deposed subservient national assemblies and governing commissions by naked violence, which culminated in a gratuitous and disastrous attack upon the French troops stationed in Peloponnesos for their common protection. The three powers realized that it was idle to liberate Greece from Ottoman government unless they found her another in its place. They decided on monarchy, and offered the crown, in February 1832, to Prince Otto, a younger son of the King of Bavaria. The negotiations dragged on many months longer than Greece could afford to wait. But in July 1832 the sultan recognized the sovereign independence of the kingdom of Hellas in consideration of a cash indemnity; and in February 1833, just a year after the first overtures had been made, the appointed king arrived at Nauplia with a decorative Bavarian staff and a substantial loan from the allies.

3.
The Consolidation of the State

Half the story of Greece is told. We have watched the nation awake and put forth its newly-found strength in a great war of independence, and we have followed the course of the struggle to its result—the foundation of the kingdom of Hellas.

It is impossible to close this chapter of Greek history without a sense of disappointment. The spirit of Greece had travailed, and only a principality was born, which gathered within its frontiers scarcely one-third of the race, and turned for its government to a foreign administration which had no bond of tradition or affinity with the population it was to rule. And yet something had been achieved. An oasis had been wrested from the Turkish wilderness, in which Hellenism could henceforth work out its own salvation untrammelled, and extend its borders little by little, until it brought within them at last the whole of its destined heritage. The fleeting glamour of dawn had passed, but it had brought the steady light of day, in which the work begun could be carried out soberly and indefatigably to its conclusion. The new kingdom, in fact, if it fulfilled its mission, might become the political nucleus and the spiritual ensample of a permanently awakened nation—an 'education of Hellas' such as Pericles hoped to see Athens become in the greatest days of Ancient Greece.

When, therefore, we turn to the history of the kingdom, our disappointment is all the more intense, for in the first fifty years of its existence there is little development to record. In 1882 King Otto's principality presented much the same melancholy spectacle as it did in 1833, when he landed in Nauplia Bay, except that Otto himself had left the scene. His Bavarian staff belonged to that reactionary generation that followed the overthrow of Napoleon in Europe, and attempted, heedless of Kapodistrias' fiasco, to impose on Greece the bureaucracy of the *ancien regime*. The Bavarians' work was entirely destructive. The local liberties which had grown up under the Ottoman dominion and been the very life of the national revival, were effectively repressed. Hydhriot and Spetziot, Suliot and Mainate, forfeited their characteristic individuality, but none of the benefits of orderly and uniform government were realized. The canker of brigandage defied all efforts to root it out, and in spite of the loans with which the royal government was supplied by the protecting powers, the public finance was subject to periodical breakdowns. In 1837 King Otto, now of age, took the government into his own hands, only to have it taken out of them again by a revolution in 1843. Thereafter he reigned as a constitutional monarch, but he never reconciled himself to the position, and in 1862 a second revolution drove him into exile, a scapegoat for the afflictions of his kingdom. Bavarian then gave place to Dane, yet the afflictions continued. In 1882 King George had been nineteen years on the throne* without any happier fortune than his predecessor's. It is true that the frontiers of the kingdom had been somewhat extended. Great Britain had presented the new sovereign with the Ionian Islands as an inaugural gift, and the Berlin Conference had recently added the province of Thessaly. Yet the major part of the Greek race still awaited liberation from the Turkish yoke, and regarded the national kingdom, chronically incapacitated by the twin plagues of brigandage and bankruptcy, with increasing disillusionment. The kingdom of Hellas seemed to have failed in its mission altogether.

What was the explanation of this failure? It was that the very nature of the mission paralysed the state from taking the steps essential to its accomplishment. The phenomenon has been, unhappily, only too familiar in the Nearer East, and any one who travelled in the Balkans in 1882, or even so recently as 1912, must at once have become aware of it.

Until a nation has completely vindicated its right to exist, it is hard for it to settle down and make its life worth living. We nations of western Europe (before disaster fell upon us) had learnt to take our existence for granted, and 'Politics' for us had come to mean an organized effort to improve the internal economy of our community. But a foreigner who picked up a Greek newspaper would have found in it none of the matter with which he was familiar in his own, no discussion of financial policy, economic development, or social reconstruction. The news-columns would have been monopolized by foreign politics, and in the cafes he would have heard the latest oscillation in the international balance of power canvassed with the same intense and minute interest that Englishmen in a railway-carriage would have been devoting to Old Age Pensions, National Health Insurance, or Land Valuation. He would have been amazed by a display of intimate knowledge such as no British quidnunc could have mustered if he had happened to stumble across these intricacies

---

*   King George, like King Otto, was only seventeen years old when he received his crown.

of international competition, and the conversation would always have terminated in the same unanswered but inconscionable challenge to the future: 'When will the oppressed majority of our race escape the Turkish yoke? If the Ottoman dominion is destroyed, what redistribution of its provinces will follow? Shall we then achieve our national unity, or will our Balkan neighbours encroach upon the inheritance which is justly ours?'

This preoccupation with events beyond the frontiers was not caused by any lack of vital problems within them. The army was the most conspicuous object of public activity, but it was not an aggressive speculation, or an investment of national profits deliberately calculated to bring in one day a larger return. It was a necessity of life, and its efficiency was barely maintained out of the national poverty. In fact, it was almost the only public utility with which the nation could afford to provide itself, and the traveller from Great Britain would have been amazed again at the miserable state of all reproductive public works. The railways were few and far between, their routes roundabout, and their rolling-stock scanty, so that trains were both rare and slow. Wheel-roads were no commoner a feature in Greece than railways are here, and such stretches as had been constructed had often never come into use, because they had just failed to reach their goal or were still waiting for their bridges, so that they were simply falling into decay and converting the outlay of capital upon them into a dead loss. The Peiraeus was the only port in the country where steamers could come alongside a quay, and discharge their cargoes directly on shore. Elsewhere, the vessel must anchor many cables' lengths out, and depend on the slow and expensive services of lighters, for lack of pier construction and dredging operations. For example, Kalamata, the economic outlet for the richest part of Peloponnesos, and the fifth largest port in the kingdom,* was and still remains a mere open roadstead, where all ships that call are kept at a distance by the silt from a mountain

---

*   The four chief ports being Peiraeus, Patras, Syra, and Volos.

torrent, and so placed in imminent danger of being driven, by the first storm, upon the rocks of a neighbouring peninsula.

These grave shortcomings were doubtless due in part to the geographical character of the country, though it was clear, from what had actually been accomplished, that it would have been both possible and profitable to attempt much more, if the nation's energy could have been secured for the work. But it is hard to tinker at details when you are kept in a perpetual fever by a question of life and death, and the great preliminary questions of national unity and self-government remained still unsettled.

Before these supreme problems all other interests paled, for they were no will-o'-the-wisps of theoretical politics. It needs a long political education to appreciate abstract ideas, and the Greeks were still in their political infancy, but the realization of Greater Greece implied for them the satisfaction of all their concrete needs at once.

So long as the *status quo* endured, they were isolated from the rest of Europe by an unbroken band of Turkish territory, stretching from the Aegean to the Adriatic Sea. What was the use of overcoming great engineering difficulties to build a line of European gauge from Athens right up to the northern frontier, if Turkey refused to sanction the construction of the tiny section that must pass through her territory between the Greek railhead and the actual terminus of the European system at Salonika? Or if, even supposing she withdrew her veto, she would have it in her power to bring pressure on Greece at any moment by threatening to sever communications along this vital artery? So long as Turkey was there, Greece was practically an island, and her only communication with continental Europe lay through her ports. But what use to improve the ports, when the recovery of Salonika, the fairest object of the national dreams, would ultimately change the country's economic centre of gravity, and make her maritime as well as her overland commerce flow along quite other channels than the present?

Thus the Greek nation's present was overshadowed by its future, and its actions paralysed by its hopes. Perhaps a nation with more power of application and less of imagination would have schooled itself to the thought that these sordid, obtrusive details were the key to the splendours of the future, and would have devoted itself to the systematic amelioration of the cramped area which it had already secured for its own. This is what Bulgaria managed to do during her short but wonderful period of internal growth between the Berlin Treaty of 1878 and the declaration of war against Turkey in 1912. But Bulgaria, thanks to her geographical situation, was from the outset freer from the tentacles of the Turkish octopus than Greece had contrived to make herself by her fifty years' start, while her temperamentally sober ambitions were not inflamed by such past traditions as Greece had inherited, not altogether to her advantage. Be that as it may, Greece, whether by fault or misfortune, had failed during this half-century to apply herself successfully to the cure of her defects and the exploitation of her assets, though she did not lack leaders strong-minded enough to summon her to the dull business of the present. Her history during the succeeding generation was a struggle between the parties of the Present and the Future, and the unceasing discomfiture of the former is typified in the tragedy of Trikoupis, the greatest modern Greek statesman before the advent of Venezelos.

Trikoupis came into power in 1882, just after the acquisition of the rich agricultural province of Thessaly under the Treaty of Berlin had given the kingdom a fresh start. There were no such continuous areas of good arable land within the original frontiers, and such rare patches as there were had been desolated by those eight years of savage warfare* which had been the price of liberty. The population had been swept away by wholesale massacres of racial minorities in every district; the dearth of industrious hands had allowed the torrents to play havoc with the cultivation-terraces on the mountain slopes; and the spectre of malaria,

---

*   1821-28

always lying in wait for its opportunity, had claimed the waterlogged plains for its own. During the fifty years of stagnation little attempt had been made to cope with the evil, until now it seemed almost past remedy.

If, however, the surface of the land offered little prospect of wealth for the moment, there were considerable treasures to be found beneath it. A metalliferous bolt runs down the whole east coast of the Greek mainland, cropping up again in many of the Aegean islands, and some of the ores, of which there is a great variety, are rare and valuable. The lack of transit facilities is partly remedied by the fact that workable veins often lie near enough to the sea for the produce to be carried straight from mine to ship, by an endless-chain system of overhead trolleys; so that, once capital is secured for installing the plant and opening the mine, profitable operations can be carried on irrespective of the general economic condition of the country. Trikoupis saw how much potential wealth was locked up in these mineral seams. The problem was how to attract the capital necessary to tap it. The nucleus round which have accumulated those immense masses of mobilised capital that are the life-blood of modern European industry and commerce, was originally derived from the surplus profits of agriculture. But a country that finds itself reduced, like Greece in the nineteenth century, to a state of agricultural bankruptcy, has obviously failed to save any surplus in the process, so that it is unable to provide from its own pocket the minimum outlay it so urgently needs in order to open for itself some new activity. If it is to obtain a fresh start on other lines, it must secure the co-operation of the foreign investor, and the capitalist with a ready market for his money will only put it into enterprises where he has some guarantee of its safety. There was little doubt that the minerals of Greece would well repay extraction; the uncertain element was the Greek nation itself. The burning question of national unity might break out at any moment into a blaze of war, and, in the probable case of disaster, involve the whole country and all interests connected with it in economic as well as political ruin. Western Europe would not commit itself to Greek mining enterprise, unless it felt confident that the statesman responsible for the government of Greece would and could restrain his country from its instinctive impulse towards political adventure.

The great merit of Trikoupis was that he managed to inspire this confidence. Greece owes most of the wheelroads, railways, and mines of which she can now boast to the dozen years of his more or less consecutive administration. But the roads are unfinished, the railway-network incomplete, the mines exploited only to a fraction of their capacity, because the forces against Trikoupis were in the end too strong for him. It may be that his eye too rigidly followed the foreign investor's point of view, and that by adopting a more conciliatory attitude towards the national ideal, he might have strengthened his position at home without impairing his reputation abroad; but his position was really made impossible by a force quite beyond his control, the irresponsible and often intolerable behaviour which Turkey, under whatever regime, has always practised towards foreign powers, and especially towards those Balkan states which have won their freedom in her despite, while perforce abandoning a large proportion of their race to the protracted outrage of Turkish misgovernment.

Several times over the Porte, by wanton insults to Greece, wrecked the efforts of Trikoupis to establish good relations between the two governments, and played the game of the chauvinist party led by Trikoupis' rival, Deliyannis. Deliyannis' tenures of office were always brief, but during them he contrived to undo most of the work accomplished by Trikoupis in the previous intervals. A particularly tense 'incident' with Turkey put him in power in 1893, with a strong enough backing from the country to warrant a general mobilization. The sole result was the ruin of Greek credit. Trikoupis was hastily recalled to office by the king, but too late. He found himself unable to retrieve the ruin, and retired altogether from politics in 1895, dying abroad next year in voluntary exile and enforced disillusionment.

With the removal of Trikoupis from the helm, Greece ran straight upon the rocks. A disastrous war with Turkey was precipitated in 1897 by events in Krete. It brought the immediate *debacle* of the army and the reoccupation of Thessaly for a year by Turkish troops, while its final penalties were the cession of the chief strategical positions along the northern frontier and the imposition of an international commission of control over the Greek finances, in view of the complete national bankruptcy entailed by the war. The fifteen years that followed 1895 were almost the blackest period in modern Greek history; yet the time was not altogether lost, and such events as the draining of the Kopais-basin by a British company, and its conversion from a malarious swamp into a rich agricultural area, marked a perceptible economic advance.

This comparative stagnation was broken at last by the Young Turk *pronunciamiento* at Salonika in 1908, which produced such momentous repercussions all through the Nearer East. The Young Turks had struck in order to forestall the dissolution of the Ottoman Empire, but the opportunity was seized by every restive element within it to extricate itself, if possible, from the Turkish coils. Now, just as in 1897, Greece was directly affected by the action of the Greek population in Krete. As a result of the revolt of 1896-7, Krete had been constituted an autonomous state subject to Ottoman suzerainty, autonomy and suzerainty alike being guaranteed by four great powers. Prince George of Greece, a son of the King of the Hellenes, had been placed at the head of the autonomous government as high commissioner; but his autocratic tendency caused great discontent among the free-spirited Kretans, who had not rid themselves of the Turkish regime in order to forfeit their independence again in another fashion. Dissension culminated in 1906, when the leaders of the opposition took to the mountains, and obtained such support and success in the guerrilla fighting that followed, that they forced Prince George to tender his resignation. He was succeeded as high commissioner by Zaimis, another citizen of the Greek kingdom, who inaugurated a more constitutional regime, and in 1908 the Kretans believed that the moment for realizing the national ideal had come. They proclaimed their union with Greece, and elected deputies to the Parliament at Athens. But the guarantor powers carried out their obligations by promptly sending a combined naval expedition, which hauled down the Greek flag at Canea, and prevented the deputies from embarking for Peiraeus. This apparently pedantic insistence upon the *status quo* was extremely exasperating to Greek nationalism. It produced a ferment in the kingdom, which grew steadily for nine months, and vented itself in July 1909 in the *coup d'etat* of the 'Military League', a second-hand imitation of the Turkish 'Committee of Union and Progress'. The royal family was cavalierly treated, and constitutional government superseded by a junta of officers. But at this point the policy of the four powers towards Krete was justified. Turkey knew well that she had lost Krete in 1897, but she could still exploit her suzerainty to prevent Greece from gaining new strength by the annexation of the island. The Young Turks had seized the reins of government, not to modify the policy of the Porte, but to intensify its chauvinism, and they accordingly intimated that they would consider any violation of their suzerain rights over Krete a *casus belli* against Greece. Greece, without army or allies, was obviously not in a position to incur another war, and the 'Military League' thus found that it had reached the end of its tether. There ensued a deadlock of another eight months, only enlivened by a naval mutiny, during which the country lay paralysed, with no programme whatsoever before it.

Then the man demanded by the situation appeared unexpectedly from the centre of disturbance, Krete. Venezelos started life as a successful advocate at Canea. He entered Kretan politics in the struggle for constitutionalism, and distinguished himself in the successful revolution of 1906, of which he was the soul. Naturally, he became one of the leading statesmen under Zaimis' regime, and he further distinguished himself by resolutely opposing the 'Unionist' agitation as premature, and yet retaining his hold over a people whose paramount political preoccupation was their national unity. The crisis of 1908-9 brought him

187

into close relations with the government of the Greek kingdom; and the king, who had gauged his calibre, now took the patriotic step of calling in the man who had expelled his son from Krete, to put his own house in order. It speaks much for both men that they worked together in harmony from the beginning. Upon the royal invitation Venezelos exchanged Kretan for Greek citizenship, and took in hand the 'Military League'. After short negotiations, he persuaded it to dissolve in favour of a national convention, which was able to meet in March 1910.

Thus Greece became a constitutional country once more, and Venezelos the first premier of the new era. During five years of continuous office he was to prove himself the good genius of his country. When he resigned his post in April 1915, he left the work of consolidating the national state on the verge of completion, and it will be his country's loss if he is baulked of achievement. Results speak for themselves, and the remainder of this pamphlet will be little more than a record of his statesmanship; but before we pass on to review his deeds, we must say a word about the character to which they are due. In March 1912 the time came for the first general election since Venezelos had taken office. Two years' experience of his administration had already won him such popularity and prestige, that the old party groups, purely personal followings infected with all the corruption, jingoism, and insincerity of the dark fifteen years, leagued themselves in a desperate effort to cast him out. Corruption on a grand scale was attempted, but Venezelos' success at the polls was sweeping. The writer happened to be spending that month in Krete. The Kretans had, of course, elected deputies in good time to the parliament at Athens, and once more the foreign warships stopped them in the act of boarding the steamer for Peiraeus, while Venezelos, who was still responsible for the Greek Government till the new parliament met, had declared with characteristic frankness that the attendance of the Kretan deputies could not possibly be sanctioned, an opening of which his opponents did not fail to take advantage. Meanwhile, every one in Krete was awaiting news of the polling in the kingdom. They might have been expected to feel, at any rate, lukewarmly towards a man who had actually taken office on the programme of deferring their cherished 'union' indefinitely; but, on the contrary, they greeted his triumph with enormous enthusiasm. Their feeling was explained by the comment of an innkeeper. 'Venezelos!' he said: 'Why, he is a man who can say "No". He won't stand any nonsense. If you try to get round him, he'll put you in irons.' And clearly he had hit the mark. Venezelos would in any case have done well, because he is a clever man with an excellent power of judgement; but acuteness is a common Greek virtue, and if he has done brilliantly, it is because he has the added touch of genius required to make the Greek take 'No' for an answer, a quality, very rare indeed in the nation, which explains the dramatic contrast between his success and Trikoupis' failure. Greece has been fortunate indeed in finding the right man at the crucial hour.

In the winter of 1911-12 and the succeeding summer, the foreign traveller met innumerable results of Venezelos' activity in every part of the country, and all gave evidence of the same thing: a sane judgement and its inflexible execution. For instance, a resident in Greece had needed an escort of soldiers four years before, when he made an expedition into the wild country north-west of the Gulf of Patras, on account of the number of criminals 'wanted' by the government who were lurking in that region as outlaws. In August 1912 an inquiry concerning this danger was met with a smile: 'Oh, yes, it was so,' said the gendarme, 'but since then Venezelos has come. He amnestied every one "out" for minor offences, and then caught the "really bad ones", so there are no outlaws in Akarnania now.' And he spoke the truth. You could wander all about the forests and mountains without molestation.

So far Venezelos had devoted himself to internal reconstruction, after the precedent of Trikoupis, but he was not the man to desert the national idea. The army and navy were reorganized by French and British missions, and when the opportunity appeared, he was ready to take full advantage of it. In the autumn of 1912, Turkey had been for a year at war with Italy; her finances had suffered a heavy drain, and the Italian command of the sea not only locked up her best troops in Tripoli, but interrupted such important lines of communication between her Asiatic and European provinces as the direct route by sea from Smyrna to Salonika, and the devious sea-passage thence round Greece to Scutari, which was the only alternative for Turkish troops to running the gauntlet of the Albanian mountaineers. Clearly the Balkan nations could find no better moment for striking the blow to settle that implacable 'preliminary question.' of national unity which had dogged them all since their birth. Their only chance of success, however, was to strike in concert, for Turkey, handicapped though she was, could still easily outmatch them singly. Unless they could compromise between their conflicting claims, they would have to let this common opportunity for making them good slip by altogether.

Of the four states concerned, two, Serbia and Montenegro, were of the same South-Slavonic nationality, and had been drawn into complete accord with each other since the formal annexation of Bosnia by Austria-Hungary in 1908, which struck a hard blow at their common national idea, while neither of them had any conflicting claims with Greece, since the Greek and South-Slavonic nationalities are at no point geographically in contact. With Bulgaria, a nation of Slavonic speech and culture, though not wholly Slavonic in origin, Serbia had quarrelled for years over the ultimate destiny of the Ueskueb district in north-western Macedonia, which was still subject to Turkey; but in the summer of 1912 the two states compromised in a secret treaty upon their respective territorial ambitions, and agreed to refer the fate of one debatable strip to the arbitration of Russia, after their already projected war with Turkey had been carried through. There was a more formidable conflict of interests between Bulgaria and Greece. These two nationalities are conterminous over a very wide extent of territory, stretching from the Black Sea on the east to the inland Lake of Okhrida on the west, and there is at no point a sharp dividing line between them. The Greek element tends to predominate towards the coast and the Bulgar towards the interior, but there are broad zones where Greek and Bulgar villages are inextricably interspersed, while purely Greek towns are often isolated in the midst of purely Bulgar rural districts. Even if the racial areas could be plotted out on a large-scale map, it was clear that no political frontier could be drawn to follow their convolutions, and that Greece and Bulgaria could only divide the spoils by both making up their minds to give and take. The actual lines this necessary compromise would follow, obviously depended on the degree of the allies' success against Turkey in the common war that was yet to be fought, and Venezelos rose to the occasion. He had the courage to offer Bulgaria the Greek alliance without stipulating for any definite minimum share in the common conquests, and the tact to induce her to accept it on the same terms. Greece and Bulgaria agreed to shelve all territorial questions till the war had been brought to a successful close; and with the negotiation of this understanding (another case in which Venezelos achieved what Trikoupis had attempted only to fail) the Balkan League was complete.

The events that followed are common knowledge. The Balkan allies opened the campaign in October, and the Turks collapsed before an impetuous attack. The Bulgarians crumpled up the Ottoman field armies in Thrace at the terrific battle of Lule Burgas; the Serbians disposed of the forces in the Macedonian interior, while the Greeks effected a junction with the Serbians from the south, and cut their way through to Salonika. Within two months of the declaration of war, the Turks on land had been driven out of the open altogether behind the shelter of the Chataldja and Gallipoli lines, and only three fortresses—Adrianople, Yannina, and Scutari—held out further to the west. Their navy, closely blockaded by the Greek fleet within the Dardanelles, had to look on passively at the successive occupation of the Aegean Islands by Greek landing-parties. With the winter came negotiations, during which an armistice reigned at Adrianople and Scutari, while the Greeks pursued the siege of Yannina and the Dardanelles blockade. The negotiations proved abortive, and the result of the renewed hostilities justified the action of the Balkan plenipotentiaries in breaking them off. By the spring of 1913 the three fortresses had fallen, and, under the treaty finally signed at London, Turkey ceded to the Balkan League, as a whole, all her European territories west of a line drawn from Ainos on the Aegean to Midia on the Black Sea, including Adrianople and the lower basin of the river Maritsa.

The time had now come for Greece and Bulgaria to settle their account, and the unexpected extent of the common gains ought to have facilitated their division. The territory in question included the whole north coast of the Aegean and its immediate hinterland, and Venezelos proposed to consider it in two sections. (1) The eastern section, conveniently known as Thrace, consisted of the lower basin of the Maritsa. As far as Adrianople the population was Bulgar, but south of that city it was succeeded by a Greek element, with a considerable sprinkling of Turkish settlements, as far as the sea. Geographically, however, the whole district is intimately connected with Bulgaria, and the railway that follows the course of the Maritsa down to the port of Dedeagatch offers a much-needed economic outlet for large regions already within the Bulgarian frontier. Venezelos, then, was prepared to resign all Greek claims to the eastern section, in return for a corresponding concession by Bulgaria in the west. (2) The western section, consisting of the lower basins of the Vardar and Struma, lay in the immediate neighbourhood of the former frontier of Greece; but the Greek population of Salonika,* and the coast-districts east of it, could not be brought within the Greek frontier without including as well a certain hinterland inhabited mainly by Bulgarians. The cession of this was the return asked for by Venezelos, and he reduced it to a minimum by abstaining from pressing the quite well-founded claims of Greece in the Monastir district, which lay further inland still.

---

*   The predominant element within the walls of Salonika itself is neither Greek nor Bulgarian, but consists of about 80,000 of those Spanish-speaking Jews who settled in Turkey as refugees during the sixteenth century.

But Venezelos' conciliatory proposals met with no response from the Bulgarian Government, which was in an 'all or nothing' mood. It swallowed Venezelos' gift of Thrace, and then proceeded to exploit the Bulgar hinterland of Salonika as a pretext for demanding the latter city as well. This uncompromising attitude made agreement impossible, and it was aggravated by the aggressive action of the Bulgarian troops in the occupied territory, who persistently endeavoured to steal ground from the Greek forces facing them. In May there was serious fighting to the east of the Struma, and peace was only restored with difficulty. Bulgarian relations with Serbia were becoming strained at the same time, though in this case Bulgaria had more justice on her side. Serbia maintained that the veto imposed by Austria upon her expansion to the Adriatic, in coincidence with Bulgaria's unexpected gains on the Maritsa to which Serbian arms had contributed, invalidated the secret treaty of the previous summer, and she announced her intention of retaining the Monastir district and the line of the Salonika railway as far as the future frontier of Greece. Bulgaria, on the other hand, shut her eyes to Serbia's necessity for an untrammelled economic outlet to one sea-board or the other, and took her stand on her strictly legal treaty-rights. However the balance of justice inclined, a lasting settlement could only have been reached by mutual forbearance and goodwill; but Bulgaria put herself hopelessly in the wrong towards both her allies by a treacherous night-attack upon them all along the line, at the end of June 1913. This disastrous act was the work of a single political party, which has since been condemned by most sections of Bulgarian public opinion; but the punishment, if not the responsibility for the crime, fell upon the whole nation. Greece and Serbia had already been drawn into an understanding by their common danger. They now declared war against Bulgaria in concert. The counter-strokes of their armies met with success, and the intervention of Rumania made Bulgaria's discomfiture certain.

The results of the one month's war were registered in the Treaty of Bucarest. Many of its provisions were unhappily, though naturally, inspired by the spirit of revenge; but the Greek premier, at any rate, showed a statesmanlike self-restraint in the negotiations. Venezelos advocated the course of taking no more after the war than had been demanded before it. He desired to leave Bulgaria a broad zone of Aegean littoral between the Struma and Maritsa rivers, including ports capable of satisfying Bulgaria's pressing need for an outlet towards the south. But, in the exasperated state of public feeling, even Venezelos' prestige failed to carry through his policy in its full moderation. King George had just been assassinated in his year of jubilee, in the streets of the long-desired Salonika; and King Constantine, his son, flushed by the victory of Kilkish and encouraged by the Machiavellian diplomacy of his Hohenzollern brother-in-law, insisted on carrying the new Greek frontier as far east as the river Mesta, and depriving Bulgaria of Kavala, the natural harbour for the whole Bulgarian hinterland in the upper basins of the Mesta and Struma.

It is true that Greece did not exact as much as she might have done. Bulgaria was still allowed to possess herself of a coastal strip east of the Mesta, containing the tolerable harbours of Porto Lagos and Dedeagatch, which had been occupied during hostilities by the Greek fleet, and thus her need for an Aegean outlet was not left unsatisfied altogether; while Greece on her part was cleverly shielded for the future from those drawbacks involved in immediate contact with Turkish territory, which she had so often experienced in the past. It is also true that the Kavala district is of great economic value in itself—it produces the better part of the Turkish Regie tobacco crop—and that on grounds of nationality alone Bulgaria has no claim to this prize, since the tobacco-growing peasantry is almost exclusively Greek or Turk, while the Greek element has been extensively reinforced during the last two years by refugees from Anatolia and Thrace.

Nevertheless, it is already clear that Venezelos' judgement was the better. The settlement at the close of the present war may even yet bring Bulgaria reparation in many quarters. If the Ruman and South Slavonic populations at present included in the complexus of Austria-Hungary are freed from their imprisonment and united with the Serbian and Rumanian national states, Bulgaria may conceivably recover from the latter those Bulgarian lands which the Treaty of Bucarest made over to them in central Macedonia and the Dobrudja, while it would be still more feasible to oust the Turk again from Adrianople, where he slipped back in the hour of Bulgaria's prostration and has succeeded in maintaining himself ever since. Yet no amount of compensation in other directions and no abstract consideration for the national principle will induce Bulgaria to renounce her claim on Greek Kavala. Access to this district is vital to Bulgaria from the geographical point of view, and she will not be satisfied here with such rights as Serbia enjoys at Salonika—free use of the port and free traffic along a railway connecting it with her own hinterland. Her heart is set on complete territorial ownership, and she will not compose her feud with Greece until she has had her way.

So long, therefore, as the question of Kavala remains unsettled, Greece will not be able to put the preliminary problem of 'national consolidation' behind her, and enter upon the long-deferred chapter of 'internal development'. To accomplish once for all this vital transition, Venezelos is taking the helm again into his hands, and it is his evident intention to close the Greek account with Bulgaria just as Serbia and Rumania hope to close theirs with the same state—by a bold territorial concession conditional upon adequate territorial compensation elsewhere.*

The possibility of such compensation is offered by certain outstanding problems directly dependent upon the issue of the European conflict, and we must glance briefly at these before passing on to consider the new chapter of internal history that is opening for the Greek nation.

---

*   The above paragraph betrays its own date; for, since it was written, the intervention of Bulgaria on the side of the Central Powers has deferred indefinitely the hope of a settlement based upon mutual agreement.

195

The problems in question are principally concerned with the ownership of islands.

The integrity of a land-frontier is guaranteed by the whole strength of the nation included within it, and can only be modified by a struggle for existence with the neighbor on whom it borders; but islands by their geographical nature constitute independent political units, easily detached from or incorporated with larger domains, according to the momentary fluctuation in the balance of sea-power. Thus it happened that the arrival of the *Goeben* and *Breslau* at the Dardanelles in August 1914 led Turkey to reopen promptly certain questions concerning the Aegean. The islands in this sea are uniformly Greek in population, but their respective geographical positions and political fortunes differentiate them into several groups.

1. The Cyclades in the south-west, half submerged vanguards of mountain ranges in continental Greece, have formed part of the modern kingdom from its birth, and their status has never since been called into question.

2. Krete, the largest of all Greek islands, has been dealt with already. She enjoyed autonomy under Turkish suzerainty for fifteen years before the Balkan War, and at its outbreak she once more proclaimed her union with Greece. This time at last her action was legalized, when Turkey expressly abandoned her suzerain rights by a clause in the Treaty of London.

3. During the war itself, the Greek navy occupied a number of islands which had remained till then under the more direct government of Turkey, The parties to the Treaty of London agreed to leave their destiny to the decision of the powers, and the latter assigned them all to Greece, with the exception of Imbros and Tenedos which command strategically the mouth of the Dardanelles.

The islands thus secured to Greece fall in turn into several sub-groups.

Two of these are *(a)* Thasos, Samothraki, and Lemnos, off the European coast, and *(b)* Samos and its satellite Nikaria, immediately off the west coast of Anatolia; and these five islands seem definitely to have been given up by Turkey for lost. The European group is well beyond the range of her present frontiers; while Samos, though it adjoins the Turkish mainland, does not mask the outlet from any considerable port, and had moreover for many years possessed the same privileged autonomy as Krete, so that the Ottoman Government did not acutely feel its final severance.

(c) A third group consists of Mitylini and Khios,* and concerning this pair Greece and Turkey have so far come to no understanding. The Turks pointed out that the littoral off which these islands lie contains not only the most indispensable ports of Anatolia but also the largest enclaves of Greek population on the Asiatic mainland, and they declared that the occupation of this group by Greece menaced the sovereignty of the Porte in its home territory. 'See', they said, 'how the two islands flank both sides of the sea-passage to Smyrna, the terminus of all the railways which penetrate the Anatolian interior, while Mitylini barricades Aivali and Edremid as well. As soon as the Greek Government has converted the harbours of these islands into naval bases, Anatolia will be subject to a perpetual Greek blockade, and this violent intimidation of the Turkish people will be reinforced by an insidious propaganda among the disloyal Greek elements in our midst.' Accordingly the Turks refused to recognize the award of the powers, and demanded the re-establishment of Ottoman sovereignty in Mitylini and Khios, under guarantee of an autonomy after the precedent of Krete and Samos.

To these arguments and demands the Greeks replied that, next to Krete; these are the two largest, most wealthy, and most populous Greek

---

* Including its famous satellite Psara.

islands in the Aegean; that their inhabitants ardently desire union with the national kingdom; and that the Greek Government would hesitate to use them as a basis for economic coercion and nationalistic propaganda against Turkey, if only because the commerce of western Anatolia is almost exclusively in the hands of the Greek element on the Asiatic continent. Greek interests were presumably bound up with the economic prosperity and political consolidation of Turkey in Asia, and the Anatolian Greeks would merely have been alienated from their compatriots by any such impolitic machinations. 'Greek sovereignty in Mitylini and Khios', the Greeks maintained, 'does not threaten Turkish sovereignty on the Continent. But the restoration of Turkish suzerainty over the islands would most seriously endanger the liberty of their inhabitants; for Turkish promises are notoriously valueless, except when they are endorsed by the guarantee of some physically stronger power.'

Negotiations were conducted between Greece and Turkey from these respective points of view without leading to any result, and the two standpoints were in fact irreconcilable, since either power required the other to leave vital national interests at the mercy of an ancient enemy, without undertaking to make corresponding sacrifices itself. The problem probably would never have been solved by compromise; but meanwhile the situation has been entirely transformed by the participation of Turkey in the European War, and the issue between Greece and Turkey, like the issue between Greece and Bulgaria, has been merged in the general problem of the European settlement.

The Balkan War of 1912 doomed the Ottoman power in Europe, but left its Asiatic future unimpaired. By making war against the Quadruple Entente, Turkey has staked her existence on both continents, and is threatened with political extinction if the Central Powers succumb in the struggle. In this event Greece will no longer have to accommodate her regime in the liberated islands to the susceptibilities of a Turkey consolidated on the opposite mainland, but will be able to stretch out her hand over the Anatolian coast and its hinterland, and compensate herself richly in this quarter for the territorial sacrifices which may still be necessary to a lasting understanding with her Bulgarian neighbour.

The shores that dominate the Dardanelles will naturally remain beyond her grasp, but she may expect to establish herself on the western littoral from a point as far north as Mount Ida and the plain of Edremid. The Greek coast-town of Aivali will be hers, and the still more important focus of Greek commerce and civilization at Smyrna; while she will push her dominion along the railways that radiate from Smyrna towards the interior. South-eastward, Aidin will be hers in the valley of the Mendere (Maiandros). Due eastward she will re-baptize the glistening city of Ala Shehr with its ancient name of Philadelphia, under which it held out heroically for Hellenism many years after Aidin had become the capital of a Moslem principality and the Turkish avalanche had rolled past it to the sea. Maybe she will follow the railway still further inland, and plant her flag on the Black Castle of Afiun, the natural railway-centre of Anatolia high up on the innermost plateau. All this and more was once Hellenic ground, and the Turkish incomer, for all his vitality, has never been able here to obliterate the older culture or assimilate the earlier population. In this western region Turkish villages are still interspersed with Greek, and under the government of compatriots the unconquerable minority would inevitably reassert itself by the peaceful weapons of its superior energy and intelligence.

4. If Greece realizes these aspirations through Venezelos' statesmanship, she will have settled in conjunction her outstanding accounts with both Bulgaria and Turkey; but a fourth group of islands still remains for consideration, and these, though formerly the property of Turkey, are now in the hands of other European powers.

(a) The first of those in question are the Sporades, a chain of islands off the Anatolian coast which continues the line of Mitylini, Khios, and Samos towards the south-east, and includes Kos, Patmos, Astypalia, Karpathos, Kasos, and, above all, Rhodes. The Sporades were occupied by Italy during her war with Turkey in 1911-12, and she stipulated in the

Peace of Lausanne that she should retain them as a pledge until the last Ottoman soldier in Tripoli had been withdrawn, after which she would make them over again to the Porte. The continued unrest in Tripoli may or may not have been due to Turkish intrigues, but in any case it deferred the evacuation of the islands by Italy until the situation was transformed here also by the successive intervention of both powers in the European War. The consequent lapse of the Treaty of Lausanne simplifies the status of the Sporades, but it is doubtful what effect it will have upon their destiny. In language and political sympathy their inhabitants are as completely Greek as all the other islanders of the Aegean, and if the Quadruple Entente has made the principle of nationality its own, Italy is morally bound, now that the Sporades are at her free disposal, to satisfy their national aspirations by consenting to their union with the kingdom of Greece. On the other hand, the prospective dissolution of the Ottoman Empire has increased Italy's stake in this quarter. In the event of a partition, the whole southern littoral of Anatolia will probably fall within the Italian sphere, which will start from the Gulf of Iskanderun, include the districts of Adana and Adalia, and march with the new Anatolian provinces of Greece along the line of the river Mendere. This continental domain and the adjacent islands are geographically complementary to one another, and it is possible that Italy may for strategical reasons insist on retaining the Sporades in perpetuity if she realizes her ambitions on the continent. This solution would be less ideal than the other, but Greece would be wise to reconcile herself to it, as Italy has reconciled herself to the incorporation of Corsica in France; for by submitting frankly to this detraction from her national unity she would give her brethren in the Sporades the best opportunity of developing their national individuality untrammelled under a friendly Italian suzerainty.

(b) The advance-guard of the Greek race that inhabits the great island of Cyprus has been subject to British government since 1878, when the provisional occupation of the island by Great Britain under a contract similar to that of Lausanne was negotiated in a secret agreement between

Great Britain and Turkey on the eve of the Conference at Berlin. The condition of evacuation was in this case the withdrawal of Russia from Kars, and here likewise it never became operative till it was abrogated by the outbreak of war. Cyprus, like the Sporades, is now at the disposal of its *de facto* possessor, and on November 5, 1914, it was annexed to the British Empire. But whatever decision Italy may take, it is to be hoped that our own government at any rate will not be influenced exclusively by strategical considerations, but will proclaim an intention of allowing Cyprus ultimately to realize its national aspirations by union with Greece.*

The whole population of the island is Greek in language, while under an excellent British administration its political consciousness has been awakened, and has expressed itself in a growing desire for national unity among the Christian majority. It is true that in Cyprus, as in Krete, there is a considerable Greek-speaking minority of Moslems** who prefer the *status quo*; but, since the barrier of language is absent, their antipathy to union may not prove permanent. However important the retention of Cyprus may be to Great Britain from the strategical point of view, we shall find that even in the balance of material interests it is not worth the price of alienating the sympathy of an awakened and otherwise consolidated nation.

This rather detailed review of problems in the islands and Anatolia brings out the fact that Greek nationalism is not an artificial conception of theorists, but a real force which impels the most scattered and down-trodden populations of Greek speech to travail unceasingly for political unity within the national state. Yet by far the most striking example of this attractive power in Hellenism is the history of it in 'Epirus'.***

---

*   Since the above was written, this intention, under a certain condition, has definitely been expressed.

**   In Cyprus about 22 per cent.

*** The name coined to include the districts of Himarra, Argyrokastro, and Koritsa.

The Epirots are a population of Albanian race, and they still speak an Albanian dialect in their homes; while the women and children, at any rate, often know no other language. But somewhat over a century ago the political organism created by the remarkable personality of Ali Pasha in the hinterland of the Adriatic coast, and the relations of Great Britain and France with this new principality in the course of their struggle for the Mediterranean, began to awaken in the Epirots a desire for civilization. Their Albanian origin opened to them no prospects, for the race had neither a literature nor a common historical tradition; and they accordingly turned to the Greeks, with whom they were linked in religion by membership of the Orthodox Church, and in politics by subjection to Ali's Government at Yannina, which had adopted Greek as its official language.

They had appealed to the right quarter; for we have seen how Greek culture accumulated a store of latent energy under the Turkish yoke, and was expending it at this very period in a vigorous national revival. The partially successful War of Liberation in the 'twenties of the nineteenth century was only the political manifestation of the new life. It has expressed itself more typically in a steady and universal enthusiasm for education, which throughout the subsequent generations of political stagnation has always opened to individual Greeks commercial and professional careers of the greatest brilliance, and often led them to spend the fortunes so acquired in endowing the nation with further educational opportunities. Public spirit is a Greek virtue. There are few villages which do not possess monuments of their successful sons, and a school is an even commoner gift than a church; while the State has supplemented the individual benefactor to an extent remarkable where public resources are so slender. The school-house, in fact, is generally the most prominent and substantial building in a Greek village, and the advantage offered to the Epirots by a *rapprochement* with the Greeks is concretely symbolized by the Greek schools established to-day in generous numbers throughout their country.

For the Epirot boy the school is the door to the future. The language he learns there makes him the member of a nation, and opens to him a world wide enough to employ all the talent and energy he may possess, if he seeks his fortune at Patras or Peiraeus, or in the great Greek commercial communities of Alexandria and Constantinople; while, if he stays at home, it still affords him a link with the life of civilized Europe through the medium of the ubiquitous Greek newspaper.* The Epirot has thus become Greek in soul, for he has reached the conception of a national life more liberal than the isolated existence of his native village through the avenue of Greek culture. 'Hellenism' and nationality have become for him identical ideas; and when at last the hour of deliverance struck, he welcomed the Greek armies that marched into his country from the south and the east, after the fall of Yannina in the spring of 1913, with the same enthusiasm with which all the enslaved populations of native Greek dialect greeted the consummation of a century's hopes.

The Greek troops arrived only just in time, for the 'Hellenism' of the Epirots had been terribly proved by murderous attacks from their Moslem neighbours on the north. The latter speak a variety of the same Albanian tongue, but were differentiated by a creed which assimilated them to the ruling race. They had been superior to their Christian kinsmen by the weight of numbers and the possession of arms, which under the Ottoman regime were the monopoly of the Moslem. At last, however, the yoke of oppression was broken and the Greek occupation seemed a harbinger of security for the future. Unluckily, however, Epirus was of interest to others besides its own inhabitants. It occupies an important geographical position facing the extreme heel of Italy, just below the narrowest point in the neck of the Adriatic, and the Italian Government insisted that the country should be included in the newly erected principality of Albania, which the powers had reserved the right to delimit in concert by a provision in the Treaty of London.

---

*   There is still practically no literature printed in the Albanian language.

Italy gave two reasons for her demand. First, she declared it incompatible with her own vital interests that both shores of the strait between Corfu and the mainland should pass into the hands of the same power, because the combination of both coasts and the channel between them offered a site for a naval base that might dominate the mouth of the Adriatic. Secondly, she maintained that the native Albanian speech of the Epirots proved their Albanian nationality, and that it was unjust to the new Albanian state to exclude from it the most prosperous and civilized branch of the Albanian nation. Neither argument is cogent.

The first argument could easily be met by the neutralization of the Corfu straits,* and it is also considerably weakened by the fact that the position which really commands the mouth of the Adriatic from the eastern side is not the Corfu channel beyond it but the magnificent bay of Avlona just within its narrowest section, and this is a Moslem district to which the Epirots have never laid claim, and which would therefore in any case fall within the Albanian frontier. The second argument is almost ludicrous. The destiny of Epirus is not primarily the concern of the other Albanians, of for that matter of the Greeks, but of the Epirots themselves, and it is hard to see how their nationality can be defined except in terms of their own conscious and expressed desire; for a nation is simply a group of men inspired by a common will to co-operate for certain purposes, and cannot be brought into existence by the external manipulation of any specific objective factors, but solely by the inward subjective impulse of its constituents. It was a travesty of justice to put the Orthodox Epirots at the mercy of a Moslem majority (which had been massacring them the year before) on the ground that they happened to speak the same language. The hardship was aggravated by the fact that all the routes connecting Epirus with the outer world run through Yannina and Salonika, from which the new frontier sundered her; while

---

*   Corfu itself is neutralized already by the agreement under which Great Britain transferred the Ionian Islands to Greece in 1863.

great natural barriers separate her from Avlona and Durazzo, with which the same frontier so ironically signalled her union.

The award of the powers roused great indignation in Greece, but Venezelos was strong enough to secure that it should scrupulously be respected; and the 'correct attitude' which he inflexibly maintained has finally won its reward. As soon as the decision of the powers was announced, the Epirots determined to help themselves. They raised a militia, and asserted their independence so successfully, that they compelled the Prince of Wied, the first (and perhaps the last) ruler of the new 'Albania', to give them home rule in matters of police and education, and to recognise Greek as the official language for their local administration. They ensured observance of this compact by the maintenance of their troops under arms. So matters continued, until a rebellion among his Moslem subjects and the outbreak of the European War in the summer of 1914 obliged the prince to depart, leaving Albania to its natural state of anarchy. The anarchy might have restored every canton and village to the old state of contented isolation, had it not been for the religious hatred between the Moslems and the Epirots, which, with the removal of all external control, began to vent itself in an aggressive assault of the former upon the latter, and entailed much needless misery in the autumn months.

The reoccupation of Epirus by Greek troops had now become a matter of life and death to its inhabitants, and in October 1914 Venezelos took the inevitable step, after serving due notice upon all the signatories to the Treaty of London. Thanks in part to the absorption of the powers in more momentous business, but perhaps even in a greater degree to the confidence which the Greek premier had justly won by his previous handling of the question, this action was accomplished without protest or opposition. Since then Epirus has remained sheltered from the vicissitudes of civil war within and punitive expeditions from without, to which the unhappy remnant of Albania has been incessantly exposed; and we may prophesy that the Epiroi, unlike their repudiated brethren of

Moslem or Catholic faith, have really seen the last of their troubles. Even Italy, from whom they had most to fear, has obtained such a satisfactory material guarantee by the occupation on her own part of Avlona, that she is as unlikely to demand the evacuation of Epirus by Greece as she is to withdraw her own force from her long coveted strategical base on the eastern shore of the Adriatic. In Avlona and Epirus the former rivals are settling down to a neighbourly contact, and there is no reason to doubt that the *de facto* line of demarcation between them will develop into a permanent and officially recognized frontier. The problem of Epirus, though not, unfortunately, that of Albania, may be regarded as definitely closed.

The reclamation of Epirus is perhaps the most honourable achievement of the Greek national revival, but it is by no means an isolated phenomenon. Western Europe is apt to depreciate modern 'Hellenism', chiefly because its ambitious denomination rather ludicrously challenges comparison with a vanished glory, while any one who has studied its rise must perceive that it has little more claim than western Europe itself to be the peculiar heir of ancient Greek culture. And yet this Hellenism of recent growth has a genuine vitality of its own. It displays a remarkable power of assimilating alien elements and inspiring them to an active pursuit of its ideals, and its allegiance supplants all others in the hearts of those exposed to its charm. The Epirots are not the only Albanians who have been Hellenized. In the heart of central Greece and Peloponnesus, on the plain of Argos, and in the suburbs of Athens, there are still Albanian enclaves, derived from those successive migrations between the fourteenth and the eighteenth centuries; but they have so entirely forgotten their origin that the villagers, when questioned, can only repeat: 'We can't say why we happen to speak "Arvanitika", but we are Greeks like everybody else.' The Vlachs again, a Romance-speaking tribe of nomadic shepherds who have wandered as far south as Akarnania and the shores of the Korinthian Gulf, are settling down there to the agricultural life of the Greek village, so that Hellenism stands to them for the transition to a higher social phase. Their still migratory brethren in the northern ranges of Pindus are already 'Hellenes' in political sympathy,* and are moving under Greek influence towards the same social evolution. In distant Cappadocia, at the root of the Anatolian peninsula, the Orthodox Greek population, submerged beneath the Turkish flood more than eight centuries ago, has retained little individuality except in its religion, and nothing of its native speech but a garbled vocabulary embedded in a Turkified syntax. Yet even this dwindling rear-guard has been overtaken just in time by the returning current of national life, bringing with it the Greek school, and with the school a community of outlook with Hellenism the world over. Whatever the fate of eastern Anatolia may be, the Greek element is now assured a prominent part in its future.

These, moreover, are the peripheries of the Greek world; and at its centre the impulse towards union in the national state readies a passionate intensity. 'Aren't you better off as you are?' travellers used to ask in Krete during the era of autonomy. 'If you get your "Union", you will have to do two years' military service instead of one year's training in the militia, and will be taxed up to half as much again.' 'We have thought of that,' the Kretans would reply, 'but what does it matter, if we are united with Greece?'

On this unity modern Hellenism has concentrated its efforts, and after nearly a century of ineffective endeavour it has been brought by the statesmanship of Venezelos within sight of its goal. Our review of outstanding problems reveals indeed the inconclusiveness of the settlement imposed at Bucarest; but this only witnesses to the wisdom of the Greek nation in reaffirming its confidence in Venezelos at the present juncture, and recalling him to power to crown the work which he has so brilliantly carried through. Under Venezelos' guidance we

---

*   Greece owed her naval supremacy in 1912-13 to the new cruiser *Georgios Averof*, named after a Vlach millionaire who made his fortune in the Greek colony at Alexandria and left a legacy for the ship's construction at his death.

cannot doubt that the heart's desire of Hellenism will be accomplished at the impending European settlement by the final consolidation of the Hellenic national state.*

Yet however attractive the sincerity of such nationalism may be, political unity is only a negative achievement. The history of a nation must be judged rather by the positive content of its ideals and the positive results which it attains, and herein the Hellenic revival displays certain grave shortcomings. The internal paralysis of social and economic life has already been noted and ascribed to the urgency of the 'preliminary question'; but we must now add to this the growing embitterment which has poisoned the relations of Greece with her Balkan neighbours during the crises through which the 'preliminary question' has been worked out to its solution. Now that this solution is at hand, will Hellenism prove capable of casting out these two evils, and adapt itself with strength renewed to the new phase of development that lies before it?

The northern territories acquired in 1913 will give a much greater impetus to economic progress than Thessaly gave a generation ago; for the Macedonian littoral west as well as east of the Struma produces a considerable proportion of the Turkish Regie tobacco, while the pine-forests of Pindus, if judiciously exploited, will go far to remedy the present deficiency of home-grown timber, even if they do not provide quantities sufficient for export abroad. If we take into account the currant-crop of the Peloponnesian plain-lands which already almost monopolizes the world-market, the rare ores of the south-eastern mountains and the Archipelago, and the vintages which scientific treatment might bring into competition with the wines of the Peninsula and France, we can see that Greece has many sources of material prosperity within her reach, if only she applies her liberated energy to their development. Yet these are all of them specialized products, and Greece will never export any staple

---

*   This paragraph, again, has been superseded by the dramatic turn of events; but the writer has left it unaltered, for the end is not yet.

commodity to rival the grain which Rumania sends in such quantities to central Europe already, and which Bulgaria will begin to send within a few years' time. Even the consolidated Greek kingdom will be too small in area and too little compact in geographical outline to constitute an independent economic unit, and the ultimate economic interests of the country demand co-operation in some organization more comprehensive than the political molecule of the national state.

Such an association should embrace the Balkans in their widest extent—from the Black Sea to the Adriatic and from the Carpathians to the Aegean; for, in sharp contrast to the inextricable chaos of its linguistic and ecclesiastical divisions, the region constitutes economically a homogeneous and indivisible whole, in which none of the parts can divest themselves of their mutual interdependence. Greece, for example, has secured at last her direct link with the railway system of the European continent, but for free transit beyond her own frontier she still depends on Serbia's good-will, just, as Serbia depends on hers for an outlet to the Aegean at Salonika. The two states have provided for their respective interests by a joint proprietorship of the section of railway between Salonika and Belgrade; and similar railway problems will doubtless bring Rumania to terms with Serbia for access to the Adriatic, and both with Bulgaria for rights of way to Constantinople and the Anatolian hinterland beyond. These common commercial arteries of the Balkans take no account of racial or political frontiers, but link the region as a whole with other regions in a common economic relation.

South-eastern and central Europe are complementary economic areas in a special degree. The industries of central Europe will draw upon the raw products of the south-east to an increasing extent, and the south-east will absorb in turn increasing quantities of manufactured plant from central Europe for the development of its own natural resources. The two areas will become parties in a vast economic nexus, and, as in all business transactions, each will try to get the best of the continually intensified bargaining. This is why co-operation is so essential to the future well-being of the Balkan States. Isolated individually and mutually competitive as they are at present, they must succumb to the economic ascendancy of Vienna and Berlin as inevitably as unorganized, unskilled labourers fall under the thraldom of a well-equipped capitalist. Central Europe will have in any event an enormous initial superiority over the Balkans in wealth, population, and business experience; and the Balkan peoples can only hope to hold their own in this perilous but essential intercourse with a stronger neighbour, if they take more active and deliberate steps towards co-operation among themselves, and find in railway conventions the basis for a Balkan zollverein. A zollverein should be the first goal of Balkan statesmanship in the new phase of history that is opening for Europe; but economic relations on this scale involve the political factor, and the Balkans will not be able to deal with their great neighbours on equal terms till the zollverein has ripened into a federation. The alternative is subjection, both political and economic; and neither the exhaustion of the Central Powers in the present struggle nor the individual consolidation of the Balkan States in the subsequent settlement will suffice by themselves to avert it in the end.

The awakening of the nation and the consolidation of the state, which we have traced in these pages, must accordingly lead on to the confederation of the Balkans, if all that has been so painfully won is not to perish again without result; and we are confronted with the question: Will Balkan nationalism rise to the occasion and transcend itself?

Many spectators of recent history will dismiss the suggestion as Utopian. 'Nationality', they will say, 'revealed itself first as a constructive force, and Europe staked its future upon it; but now that we are committed to it, it has developed a sinister destructiveness which we cannot remedy. Nationality brought the Balkan States into being and led them to final victory over the Turk in 1912, only to set them tearing one another to pieces again in 1913. In the present catastrophe the curse of the Balkans has descended upon the whole of Europe, and laid bare unsuspected depths of chaotic hatred; yet Balkan antagonisms still remain more ineradicable than ours. The cure for nationality is forgetfulness, but Balkan nationalism is rooted altogether in the past. The Balkan peoples have suffered one shattering experience in common—the Turk, and the waters of Ottoman oppression that have gone over their souls have not been waters of Lethe. They have endured long centuries of spiritual exile by the passionate remembrance of their Sion, and when they have vindicated their heritage at last, and returned to build up the walls of their city and the temple of their national god, they have resented each other's neighbourhood as the repatriated Jew resented the Samaritan. The Greek dreams with sullen intensity of a golden age before the Bulgar was found in the land, and the challenge implied in the revival of the Hellenic name, so far from being a superficial vanity, is the dominant characteristic of the nationalism which has adopted it for its title. Modern Hellenism breathes the inconscionable spirit of the *emigre.*'

This is only too true. The faith that has carried them to national unity will suffice neither the Greeks nor any other Balkan people for the new era that has dawned upon them, and the future would look dark indeed, but for a strange and incalculable leaven, which is already potently at work in the land.

Since the opening of the present century, the chaotic, unneighbourly races of south-eastern Europe, whom nothing had united before but the common impress of the Turk, have begun to share another experience in common—America. From the Slovak villages in the Carpathians to the Greek villages in the Laconian hills they have been crossing the Atlantic in their thousands, to become dockers and navvies, boot-blacks and waiters, confectioners and barbers in Chicago, St. Louis, Omaha, and all the other cities that have sprung up like magic to welcome the immigrant to the hospitable plains of the Middle West. The intoxication of his new environment stimulates all the latent industry and vitality of the Balkan peasant, and he abandons himself whole-heartedly to American life; yet he does not relinquish the national tradition in which he grew up. In America work brings wealth, and the Greek or Slovak soon worships

211

his God in a finer church and reads his language in a better-printed newspaper than he ever enjoyed in his native village. The surplus flows home in remittances of such abundance that they are steadily raising the cost of living in the Balkans themselves, or, in other words, the standard of material civilization; and sooner or later the immigrant goes the way of his money orders, for home-sickness, if not a mobilization order, exerts its compulsion before half a dozen years are out.

It is a strange experience to spend a night in some remote mountain-village of Greece, and see Americanism and Hellenism face to face. Hellenism is represented by the village schoolmaster. He wears a black coat, talks a little French, and can probably read Homer; but his longest journey has been to the normal school at Athens, and it has not altered his belief that the ikon in the neighbouring monastery was made by St. Luke and the Bulgar beyond the mountains by the Devil. On the other side of you sits the returned emigrant, chattering irrepressibly in his queer version of the 'American language', and showing you the newspapers which are mailed to him every fortnight from the States. His clean linen collar and his well-made American boots are conspicuous upon him, and he will deprecate on your behalf and his own the discomfort and squalor of his native surroundings. His home-coming has been a disillusionment, but it is a creative phenomenon; and if any one can set Greece upon a new path it is he. He is transforming her material life by his American savings, for they are accumulating into a capital widely distributed in native hands, which will dispense the nation from pawning its richest mines and vineyards to the European exploiter, and enable it to carry on their development on its own account at this critical juncture when European sources of capital are cut off for an indefinite period by the disaster of the European War. The emigrant will give Greece all Trikoupis dreamed of, but his greatest gift to his country will be his American point of view. In the West he has learnt that men of every language and religion can live in the same city and work at the same shops and sheds and mills and switch-yards without desecrating each other's churches or even suppressing each other's newspapers, not to speak of cutting each other's throats; and when next he meets Albanian or Bulgar on Balkan ground, he may remember that he has once dwelt with him in fraternity at Omaha or St. Louis or Chicago. This is the gospel of Americanism, and unlike Hellenism, which spread downwards from the patriarch's residence and the merchant's counting-house, it is being preached in all the villages of the land by the least prejudiced and most enterprising of their sons (for it is these who answer America's call); and spreading upward from the peasant towards the professor in the university and the politician in parliament.

Will this new leaven conquer, and cast out the stale leaven of Hellenism before it sours the loaf? Common sense is mighty, but whether it shall prevail in Greece and the Balkans and Europe lies on the knees of the gods.

RUMANIA:
HER HISTORY AND POLITICS

1.

Introduction

The problem of the origin and formation of the Rumanian nation has always provided matter for keen disputation among historians, and the theories which have been advanced are widely divergent. Some of these discussions have been undertaken solely for political reasons, and in such cases existing data prove conveniently adaptable. This elastic treatment of the historical data is facilitated by the fact that a long and important period affecting the formation and the development of the Rumanian nation (270-1220) has bequeathed practically no contemporary evidence. By linking up, however, what is known antecedent to that period with the precise data available regarding the following it, and by checking the inferred results with what little evidence exists respecting the obscure epoch of Rumanian history, it has been possible to reconstruct, almost to a certainty, the evolution of the Rumanians during the Middle Ages.

A discussion of the varying theories would be out of proportion, and out of place, in this essay. Nor is it possible to give to any extent a detailed description of the epic struggle which the Rumanians carried on for centuries against the Turks. I shall have to deal, therefore, on broad lines, with the historical facts—laying greater stress only upon the

214

three fundamental epochs of Rumanian history: the formation of the Rumanian nation; its initial casting into a national polity (foundation of the Rumanian principalities); and its final evolution into the actual unitary State; and shall then pass on to consider the more recent internal and external development of Rumania, and her present attitude.

2.
Formation of the Rumanian Nation

About the fifth century B.C., when the population of the Balkan-Carpathian region consisted of various tribes belonging to the Indo-European family, the northern portion of the Balkan peninsula was conquered by the Thracians and the Illyrians. The Thracians spread north and south, and a branch of their race, the Dacians, crossed the Danube. The latter established themselves on both sides of the Carpathian ranges, in the region which now comprises the provinces of Oltenia (Rumania), and Banat and Transylvania (Hungary). The Dacian Empire expanded till its boundaries touched upon those of the Roman Empire. The Roman province of Moesia (between the Danube and the Balkans) fell before its armies, and the campaign that ensued was so successful that the Dacians were able to compel Rome to an alliance.

Two expeditions undertaken against Dacia by the Emperor Trajan (98-117) released Rome from these ignominious obligations, and brought Dacia under Roman rule (A.D. 106). Before his second expedition Trajan erected a stone bridge over the Danube, the remains of which can still be seen at Turnu-Severin, a short distance below the point where the Danube enters Rumanian territory. Trajan celebrated his victory by erecting at Adam Klissi (in the province of Dobrogea) the recently discovered *Tropaeum Traiani*, and in Rome the celebrated 'Trajan's Column', depicting in marble reliefs various episodes of the Dacian wars.

The new Roman province was limited to the regions originally inhabited by the Dacians, and a strong garrison, estimated by historians at 25,000 men, was left to guard it. Numerous colonists from all parts of the Roman Empire were brought here as settlers, and what remained of the Dacian population completely amalgamated with them. The new province quickly developed under the impulse of Roman civilization, of which numerous inscriptions and other archaeological remains are evidence. It became one of the most flourishing dependencies of the Roman Empire, and was spoken of as *Dacia Felix*.

About a century and a half later hordes of barbarian invaders, coming from the north and east, swept over the country. Under the strain of those incursions the Roman legions withdrew by degrees into Moesia, and in A.D. 271 Dacia was finally evacuated. But the colonists remained, retiring into the Carpathians, where they lived forgotten of history.

The most powerful of these invaders were the Goths (271-375), who, coming from the shores of the Baltic, had shortly before settled north of the Black Sea. Unaccustomed to mountain life, they did not penetrate beyond the plains between the Carpathians and the Dnjester. They had consequently but little intercourse with the Daco-Roman population, and the total absence in the Rumanian language and in Rumanian place-names of words of Gothic origin indicates that their stay had no influence upon country or population. Material evidence of their occupation is afforded, however, by a number of articles made of gold found in 1837 at Petroasa (Moldavia), and now in the National Museum at Bucarest.

After the Goths came the Huns (375-453), under Attila, the Avars (566-799), both of Mongolian race, and the Gepidae (453-566), of Gothic race—all savage, bloodthirsty raiders, passing and repassing over the Rumanian regions, pillaging and burning everywhere. To avoid destruction the Daco-Roman population withdrew more and more into the inaccessible wooded regions of the mountains, and as a result were in no wise influenced by contact with the invaders.

But with the coming of the Slavs, who settled in the Balkan peninsula about the beginning of the seventh century, certain fundamental changes took place in the ethnical conditions prevailing on the Danube. The Rumanians were separated from the Romans, following the occupation by the Slavs of the Roman provinces between the Adriatic and the Black Sea. Such part of the population as was not annihilated during the raids of the Avars was taken into captivity, or compelled to retire southwards towards modern Macedonia and northwards towards the Dacian regions.

Parts of the Rumanian country became dependent upon the new state founded between the Balkans and the Danube in 679 by the Bulgarians, a people of Turanian origin, who formerly inhabited the regions north of the Black Sea between the Volga and the mouth of the Danube.

After the conversion of the Bulgarians to Christianity (864) the Slovenian language was introduced into their Church, and afterwards also into the Church of the already politically dependent Rumanian provinces.[*] This finally severed the Daco-Rumanians from the Latin world. The former remained for a long time under Slav influence, the extent of which is shown by the large number of words of Slav origin contained in the Rumanian language, especially in geographical and agricultural terminology.

The coming of the Hungarians (a people of Mongolian race) about the end of the ninth century put an end to the Bulgarian domination in Dacia. While a few of the existing Rumanian duchies were subdued by Stephen the Saint, the first King of Hungary (995-1038), the 'land of the Vlakhs' *(Terra Blacorum)*, in the south-eastern part of Transylvania, enjoyed under the Hungarian kings a certain degree of national autonomy. The Hungarian chronicles speak of the Vlakhs as 'former colonists of

---

[*]   The Rumanians north and south of the Danube embraced the Christian faith after its introduction into the Roman Empire by Constantine the Great (325), with Latin as religious language and their church organization under the rule of Rome. A Christian basilica, dating from that period, has been discovered by the Rumanian; archaeologist, Tocilescu, at Adam Klissi (Dobrogea).

217

the Romans'. The ethnological influence of the Hungarians upon the Rumanian population has been practically nil. They found the Rumanian nation firmly established, race and language, and the latter remained pure of Magyarisms, even in Transylvania. Indeed, it is easy to prove—and it is only what might be expected, seeing that the Rumanians had attained a higher state of civilization than the Hungarian invaders—that the Hungarians were largely influenced by the Daco-Romans. They adopted Latin as their official language, they copied many of the institutions and customs of the Rumanians, and recruited a large number of their nobles from among the Rumanian nobility, which was already established on a feudal basis when the Hungarians arrived.

A great number of the Rumanian nobles and freemen were, however, inimical to the new masters, and migrated to the regions across the mountains. This the Hungarians used as a pretext for bringing parts of Rumania under their domination, and they were only prevented from further extending it by the coming of the Tartars (1241), the last people of Mongolian origin to harry these regions. The Hungarians maintained themselves, however, in the parts which they had already occupied, until the latter were united into the principality of the 'Rumanian land'.

To sum up: 'The Rumanians are living to-day where fifteen centuries ago their ancestors were living. The possession of the regions on the Lower Danube passed from one nation to another, but none endangered the Rumanian nation as a national entity. "The water passes, the stones remain"; the hordes of the migration period, detached from their native soil, disappeared as mist before the sun. But the Roman element bent their heads while the storm passed over them, clinging to the old places until the advent of happier days, when they were able to stand up and stretch their limbs.'*

---

*   Traugott Tamm, *Ueber den Ursprung der Rumaenen*, Bonn, 1891.

3.

The Foundation and Development of the Rumanian Principalities

The first attempt to organize itself into a political entity was made by the Rumanian nation in the thirteenth century, when, under the impulse of the disaffected nobles coming from Hungary, the two principalities of 'Muntenia' (Mountain Land), commonly known as Wallachia and 'Moldavia', came into being. The existence of Rumanians on both sides of the Carpathians long before Wallachia was founded is corroborated by contemporary chroniclers. We find evidence of it in as distant a source as the *History of the Mongols,* of the Persian chronicler, Rashid Al-Din, who, describing the invasion of the Tartars, says: 'In the middle of spring (1240) the princes (Mongols or Tartars) crossed the mountains in order to enter the country of the Bulares (Bulgarians) and of the Bashguirds (Hungarians). Orda, who was marching to the right, passed through the country of the Haute (Olt), where Bazarambam met him with an army, but was beaten. Boudgek crossed the mountains to enter the Kara-Ulak, and defeated the Ulak (Vlakh) people.'* Kara-Ulak means Black Wallachia; Bazarambam is certainly the corrupted name of the Ban Bassarab, who ruled as vassal of Hungary over the province of Oltenia, and whose dynasty founded the principality of Muntenia. The early history of this principality was marked by efforts to free it from Hungarian domination, a natural development of the desire for emancipation which impelled the Rumanians to migrate from the subdued provinces in Hungary.

The foundation of Moldavia dates from after the retreat of the Tartars, who had occupied the country for a century (1241-1345). They were driven out by an expedition under Hungarian leadership, with the aid of Rumanians from the province of Maramuresh. It was the latter who then

---

*   Xenopol, *Histoire des Roumains,* Paris, 1896, i, 168.

founded the principality of Moldavia under the suzerainty of Hungary, the chroniclers mentioning as its first ruler the Voivod Dragosh.*

The rudimentary political formations which already existed before the foundation of the principalities were swept away by the invasion of the Tartars, who destroyed all trace of constituted authority in the plains below the Carpathians. In consequence the immigrants from Transylvania did not encounter any resistance, and were even able to impose obedience upon the native population, though coming rather as refugees than as conquerors. These new-comers were mostly nobles (boyards). Their emigration deprived the masses of the Rumanian population of Transylvania of all moral and political support—especially as a part of the nobility had already been won over by their Hungarian masters—and with time the masses fell into servitude. On the other hand the immigrating nobles strengthened and secured the predominance of their class in the states which were to be founded. In both cases the situation of the peasantry became worse, and we have, curiously enough, the same social fact brought about by apparently contrary causes.

Though the Rumanians seem to have contributed but little, up to the nineteenth century, to the advance of civilization, their part in European history is nevertheless a glorious one, and if less apparent, perhaps of more fundamental importance. By shedding their blood in the struggle against the Ottoman invasion, they, together with the other peoples of Oriental Europe, procured that security which alone made possible the development of western civilization. Their merit, like that of all with

---

*   The legend as to the foundation of Moldavia tells us that Dragosh, when hunting one day in the mountains, was pursuing a bison through the dense forest. Towards sunset, just when a successful shot from his bow had struck and killed the animal, he emerged at a point from which the whole panorama of Moldavia was unfolded before his astonished eyes. Deeply moved by the beauty of this fair country, he resolved to found a state there. It is in commemoration of this event that Moldavia bears the head of a wild bison on her banner.

whom they fought, 'is not to have vanquished time and again the followers of Mohammed, who always ended by gaining the upper hand, but rather to have resisted with unparalleled energy, perseverance, and bravery the terrible Ottoman invaders, making them pay for each step advanced such a heavy price, that their resources were drained, they were unable to carry on the fight, and thus their power came to an end'.*

From the phalanx of Christian warriors stand out the names of a few who were the bravest of a time when bravery was common; but while it is at least due that more tribute than a mere mention of their names should be paid to the patriot princes who fought in life-long conflict against Turkish domination, space does not permit me to give more than the briefest summary of the wars which for centuries troubled the country.

It was in 1389, when Mircea the Old was Prince of Wallachia, that the united Balkan nations attempted for the first time to check Ottoman invasion. The battle of Kosovo, however, was lost, and Mircea had to consent to pay tribute to the Turks. For a short space after the battle of Rovine (1398), where Mircea defeated an invading Turkish army, the country had peace, until Turkish victories under the Sultan Mohammed resulted, in 1411, in further submissions to tribute.

It is worthy of mention that it was on the basis of tribute that the relations between Turkey and Rumania rested until 1877, the Rumanian provinces becoming at no time what Hungary was for a century and a half, namely, a Turkish province.

In a battle arising following his frustration—by means not unconnected with his name—of a Turkish plot against his person, Vlad the Impaler (1458-62) completely defeated the Turks under Mohammed II; but an unfortunate feud against Stephen the Great, Prince of Moldavia, put an end to the reign of Vlad—a fierce but just prince.

A period of the most lamentable decadence followed, during which Turkish domination prevailed more and more in the country. During

---

*   Xenopol, op. cit., i. 266.

an interval of twenty-five years (1521-46) no less than eleven princes succeeded one another on the throne of Muntenia, whilst of the nineteen princes who ruled during the last three-quarters of the sixteenth century, only two died a natural death while still reigning.

In Moldavia also internal struggles were weakening the country. Not powerful enough to do away with one another, the various aspirants to the throne contented themselves with occupying and ruling over parts of the province. Between 1443-7 there were no less than three princes reigning simultaneously, whilst one of them, Peter III, lost and regained the throne three times.

For forty-seven years (1457-1504) Stephen the Great fought for the independence of Moldavia. At Racova, in 1475, he annihilated an Ottoman army in a victory considered the greatest ever secured by the Cross against Islam. The Shah of Persia, Uzun Hasan, who was also fighting the Turks, offered him an alliance, urging him at the same time to induce all the Christian princes to unite with the Persians against the common foe. These princes, as well as Pope Sixtus IV, gave him great praise; but when Stephen asked from them assistance in men and money, not only did he receive none, but Vladislav, King of Hungary, conspired with his brother Albert, King of Poland, to conquer and divide Moldavia between them. A Polish army entered the country, but was utterly destroyed by Stephen in the forest of Kosmin.

Having had the opportunity of judging at its right value the friendship of the Christian princes, on his death-bed Stephen advised his son Bogdan to make voluntary submission to the Turks. Thus Moldavia, like Wallachia, came under Turkish suzerainty.

For many years after Stephen's death the Turks exploited the Rumanian countries shamelessly, the very candidates for the throne having to pay great sums for Turkish support. The country groaned under the resultant taxation and the promiscuousness of the tribute exacted till, in 1572, John the Terrible ascended the Moldavian throne. This prince refused to pay tribute, and repeatedly defeated the Turks. An army of 100,000 men advanced against John; but his cavalry, composed of nobles not over-loyal to a prince having the peasant cause so much at heart, deserted to the enemy, with the result that, after a gallant and prolonged resistance, he suffered defeat.

Michael the Brave, Prince of Muntenia (1593-1601), was the last of the Vlakhs to stand up against Turkish aggression. This prince not only succeeded in crushing a Turkish army sent against him, but he invaded Transylvania, whose prince had leanings towards Turkey, pushed further into Moldavia, and succeeded in bringing the three Rumanian countries under his rule. Michael is described in the documents of the time as 'Prince of the whole land of Hungro-Wallachia, of Transylvania, and of Moldavia'. He ruled for eight years. 'It was not the Turkish sword which put an end to the exploits of Michael the Brave. The Magyars of Transylvania betrayed him; the German emperor condemned him; and a Greek in Austria's service, General Basta, had him sabred: as though it were fated that all the enemies of the Rumanian race, the Magyar, the German, and the Greek, should unite to dip their hands in the blood of the Latin hero.'[*] The union of the Rumanian lands which he realized did not last long; but it gave form and substance to the idea which was from that day onward to be the ideal of the Rumanian nation.

The fundamental cause of all the sufferings of the Rumanian principalities was the hybrid 'hereditary-elective' system of succession to the throne, which prevailed also in most of the neighbouring countries. All members of the princely family were eligible for the succession; but the right of selecting among them lay with an assembly composed of the higher nobility and clergy. All was well if a prince left only one successor. But if there were several, even if illegitimate children, claiming the right to rule, then each endeavoured to gain over the nobility with promises, sometimes, moreover, seeking the support of neighbouring countries. This system rendered easier and hastened the establishment of Turkish

---

[*]   Alfred Rumbaud, Introduction to Xenopol, op, cit., i. xix.

domination; and corruption and intrigues, in which the Sultan's harem had a share, became capital factors in the choice and election of the ruler.

Economically and intellectually all this was disastrous. The Rumanians were an agricultural people. The numerous class of small freeholders (moshneni and razeshi), not being able to pay the exorbitant taxes, often had their lands confiscated by the princes. Often, too, not being able to support themselves, they sold their property and their very selves to the big landowners. Nor did the nobles fare better. Formerly free, quasi-feudal warriors, seeking fortune in reward for services rendered to their prince, they were often subjected to coercive treatment on his part now that the throne depended upon the goodwill of influential personages at Constantinople. Various civil offices were created at court, either necessitated by the extension of the relations of the country or intended to satisfy some favourite of the prince. Sources of social position and great material benefit, these offices were coveted greedily by the boyards, and those who obtained none could only hope to cheat fortune by doing their best to undermine the position of the prince.

4.

The Phanariote Rule

These offices very presently fell to the lot of the Phanariotes (Greek merchants and bankers inhabiting the quarter of Phanar), who had in some way or another assisted the princes to their thrones, these being now practically put up to auction in Constantinople. As a natural consequence of such a state of affairs the thoughts of the Rumanian princes turned to Russia as a possible supporter against Ottoman oppression. A formal alliance was entered into in 1711 with Tsar Peter the Great, but a joint military action against the Turks failed, the Tsar returned to Russia, and the Porte threatened to transform Moldavia, in order to secure her against incipient Russian influence, into a Turkish province with a pasha as administrator. The nobles were preparing to leave the country, and the people to retire into the mountains, as their ancestors had done in times of danger. It is not to be wondered at that, under the menace of losing their autonomy, the Rumanians 'welcomed the nomination of the dragoman of the Porte, Nicholas Mavrocordato, though he was a Greek. The people greeted with joy the accession of the first Phanariote to the throne of the principality of Moldavia'* (1711).

Knowledge of foreign languages had enabled the Phanariotes to obtain important diplomatic positions at Constantinople, and they ended by acquiring the thrones of the Rumanian principalities as a recompense for their services. But they had to pay for it, and to make matters more profitable the Turks devised the ingenious method of transferring the princes from one province to another, each transference being considered as a new nomination. From 1730 to 1741 the two reigning princes interchanged thrones in this way three times. They acquired the throne by gold, and they could only keep it by gold. All depended upon how much they wore able to squeeze out of the country. The princes soon became past masters in the art of spoliation. They put taxes upon chimneys, and the starving peasants pulled their cottages down and went to live in mountain caves; they taxed the animals, and the peasants preferred to kill the few beasts they possessed. But this often proved no remedy, for we are told that the Prince Constantin Mavrocordato, having prescribed a tax on domestic animals at a time when an epidemic had broken out amongst them, ordered the tax to be levied on the carcasses. 'The Administrative regime during the Phanariote period was, in general, little else than organized brigandage,' says Xenopol**. In fact the Phanariote rule was instinct with corruption, luxury, and intrigue. Though individually some of them may not deserve blame, yet considering what the Phanariotes

---

*   Xenopol, op. cit., ii. 138
** Ibid, op. cit., ii. 308

took out of the country, what they introduced into it, and to what extent they prevented its development, their era was the most calamitous in Rumanian history.

The war of 1768 between Russia and Turkey gave the former power a vague protectorate over the Rumanian provinces (Treaty of Kutchuk Kainardji). In 1774 Austria acquired from the Turks, by false promises, the northern part of Moldavia, the pleasant land of Bucovina. During the new conflict between Turkey and Russia, the Russian armies occupied and battened upon the Rumanian provinces for six years. Though they had again to abandon their intention of making the Danube the southern boundary of their empire—to which Napoleon had agreed by the secret treaty with Tsar Alexander (Erfurt, September 27, 1808)—they obtained from Turkey the cession of Bessarabia (Treaty of Bucarest, May 28, 1812), together with that part of Moldavia lying between the Dnjester and the Pruth, the Russians afterwards giving to the whole region the name of Bessarabia.

5.
Modern Period to 1866

In 1821 the Greek revolution, striving to create an independent Greece, broke out on Rumanian ground, supported by the princes of Moldavia and Muntenia. Of this support the Rumanians strongly disapproved, for, if successful, the movement would have strengthened the obnoxious Greek domination; If unsuccessful, the Turks were sure to take a terrible revenge for the assistance given by the Rumanian countries. The movement, which was started about the same time by the ennobled peasant, Tudor Vladimirescu, for the emancipation of the lower classes, soon acquired, therefore, an anti-Greek tendency. Vladimirescu was assassinated at the instigation of the Greeks; the latter were completely checked by the Turks, who, grown suspicious after the Greek rising and confronted

226

with the energetic attitude of the Rumanian nobility, consented in 1822 to the nomination of two native boyards, Jonitza Sturdza and Gregory Ghica, recommended by their countrymen, as princes of Moldavia and Wallachia. The iniquitous system of 'the throne to the highest bidder' had come to an end.

The period which marks the decline of Greek influence in the Rumanian principalities also marks the growth of Russian influence; the first meant economic exploitation, the second was a serious menace to the very existence of the Rumanian nation. But if Russia seemed a possible future danger, Turkey with its Phanariote following was a certain and immediate menace. When, therefore, at the outbreak of the conflict with Turkey in 1828 the Russians once more passed the Pruth, the country welcomed them. Indeed, the Rumanian boyards, who after the rising of 1821 and the Turkish occupation had taken refuge in Transylvania, had even more than once invited Russian intervention.* Hopes and fears alike were realized. By the Treaty of Adrianople (1829) the rights of Turkey as suzerain were limited to the exaction of a monetary tribute and the right of investiture of the princes, one important innovation being that these last were to be elected by national assemblies for life. But, on the other hand, a Russian protectorate was established, and the provinces remained in Russian military occupation up to 1834, pending the payment of the war indemnity by Turkey. The ultimate aim of Russia may be open to discussion. Her immediate aim was to make Russian influence paramount in the principalities; this being the only possible explanation of the anomalous fact that, pending the payment of the war indemnity, Russia herself was occupying the provinces whose autonomy she had but now forcibly retrieved from Turkey. The *Reglement Organique*, the new constitutional law given to the principalities by their Russian governor, Count Kisseleff, truly reflected the tendency. From the administrative point of view it was meant to make for progress; from the political point

---

*   Sec P. Eliade, *Histoire de l'Esprit Public en Roumanie*, i, p. 167 et seq.

of view it was meant to bind the two principalities to the will of the Tsar. The personal charm of Count Kisseleff seemed to have established as it were an unbreakable link between Russians and Rumanians. But when he left the country in 1834 'the liking for Russia passed away to be replaced finally by the two sentiments which always most swayed the Rumanian heart: love for their country, and affection towards France'.

French culture had been introduced into the principalities by the Phanariote princes who, as dragomans of the Porte, had to know the language, and usually employed French secretaries for themselves and French tutors for their children. With the Russian occupation a fresh impetus was given to French culture, which was pre-eminent in Russia at the time; and the Russian officials, not speaking the language of the country, generally employed French in their relations with the Rumanian authorities, French being already widely spoken in Rumania. The contact with French civilization, at an epoch when the Rumanians were striving to free themselves from Turkish, Greek, and Russian political influence, roused in them the sleeping Latin spirit, and the younger generation, in constantly increasing numbers, flocked to Paris in search of new forms of civilization and political life. At this turning-point in their history the Rumanians felt themselves drawn towards France, no less by racial affinity than by the liberal ideas to which that country had so passionately given herself during several decades.

By the Treaty of Adrianople the Black Sea was opened to the commercial vessels of all nations. This made for the rapid economic development of the principalities by providing an outlet for their agricultural produce, the chief source of their wealth. It also brought them nearer to western Europe, which began to be interested in a nation whose spirit centuries of sufferings had failed to break. Political, literary, and economic events thus prepared the ground for the Rumanian Renascence, and when in 1848 the great revolution broke out, it spread at once over the Rumanian countries, where the dawn of freedom had been struggling to break since 1821. The Rumanians of Transylvania rose against the tyranny of

228

the Magyars; those of Moldavia and Muntenia against the oppressive influence of Russia. The movement under the gallant, but inexperienced, leadership of a few patriots, who, significantly enough, had almost all been educated in France, was, however, soon checked in the principalities by the joint action of Russian and Turkish forces which remained in occupation of the country. Many privileges were lost (Convention of Balta Liman, May 1, 1849); but the revolution had quickened the national sentiment of the younger generation in all classes of society, and the expatriated leaders, dispersed throughout the great capitals of Europe, strenuously set to work to publish abroad the righteous cause of their country. In this they received the enthusiastic and invaluable assistance of Edgar Quinet, Michelet, Saint-Marc Girardin, and others.

This propaganda had the fortune to be contemporaneous and in agreement with the political events leading to the Crimean War, which was entered upon to check the designs of Russia. A logical consequence was the idea, raised at the Paris Congress of 1856, of the union of the Rumanian principalities as a barrier to Russian expansion. This idea found a powerful supporter in Napoleon III, ever a staunch upholder of the principle of nationality. But at the Congress the unexpected happened. Russia favoured the idea of union, 'to swallow the two principalities at a gulp,' as a contemporary diplomatist maliciously suggested; while Austria opposed it strongly. So, inconceivably enough, did Turkey, whose attitude, as the French ambassador at Constantinople, Thouvenel, put it, 'was less influenced by the opposition of Austria than by the approval of Russia'.* Great Britain also threw in her weight with the powers which opposed the idea of union, following her traditional policy of preserving the European equilibrium. The treaty of March 30, 1856, re-incorporated with Moldavia the southern part of Bessarabia, including the delta of the Danube, abolished the Russian protectorate, but confirmed the suzerainty of

---

*   A. Xenopol, *Unionistii si Separatistii* (Paper read before the Rumanian Academy), 1909.

Turkey—not unnaturally, since the integrity of the Ottoman Empire had been the prime motive of the war. By prohibiting Turkey, however, from entering Rumanian territory, save with the consent of the great powers, it was recognized indirectly that the suzerainty was merely a nominal one. Article 23 of the treaty, by providing that the administration of the principalities was to be on a national basis, implicitly pointed to the idea of union, as the organization of one principality independently of the other would not have been national. But as the main argument of Turkey and Austria was that the Rumanians themselves did not desire the union, it was decided to convene in both principalities special assemblies (divans *ad hoc*) representing all classes of the population, whose wishes were to be embodied, by a European commission, in a report for consideration by the Congress.

To understand the argument of the two powers concerned and the decision to which it led, it must be borne in mind that the principalities were in the occupation of an Austrian army, which had replaced the Russian armies withdrawn in 1854, and that the elections for the assemblies were to be presided over by Turkish commissaries. Indeed, the latter, in collaboration with the Austrian consuls, so successfully doctored the election lists,* that the idea of union might once more have fallen through, had it not been for the invaluable assistance which Napoleon III gave the Rumanian countries. As Turkish policy was relying mainly on England's support, Napoleon brought about a personal meeting with Queen Victoria and Prince Albert, at Osborne (August 1857), the result of which was a compromise: Napoleon agreed to defer for the time being the idea of an effective union of the two principalities, England undertaking, on the other hand, to make the Porte cancel the previous elections, and proceed to new ones after revision of the electoral lists. The corrupt Austrian

---

* The edifying correspondence between the Porte and its commissary Vorgorides regarding the arrangements for the Rumanian elections fell into the hands of Rumanian politicians, and caused a great sensation when it appeared in *L'Etoile du Danube*, published in Brussels by Rumanian *emigres*.

and Turkish influence on the old elections was best demonstrated by the fact that only three of the total of eighty-four old members succeeded in securing re-election. The assemblies met and proclaimed as imperatively necessary to the future welfare of the provinces, their union, 'for no frontier divides us, and everything tends to bring us closer, and nothing to separate us, save the ill-will of those who desire to see us disunited and weak'; further, a foreign hereditary dynasty, because 'the accession to the throne of princes chosen from amongst us has been a constant pretext for foreign interference, and the throne has been the cause of unending feud among the great families of this country'. Moreover, if the union of the two principalities was to be accomplished under a native prince, it is obvious that the competition would have become doubly keen; not to speak of the jealousies likely to be arousal between Moldavians and Muntenians.

Such were the indisputable wishes of the Rumanians, based on knowledge of men and facts, and arising out of the desire to see their country well started on the high road of progress. But Europe had called for the expression of these wishes only to get the question shelved for the moment, as in 1856 everybody was anxious for a peace which should at all costs be speedy. Consequently, when a second Congress met in Paris, in May 1858, three months of discussion and the sincere efforts of France only resulted in a hybrid structure entitled the 'United Principalities'. These were to have a common legislation, a common army, and a central committee composed of representatives of both assemblies for the discussion of common affairs; but were to continue to form two separate states, with independent legislative and executive institutions, each having to elect a prince of Rumanian descent for life.

Disappointed in their hopes and reasonable expectations, the Rumanians adopted the principle of 'help yourself and God will help you', and proceeded to the election of their rulers. Several candidates competed in Moldavia. To avoid a split vote the name of an outsider was put forward the day before the election, and on January 17, 1859,

Colonel Alexander Ioan Cuza was unanimously elected. In Wallachia the outlook was very uncertain when the assembly met, amid great popular excitement, on February 5. The few patriots who had realized that the powers, seeking only their own interests, were consciously and of set purpose hampering the emancipation of a long-suffering nation, put forth and urged the election of Cuza, and the assembly unanimously adopted this spirited suggestion. By this master-stroke the Rumanians had quietly accomplished the reform which was an indispensable condition towards assuring a better future. The political moment was propitious. Italy's military preparation prevented Austria from intervening, and, as usual when confronted with an accomplished fact, the great powers and Turkey finished by officially recognizing the action of the principalities in December 1861. The central commission was at once abolished, the two assemblies and cabinets merged into one, and Bucarest became the capital of the new state 'Rumania'.

If the unsympathetic attitude of the powers had any good result, it was to bring home for the moment to the Rumanians the necessity for national unity. When the danger passed, however, the wisdom which it had evoked followed suit. Cuza cherished the hope of realizing various ideal reforms. Confronted with strong opposition, he did not hesitate to override the constitution by dissolving the National Assembly (May 2, 1864) and arrogating to himself the right, till the formation of a new Chamber, to issue decrees which had all the force of law. He thus gave a dangerous example to the budding constitutional polity; political passions were let loose, and a plot organized by the Opposition led to the forced abdication of Cuza on February 23, 1866. The prince left the country for ever a few days later. No disturbance whatever took place, not one drop of blood was shed.

A series of laws, mostly adapted from French models, was introduced by Cuza. Under the Education Act of 1864 all degrees of education were free, and elementary education compulsory. A large number of special and technical schools were founded, as well as two universities, one at

Jassy (1860) and one at Bucarest (1864). After the *coup d'etat* of 1864 universal suffrage was introduced, largely as an attempt to 'swamp' the fractious political parties with the peasant vote; while at the same time a 'senate' was created as a 'moderating assembly' which, composed as it was of members by right and members nominated by the prince, by its very nature increased the influence of the crown. The chief reforms concerned the rural question. Firstly, Cuza and his minister, Cogalniceanu, secularized and converted to the state the domains of the monasteries, which during the long period of Greek influence had acquired one-fifth of the total area of the land, and were completely in the hands of the Greek clergy (Law of December 13, 1863). More important still, as affecting fundamentally the social structure of the country, was the Rural Law (promulgated on August 26, 1864), which had been the cause of the conflict between Cuza and the various political factions, the Liberals clamouring for more thorough reforms, the Conservatives denouncing Cuza's project as revolutionary. As the peasant question is the most important problem left for Rumania to solve, and as I believe that, in a broad sense, it has a considerable bearing upon the present political situation in that country, it may not be out of place here to devote a little space to its consideration.

Originally the peasant lived in the village community as a free land-owner. He paid a certain due (one-tenth of his produce and three days' labour yearly) to his leader *(cneaz)* as recompense for his leadership in peace and war. The latter, moreover, solely enjoyed the privilege of carrying on the occupations of miller and innkeeper, and the peasant was compelled to mill with him. When after the foundation of the principalities the upper class was established on a feudal basis, the peasantry were subjected to constantly increasing burdens. Impoverished and having in many cases lost their land, the peasants were also deprived at the end of the sixteenth century of their freedom of movement. By that time the cneaz, from being the leader of the community, had become the actual lord of the village, and his wealth was estimated by the number of villages he possessed. The peasant owners paid their dues to him in labour and in kind. Those peasants who owned no land were his serfs, passing with the land from master to master.

Under the Turkish domination the Rumanian provinces became the granary of the Ottoman Empire. The value of land rose quickly, as did also the taxes. To meet these taxes—from the payment of which the boyards (the descendants of the cneazi) were exempt—the peasant owners had frequently to sacrifice their lands; while, greedy after the increased benefits, the boyards used all possible means to acquire more land for themselves. With the increase of their lands they needed more labour, and they obtained permission from the ruler not only to exact increased labour dues from the peasantry, but also to determine the amount of work that should be done in a day. This was effected in such a way that the peasants had, in fact, to serve three and four times the number of days due.

The power to acquire more land from the freeholders, and to increase the amount of labour due by the peasants, was characteristic of the legislation of the eighteenth century. By a decree of Prince Moruzi, in 1805, the lords were for the first time empowered to reserve to their own use part of the estate, namely, one-fourth of the meadow land, and this privilege was extended in 1828 to the use of one-third of the arable land. The remaining two-thirds were reserved for the peasants, every young married couple being entitled to a certain amount of land, in proportion to the number of traction animals they owned. When the Treaty of Adrianople of 1829 opened the western markets to Rumanian corn, in which markets far higher prices were obtainable than from the Turks, Rumanian agriculture received an extraordinary impetus. Henceforth the efforts of the boyards were directed towards lessening the amount of land to which the peasants were entitled. By the *Reglement Organique* they succeeded in reducing such land to half its previous area, at the same time maintaining and exacting from the peasant his dues in full. It is in the same Act that there appears for the first time the fraudulent title 'lords of the land', though the boyards had no exclusive right of property; they had the use of one-third of the estate, and a right to a due in labour and in kind from the peasant holders, present or prospective, of the other two-thirds.

With a view to ensuring, on the one hand, greater economic freedom to the land-owners, and, on the other, security for the peasants from the enslaving domination of the upper class, the rural law of 1864 proclaimed the peasant-tenants full proprietors of their holdings, and the land-owners full proprietors of the remainder of the estate. The original intention of creating common land was not carried out in the Bill. The peasant's holding in arable land being small, he not infrequently ploughed his pasture, and, as a consequence, had either to give up keeping beasts, or pay a high price to the land-owners for pasturage. Dues in labour and in kind were abolished, the land-owners receiving an indemnity which was to be refunded to the state by the peasants in instalments within a period of fifteen years. This reform is characteristic of much of the legislation of Cuza: despotically pursuing the realization of some ideal reform, without adequate study of and adaptation to social circumstances, his laws provided no practical solution of the problem with which they dealt. In this case, for example, the reform benefited the upper class solely, although generally considered a boon to the peasantry. Of ancient right two-thirds of the estate were reserved for the peasants; but the new law gave them possession of no more than the strip they were holding, which barely sufficed to provide them with the mere necessaries of life. The remainder up to two-thirds of the estate went as a gift, with full proprietorship; to the boyard. For the exemption of their dues in kind and in labour, the peasants had to pay an indemnity, whereas the right of their sons to receive at their marriage a piece of land in proportion to the number of traction animals they possessed was lost without compensation. Consequently, the younger peasants had to sell their labour, contracting for periods of a year and upwards, and became a much easier prey to the spoliation of the upper class than when they had at least a strip of land on which to build a hut, and from which to procure their daily bread; the more so as the country had no industry which could compete with agriculture in the labour market. An investigation undertaken by the Home Office showed that out of 1,265 labour contracts for 1906, chosen at random, only 39.7 per cent, were concluded at customary wages; the others were lower in varying degrees, 13.2 per cent. of the cases showing wages upwards of 75 per cent. below the usual rates.

Under these conditions of poverty and economic serfdom the peasantry was not able to participate in the enormous development of Rumanian agriculture, which had resulted from increased political security and the establishment of an extensive network of railways. While the boyards found an increasing attraction in politics, a new class of middlemen came into existence, renting the land from the boyards for periods varying generally from three to five years. Owing to the resultant competition, rents increased considerably, while conservative methods of cultivation kept production stationary. Whereas the big cultivator obtained higher prices to balance the increased cost of production, the peasant, who produced for his own consumption, could only face such increase by a corresponding decrease in the amount of food consumed. To show how much alive the rural question is, it is enough to state that peasant risings occurred in 1888, 1889, 1894, 1900, and 1907; that new distributions of land took place in 1881 and 1889; that land was promised to the peasants as well at the time of the campaign of 1877 as at that of 1913; and that more or less happily conceived measures concerning rural questions have been passed in almost every parliamentary session. The general tendency of such legislation partook of the 'free contract' nature, though owing to the social condition of the peasantry the acts in question had to embody protective measures providing for a maximum rent for arable and pasture land, and a minimum wage for the peasant labourer.

Solutions have been suggested in profusion. That a solution is possible no one can doubt. One writer, basing his arguments on official statistics which show that the days of employment in 1905 averaged only ninety-one for each peasant, claims that only the introduction of circulating capital and the creation of new branches of activity can bring about a change. The suggested remedy may be open to discussion; but our author is undoubtedly right when, asking himself why this solution has not yet been attempted, he says: 'Our country is governed at present by an agrarian class . . . Her whole power rests in her ownership of the land, our only wealth. The introduction of circulating capital would result in the disintegration of that wealth, in the loss of its unique quality, and, as a consequence, in the social decline of its possessors.'* This is the fundamental evil which prevents any solution of the rural question. A small class of politicians, with the complicity of a large army of covetous and unscrupulous officials, live in oriental indolence out of the sufferings of four-fifths of the Rumanian nation. Though elementary education is compulsory, more than 60 per cent. of the population are still illiterate, mainly on account of the inadequacy of the educational budget. Justice is a myth for the peasant. Of political rights he is, in fact, absolutely deprived. The large majority, and by far the sanest part of the Rumanian nation, are thus fraudulently kept outside the political and social life of the country. It is not surmising too much, therefore, to say that the opportunity of emancipating the Transylvanians would not have been wilfully neglected, had that part of the Rumanian nation in which the old spirit still survives had any choice in the determination of their own fate.

6.
Contemporary Period: Internal Development

In order to obviate internal disturbances or external interference, the leaders of the movement which had dethroned Prince Cuza caused parliament to proclaim, on the day of Cuza's abdication, Count Philip

---

*   St. Antim, *Chestiunea Social[)a] [^i]n Rom[^a]nia*, 1908, p. 214.

of Flanders—the father of King Albert of Belgium—Prince of Rumania. The offer was, however, not accepted, as neither France nor Russia favoured the proposal. Meanwhile a conference had met again in Paris at the instance of Turkey and vetoed the election of a foreign prince. But events of deeper importance were ripening in Europe, and the Rumanian politicians rightly surmised that the powers would not enforce their protests if a candidate were found who was likely to secure the support of Napoleon III, then 'schoolmaster' of European diplomacy. This candidate was found in the person of Prince Carol of Hohenzollern-Sigmaringen, second son of the head of the elder branch of the Hohenzollerns (Catholic and non-reigning). Prince Carol was cousin to the King of Prussia, and related through his grandmother to the Bonaparte family. He could consequently count upon the support of France and Prussia, while the political situation fortunately secured him from the opposition of Russia, whose relations with Prussia were at the time friendly, and also from that of Austria, whom Bismarck proposed to 'keep busy for some time to come'. The latter must have viewed with no little satisfaction the prospect of a Hohenzollern occupying the throne of Rumania at this juncture; and Prince Carol, allowing himself to be influenced by the Iron Chancellor's advice, answered the call of the Rumanian nation, which had proclaimed him as 'Carol I, Hereditary Prince of Rumania'. Travelling secretly with a small retinue, the prince second class, his suite first, Prince Carol descended the Danube on an Austrian steamer, and landed on May 8 at Turnu-Severin, the very place where, nearly eighteen centuries before, the Emperor Trajan had alighted and founded the Rumanian nation.

By independent and energetic action, by a conscious neglect of the will of the powers, which only a young constitutional polity would have dared, by an active and unselfish patriotism, Rumania had at last chosen and secured as her ruler the foreign prince who alone had a chance of putting a stop to intrigues from within and from without. And the Rumanians had been extremely fortunate in their hasty and not quite independent choice. A prince of Latin origin would probably have been more warmly welcomed to the hearts of the Rumanian people; but after so many years of political disorder, corrupt administration, and arbitrary rule, a prince possessed of the German spirit of discipline and order was best fitted to command respect and impose obedience and sobriety of principle upon the Rumanian politicians.

Prince Carol's task was no easy one. The journal compiled by the provisional government, which held the reins for the period elapsing between the abdication of Cuza and the accession of Prince Carol, depicts in the darkest colours the economic situation to which the faults, the waste, the negligence, and short-sightedness of the previous regime had reduced the country, 'the government being in the humiliating position of having brought disastrous and intolerable hardship alike upon its creditors, its servants, its pensioners, and its soldiers'.* Reforms were badly needed, and the treasury had nothing in hand but debts. To increase the income of the state was difficult, for the country was poor and not economically independent. Under the Paris Convention of 1858, Rumania remained bound, to her detriment, by the commercial treaties of her suzerain, Turkey, the powers not being willing to lose the privileges they enjoyed under the Turkish capitulations. Moreover, she was specially excluded from the arrangement of 1860, which allowed Turkey to increase her import taxes. The inheritance of ultra-liberal measures from the previous regime made it difficult to cope with the unruly spirit of the nation. Any attempt at change in this direction would have savoured of despotism to the people, who, having at last won the right to speak aloud, believed that to clamour against anything that meant 'rule' was the only real and full assertion of liberty. And the dissatisfied were always certain of finding a sympathetic ear and an open purse in the Chancellories of Vienna and St. Petersburg.

---

*   D.A. Sturdza, *Treizeci de ani de Domnie ai Regelui Carol*, 1900, i.82.

Prince Carol, not being sufficiently well acquainted with the conditions of the country nor possessing as yet much influence with the governing class, had not been in a position to influence at their inception the provisions of the extremely liberal constitution passed only a few weeks after his accession to the throne. The new constitution, which resembled that of Belgium more nearly than any other, was framed by a constituent assembly elected on universal suffrage, and, except for slight modifications introduced in 1879 and 1884, is in vigour to-day. It entrusts the executive to the king and his ministers, the latter alone being responsible for the acts of the government.* The legislative power is vested in the king and two assemblies—a senate and a chamber—the initiative resting with any one of the three.** The budget and the yearly bills fixing the strength of the army, however, must first be passed by the Chamber. The agreement of the two Chambers and the sanction of the king are necessary before any bill becomes law. The king convenes, adjourns, and dissolves parliament. He promulgates the laws and is invested with the right of absolute veto. The constitution proclaims the inviolability of domicile, the liberty of the press and of assembly, and absolute liberty of creed and religion, in so far as its forms of celebration do not come into conflict with public order and decency. It recognizes no distinction of class and privilege; all the citizens share equally rights and duties within the law. Education is

---

*   There are at present nine departments: Interior, Foreign Affairs, Finance, War, Education and Religion, Domains and Agriculture, Public Works, Justice, and Industry and Commerce. The President of the Cabinet is Prime Minister, with or without portfolio.

**   All citizens of full age paying taxes, with various exemptions, are electors, voting according to districts and census. In the case of the illiterate country inhabitants, with an income from land of less than L12 a year, fifty of them choose one delegate having one vote in the parliamentary election. The professorial council of the two universities of Jassy and Bucarest send one member each to the Senate, the heir to the throne and the eight bishops being members by right.

free in the state schools, and elementary education compulsory wherever state schools exist. Individual liberty and property are guaranteed; but only Rumanian citizens can acquire rural property. Military service is compulsory, entailing two years in the infantry, three years in the cavalry and artillery, one year in all arms for those having completed their studies as far as the university stage. Capital punishment does not exist, except for military offences in time of war.

The state religion is Greek Orthodox. Up to 1864 the Rumanian Church was subordinate to the Patriarchate of Constantinople. In that year it was proclaimed independent, national, and autocephalous, though this change was not recognized by the Patriarchate till 1885, while the secularization of the property of the monasteries put an end *de facto* to the influence of the Greek clergy. Religious questions of a dogmatic nature are settled by the Holy Synod of Bucarest, composed of the two metropolitans of Bucarest and Jassy and the eight bishops; the Minister for Education, with whom the administrative part of the Church rests, having only a deliberative vote. The maintenance of the Church and of the clergy is included in the general budget of the country, the ministers being state officials (Law of 1893).

Religion has never played an important part in Rumanian national life, and was generally limited to merely external practices. This may be attributed largely to the fact that as the Slavonic language had been used in the Church since the ninth century and then was superseded by Greek up to the nineteenth century, the clergy was foreign, and was neither in a position nor did it endeavour to acquire a spiritual influence over the Rumanian peasant. There is no record whatever in Rumanian history of any religious feuds or dissensions. The religious passivity remained unstirred even during the domination of the Turks, who contented themselves with treating the unbelievers with contempt, and squeezing as much money as possible out of them. Cuza having made no provision for the clergy when he converted the wealth of the monasteries to the state, they were left for thirty years in complete destitution, and remained as a consequence outside the general intellectual development of the country. Though the situation has much improved since the Law of 1893, which incorporated the priests with the other officials of the Government, the clergy, recruited largely from among the rural population, are still greatly inferior to the Rumanian priests of Bucovina and Transylvania. Most of them take up Holy orders as a profession: 'I have known several country parsons who were thorough atheists.'*

However difficult his task, Prince Carol never deviated from the strictly constitutional path: his opponents were free to condemn the prince's opinions; he never gave them the chance of questioning his integrity.

Prince Carol relied upon the position in which his origin and family alliances placed him in his relations with foreign rulers to secure him the respect of his new subjects. Such considerations impressed the Rumanians. Nor could they fail to be aware of 'the differences between the previously elected princes and the present dynasty, and the improved position which the country owed to the latter'.**

To inculcate the Rumanians with the spirit of discipline the prince took in hand with energy and pursued untiringly, in spite of all obstacles, the organization of the army. A reliable and well-organized armed force was the best security against internal trouble-mongers, and the best argument in international relations, as subsequent events amply proved.

The Rumanian political parties were at the outset personal parties, supporting one or other of the candidates to the throne. When Greek influence, emanating from Constantinople, began to make itself felt, in the seventeenth century, a national party arose for the purpose of opposing it. This party counted upon the support of one of the neighbouring powers, and its various groups were known accordingly as the Austrian, the Russian, &c., parties. With the election of Cuza the external danger diminished, and the politicians divided upon principles of internal reform.

---

*   R. Rosetti, *Pentru ce s-au r[]a]sculat [t']]a]ranii*, 1907, p. 600
**   Augenzeuge, *Aus dem Leben Koenig Karls von Rum[]a]nien, 1894-1900,* iii. 177.

Cuza not being in agreement with either party, they united to depose him, keeping truce during the period preceding the accession of Prince Carol, when grave external dangers were threatening, and presiding in a coalition ministry at the introduction of the new constitution of 1866. But this done, the truce was broken. Political strife again awoke with all the more vigour for having been temporarily suppressed.

The reforms which it became needful to introduce gave opportunity for the development of strong divergence of views between the political parties. The Liberals—the Red Party, as they were called at the time—(led by C.A. Rosetti and Ioan Bratianu, both strong Mazzinists, both having taken an important part in the revolutionary movements of 1848 and in that which led to the deposition of Cuza) were advocating reforms hardly practicable even in an established democracy; the Conservatives (led by Lascar Catargiu) were striving to stem the flood of ideal liberal measures on which all sense of reality was being carried away.* In little more than a year there were four different Cabinets, not to mention numerous changes in individual ministers. 'Between the two extreme tendencies Prince Carol had to strive constantly to preserve unity of direction, he himself being the only stable element in that ever unstable country.' It was not without many untoward incidents that he succeeded. His person was the subject of more than one unscrupulous attack by politicians in opposition, who did not hesitate to exploit the German origin and the German sympathies of the prince in order to inflame the masses. These internal conflicts entered upon an acute phase at the time of the Franco-German conflict of 1870. Whilst, to satisfy public opinion, the Foreign Secretary of the time, M.P.P. Carp, had to declare in parliament, that 'wherever the colours of France are waving, there are our interests and sympathies', the prince wrote to the King of Prussia assuring him that 'his sympathies will always

---

*   A few years ago a group of politicians, mainly of the old Conservative party, detached themselves and became the Conservative-Democratic party under the leadership of M. Take Ionescu.

be where the black and white banner is waving'. In these so strained circumstances a section of the population of Bucarest allowed itself to be drawn into anti-German street riots. Disheartened and despairing of ever being able to do anything for that 'beautiful country', whose people 'neither know how to govern themselves nor will allow themselves to be governed', the prince decided to abdicate.

So strong was the feeling in parliament roused by the prince's decision that one of his most inveterate opponents now declared that it would be an act of high treason for the prince to desert the country at such a crisis. We have an inkling of what might have resulted in the letter written by the Emperor of Austria to Prince Carol at the time, assuring him that 'my Government will eagerly seize any opportunity which presents itself to prove by deeds the interest it takes in a country connected by so many bonds to my empire'. Nothing but the efforts of Lascar Catargiu and the sound patriotism of a few statesmen saved the country from what would have been a real misfortune. The people were well aware of this, and cheers lasting several minutes greeted that portion of the message from the throne which conveyed to the new parliament the decision of the prince to continue reigning.

The situation was considerably strengthened during a period of five years' Conservative rule. Prince Carol's high principles and the dignified example of his private life secured for him the increasing respect of politicians of all colours; while his statesmanlike qualities, his patience and perseverance, soon procured him an unlimited influence in the affairs of the state. This was made the more possible from the fact that, on account of the political ignorance of the masses, and of the varied influence exercised on the electorate by the highly centralized administration, no Rumanian Government ever fails to obtain a majority at an election. Any statesman can undertake to form a Cabinet if the king assents to a dissolution of parliament. Between the German system, where the emperor chooses the ministers independently of parliament, and the English system, where the members of the executive are indicated by the electorate through the medium of parliament, independently of the Crown, the Rumanian system takes a middle path. Neither the crown, nor the electorate, nor parliament possesses exclusive power in this direction. The Government is not, generally speaking, defeated either by the electorate or by parliament. It is the Crown which has the final decision in the changes of regime, and upon the king falls the delicate task of interpreting the significance of political or popular movements. The system—which comes nearest to that of Spain—undoubtedly has its advantages in a young and turbulent polity, by enabling its most stable element, the king, to ensure a continuous and harmonious policy. But it also makes the results dangerously dependent on the quality of that same element. Under the leadership of King Carol it was an undoubted success; the progress made by the country from an economic, financial, and military point of view during the last half-century is really enormous. Its position was furthermore strengthened by the proclamation of its independence, by the final settlement of the dynastic question,* and by its elevation on May 10, 1881, to the rank of kingdom, when upon the head of the first King of Rumania was placed a crown of steel made from one of the guns captured before Plevna from an enemy centuries old.

From the point of view of internal politics progress has been less satisfactory. The various reforms once achieved, the differences of principle between the political parties degenerated into mere opportunism, the Opposition opposing, the Government disposing. The parties, and especially the various groups within the parties, are generally known by the names of their leaders, these denominations not implying any definite political principle or Government programme. It is, moreover, far from

---

* In the absence of direct descendants and according to the constitution, Prince Ferdinand (born 1865), second son of King Carol's elder brother, was named Heir Apparent to the Rumanian throne. He married in 1892 Princess Marie of Coburg, and following the death of King Carol in 1914, he acceded to the throne as Ferdinand I.

245

edifying that the personal element should so frequently distort political discussion. 'The introduction of modern forms of state organization has not been followed by the democratization of all social institutions ... The masses of the people have remained all but completely outside political life. Not only are we yet far from government of the people by the people, but our liberties, though deeply graven on the facade of our constitution, have not permeated everyday life nor even stirred in the consciousness of the people.'[*]

It is strange that King Carol, who had the welfare of the people sincerely at heart, should not have used his influence to bring about a solution of the rural question; but this may perhaps be explained by the fact that, from Cuza's experience, he anticipated opposition from all political factions. It would almost seem as if, by a tacit understanding, and anxious to establish Rumania's international position, King Carol gave his ministers a free hand in the rural question, reserving for himself an equally free hand in foreign affairs. This seems borne out by the fact that, in the four volumes in which an 'eyewitness', making use of the king's private correspondence and personal notes, has minutely described the first fifteen years of the reign, the peasant question is entirely ignored.[**]

Addressing himself, in 1871, to the Rumanian representative at the Porte, the Austrian ambassador, von Prokesch-Osten, remarked: 'If Prince Carol manages to pull through without outside help, and make Rumania governable, it will be the greatest *tour de force* I have ever witnessed in my diplomatic career of more than half a century. It will be nothing less than a conjuring trick.' King Carol succeeded; and only those acquainted with Rumanian affairs can appreciate the truth of the ambassador's words.

---

[*]   C. Stere, *Social-democratizm sau Poporanizm*, Jassy.
[**]   The 'eyewitness' was Dr. Schaeffer, formerly tutor to Prince Carol.

7.

Contemporary Period: Foreign Affairs

Up to 1866 Rumanian foreign politics may be said to have been non-existent. The offensive or defensive alliances against the Turks concluded by the Rumanian rulers with neighbouring princes during the Middle Ages were not made in pursuance of any definite policy, but merely to meet the moment's need. With the establishment of Turkish suzerainty Rumania became a pawn in the foreign politics of the neighbouring empires, and we find her repeatedly included in their projects of acquisition, partition, or compensation (as, for instance, when she was put forward as eventual compensation to Poland for the territories lost by that country in the first partition).* Rumania may be considered fortunate in not having lost more than Bucovina to Austria (1775), Bessarabia to Russia (1812), and, temporarily, to Austria the region between the Danube and the Aluta, called Oltenia (lost by the Treaty of Passarowitz, 1718; recovered by the Treaty of Belgrade, 1739).

While her geographical position made of Rumania the cynosure of many covetous eyes, it at the same time saved her from individual attack by exciting countervailing jealousies. Moreover, the powers came at last to consider her a necessary rampart to the Ottoman Empire, whose dissolution all desired but none dared attempt. Austria and Russia, looking to the future, were continually competing for paramount influence in Rumania, though it is not possible to determine where their policy of acquisition ended and that of influence began.

The position of the principalities became more secure after the Paris Congress of 1858, which placed them under the collective guarantee of the great powers; but this fact, and the maintenance of Turkish suzerainty,

---

*   See Albert Sorel, *The Eastern Question in the Eighteenth Century* (Engl. ed.), 1898, pp. 141, 147 &c.

coupled with their own weakness, debarred them from any independence in their foreign relations.

A sudden change took place with the accession of Prince Carol; a Hohenzollern prince related to the King of Prussia and to Napoleon III could not be treated like one of the native boyards. The situation called for the more delicacy of treatment by the powers in view of the possibility of his being able to better those internal conditions which made Rumania 'uninteresting' as a factor in international politics. In fact, the prince's personality assured for Rumania a status which she could otherwise have attained only with time, by a political, economic, and military consolidation of her home affairs; and the prince does not fail to remark in his notes that the attentions lavished upon him by other sovereigns were meant rather for the Hohenzollern prince than for the Prince of Rumania. Many years later even, after the war of 1878, while the Russians were still south of the Danube with their lines of communication running through Rumania, Bratianu begged of the prince to give up a projected journey on account of the difficulties which might at any moment arise, and said: 'Only the presence of your Royal Highness keeps them [the Russians] at a respectful distance.' It was but natural under these circumstances that the conduct of foreign affairs should have devolved almost exclusively on the prince. The ascendancy which his high personal character, his political and diplomatic skill, his military capacity procured for him over the Rumanian statesmen made this situation a lasting one; indeed it became almost a tradition. Rumania's foreign policy since 1866 may be said, therefore, to have been King Carol's policy. Whether one agrees with it or not, no one can deny with any sincerity that it was inspired by the interests of the country, as the monarch saw them. Rebuking Bismarck's unfair attitude towards Rumania in a question concerning German investors, Prince Carol writes to his father in 1875: 'I have to put Rumania's interests above those of Germany. My path is plainly mapped out, and I must follow It unflinchingly, whatever the weather.'

Prince Carol was a thorough German, and as such naturally favoured the expansion of German influence among his new subjects. But if he desired Rumania to follow in the wake of German foreign policy, it was because of his unshaken faith in the future of his native country, because he considered that Rumania had nothing to fear from Germany, whilst it was all in the interest of that country to see Rumania strong and firmly established. At the same time, acting on the advice of Bismarck, he did not fail to work toward a better understanding with Russia, 'who might become as well a reliable friend as a dangerous enemy to the Rumanian state'. The sympathy shown him by Napoleon III was not always shared by the French statesmen,* and the unfriendly attitude of the French ambassador in Constantinople caused Prince Carol to remark that 'M. de Moustier is considered a better Turk than the Grand Turk himself'. Under the circumstances a possible alliance between France and Russia, giving the latter a free hand in the Near East, would have proved a grave danger to Rumania; 'it was, consequently, a skilful, if imperious act, to enter voluntarily, and without detriment to the existing friendly relations with France, within the Russian sphere of influence, and not to wait till compelled to do so.'

The campaigns of 1866 and 1870 having finally established Prussia's supremacy in the German world, Bismarck modified his attitude towards Austria. In an interview with the Austrian Foreign Secretary, Count Beust (Gastein, October 1871), he broached for the first time the question of an alliance and, touching upon the eventual dissolution of the Ottoman Empire, 'obligingly remarked that one could not conceive of a great power not making of its faculty for expansion a vital question'.** Quite in keeping with that change were the counsels henceforth tendered to Prince Carol. Early that year Bismarck wrote of his sorrow at having

---

*   See *Revue des Deux Mondes*, June 15, 1866, article by Eugene Forcade.
**   Gabriel Hanotaux, *La Guerre des Balkans et l'Europe* (Beust, Memoires), Paris, 1914, p. 297.

been forced to the conclusion that Rumania had nothing to expect from Russia, while Prince Anthony, Prince Carol's father and faithful adviser, wrote soon after the above interview (November 1871), that 'under certain circumstances it would seem a sound policy for Rumania to rely upon the support of Austria'. Persevering in this crescendo of suggestion, Austria's new foreign secretary, Count Andrassy, drifted at length to the point by plainly declaring not long afterwards that 'Rumania is not so unimportant that one should deprecate an alliance with her'.

Prince Carol had accepted the throne with the firm intention of shaking off the Turkish suzerainty at the first opportunity, and not unnaturally he counted upon Germany's support to that end. He and his country were bitterly disappointed, therefore, when Bismarck appealed directly to the Porte for the settlement of a difference between the Rumanian Government and a German company entrusted with the construction of the Rumanian railways; the more so as the Paris Convention had expressly forbidden any Turkish interference in Rumania's internal affairs. It thus became increasingly evident that Rumania could not break away from Russia, the coming power in the East. The eyes of Russia were steadfastly fixed on Constantinople: by joining her, Rumania had the best chance of gaining her independence; by not doing so, she ran the risk of being trodden upon by Russia on her way to Byzantium. But though resolved to co-operate with Russia in any eventual action in the Balkans, Prince Carol skilfully avoided delivering himself blindfold into her hands by deliberately cutting himself away from the other guaranteeing powers. To the conference which met in Constantinople at the end of 1876 to settle Balkan affairs he addressed the demand that 'should war break out between one of the guaranteeing powers and Turkey, Rumania's line of conduct should be dictated, and her neutrality and rights guaranteed, by the other powers'. This *demarche* failed. The powers had accepted the invitation to the conference as one accepts an invitation to visit a dying man. Nobody had any illusions on the possibility of averting war, least of all the two powers principally interested. In November 1876 Ali Bey and M. de Nelidov arrived simultaneously and secretly in Bucarest to sound Rumania as to an arrangement with their respective countries, Turkey and Russia. In opposition to his father and Count Andrassy, who counselled neutrality and the withdrawal of the Rumanian army into the mountains, and in sympathy with Bismarck's advice, Prince Carol concluded a Convention with Russia on April 16, 1877. Rumania promised to the Russian army 'free passage through Rumanian territory and the treatment due to a friendly army'; whilst Russia undertook to respect Rumania's political rights, as well as 'to maintain and defend her actual integrity'. 'It is pretty certain', wrote Prince Carol to his father, 'that this will not be to the liking of most of the great powers; but as they neither can nor will offer us anything, we cannot do otherwise than pass them by. A successful Russian campaign will free us from the nominal dependency upon Turkey, and Europe will never allow Russia to take her place.'

On April 23 the Russian armies passed the Pruth. An offer of active participation by the Rumanian forces in the forthcoming campaign was rejected by the Tsar, who haughtily declared that 'Russia had no need for the cooperation of the Rumanian army', and that 'it was only under the auspices of the Russian forces that the foundation of Rumania's future destinies could be laid'. Rumania was to keep quiet and accept in the end what Russia would deign to give her, or, to be more correct, take from her. After a few successful encounters, however, the Tsar's soldiers met with serious defeats before Plevna, and persistent appeals were now urged for the participation of the Rumanian army in the military operations. The moment had come for Rumania to bargain for her interests. But Prince Carol refused to make capital out of the serious position of the Russians; he led his army across the Danube and, at the express desire of the Tsar, took over the supreme command of the united forces before Plevna. After a glorious but terrible struggle Plevna, followed at short intervals by other strongholds, fell, the peace preliminaries were signed, and Prince Carol returned to Bucarest at the head of his victorious army.

Notwithstanding the flattering words in which the Tsar spoke of the Rumanian share in the success of the campaign, Russia did not admit Rumania to the Peace Conference. By the Treaty of San Stefano (March 3,1878) Rumania's independence was recognized; Russia obtained from Turkey the Dobrudja and the delta of the Danube, reserving for herself the right to exchange these territories against the three southern districts of Bessarabia, restored to Rumania by the Treaty of Paris, 1856. This stipulation was by no means a surprise to Rumania, Russia's intention to recover Bessarabia was well known to the Government, who hoped, however, that the demand would not be pressed after the effective assistance rendered by the Rumanian army. 'If this be not a ground for the extension of our territory, it is surely none for its diminution,' remarked Cogalniceanu at the Berlin Congress. Moreover, besides the promises of the Tsar, there was the Convention of the previous year, which, in exchange for nothing more than free passage for the Russian armies, guaranteed Rumania's integrity. But upon this stipulation Gorchakov put the jesuitical construction that, the Convention being concluded in view of a war to be waged against Turkey, it was only against Turkey that Russia undertook to guarantee Rumania's integrity; as to herself, she was not in the least bound by that arrangement. And should Rumania dare to protest against, or oppose the action of the Russian Government, 'the Tsar will order that Rumania be occupied and the Rumanian army disarmed'. 'The army which fought at Plevna', replied Prince Carol through his minister, 'may well be destroyed, but never disarmed.'

There was one last hope left to Rumania: that the Congress which met in Berlin in June 1878 for the purpose of revising the Treaty of San Stefano, would prevent such an injustice. But Bismarck was anxious that no 'sentiment de dignite blessee' should rankle in Russia's future policy; the French representative, Waddington, was 'above all a practical man'; Corti, the Italian delegate, was 'nearly rude' to the Rumanian delegates; while Lord Beaconsfield, England's envoy, receiving the Rumanian delegates privately, had nothing to say but that 'in politics the best services are often rewarded with ingratitude'. Russia strongly opposed even the idea that the Rumanian delegates should be allowed to put their case before the Congress, and consent was obtained only with difficulty after Lord Salisbury had ironically remarked that 'having heard the representatives of Greece, which was claiming foreign provinces, it would be but fair to listen also to the representatives of a country which was only seeking to retain what was its own'. Shortly before, Lord Salisbury, speaking in London to the Rumanian special envoy, Callimaki Catargiu, had assured him of England's sympathy and of her effective assistance in case either of war or of a Congress. 'But to be quite candid he must add that there are questions of more concern to England, and should she be able to come to an understanding with Russia with regard to them, she would not wage war for the sake of Rumania.' Indeed, an understanding came about, and an indiscretion enabled the *Globe* to make its tenor public early in June 1878. 'The Government of her Britannic Majesty', it said, 'considers that it will feel itself bound to express its deep regret should Russia persist in demanding the retrocession of Bessarabia . . . England's interest in this question is not such, however, as to justify her taking upon herself alone the responsibility of opposing the intended exchange.' So Bessarabia was lost, Rumania receiving instead Dobrudja with the delta of the Danube. But as the newly created state of Bulgaria was at the time little else than a detached Russian province, Russia, alone amongst the powers, opposed and succeeded in preventing the demarcation to the new Rumanian province of a strategically sound frontier. Finally, to the exasperation of the Rumanians, the Congress made the recognition of Rumania's independence contingent upon the abolition of Article 7 of the Constitution—which denied to non-Christians the right of becoming Rumanian citizens—and the emancipation of the Rumanian Jews.*

---

* Rumania only partially gave way to this intrusion of the powers into her internal affairs. The prohibition was abolished; but only individual naturalization was made possible, and that by special Act of Parliament. Only a very small proportion of the Jewish population has since been naturalized. The Jewish question in Rumania is undoubtedly a very serious one; but the matter is too

It was only after innumerable difficulties and hardships that, at the beginning of 1880, Rumania secured recognition of an independence which she owed to nobody but herself. Whilst Russia was opposing Rumania at every opportunity in the European conferences and commissions, she was at pains to show herself more amenable in *tete-a-tete*, and approached Rumania with favourable proposals. 'Rather Russia as foe than guardian,' wrote Prince Carol to his father; and these words indicate an important turning-point in Rumania's foreign policy.

In wresting Bessarabia from Rumania merely as a sop to her own pride, and to make an end of all that was enacted by the Treaty of Paris, 1856, Russia made a serious political blunder. By insisting that Austria should share in the partition of Poland, Frederick the Great had skilfully prevented her from remaining the one country towards which the Poles would naturally have turned for deliverance. Such an opportunity was lost by Russia through her short-sighted policy in Bessarabia—that of remaining the natural ally of Rumania against Rumania's natural foe, Austria-Hungary.

Rumania had neither historical, geographical, nor any important ethnographical points of contact with the region south of the Danube; the aims of a future policy could only have embraced neighbouring tracts of foreign territory inhabited by Rumanians. Whereas up to the date of the Berlin Congress such tracts were confined to Austria-Hungary, by that Congress a similar sphere of attraction for Rumanian aspirations was created in Russia.* The interests of a peaceful development demanded that Rumania should maintain friendly relations with both the powers striving for domination in the Near East; it was a vital necessity for her, however, to be able to rely upon the effective support of at least one

---

controversial to be dealt with in a few lines without risking misrepresentation or doing an injustice to one or other of the parties. For which reason it has not been included in this essay.

*   It is probable that this confederation had much to do with the readiness with which Bismarck supported the demands of his good friend, Gorchakov.

of them in a case of emergency. Russia's conduct had aroused a deep feeling of bitterness and mistrust in Rumania, and every lessening of her influence was a step in Austria's favour. Secondary considerations tended to intensify this: on the one hand lay the fact that through Russia's interposition Rumania had no defendable frontier against Bulgaria; on the other hand was the greatly strengthened position created for Austria by her alliance with Germany, in whose future Prince Carol had the utmost confidence.

Germany's attitude towards Rumania had been curiously hostile during these events; but when Prince Carol's father spoke of this to the German Emperor, the latter showed genuine astonishment: Bismarck had obviously not taken the emperor completely into his confidence. When, a few days later, Sturdza had an interview with Bismarck at the latter's invitation, the German Chancellor discovered once more that Rumania had nothing to expect from Russia. Indeed, Rumania's position between Russia and the new Slav state south of the Danube might prove dangerous, were she not to seek protection and assistance from her two 'natural friends', France and Germany. And, with his usual liberality when baiting his policy with false hopes, Bismarck went on to say that 'Turkey is falling to pieces; nobody can resuscitate her; Rumania has an important role to fulfil, but for this she must be wise, cautious, and strong'. This new attitude was the natural counterpart of the change which was at that time making itself felt in Russo-German relations. While a Franco-Russian alliance was propounded by Gorchakov in an interview with a French journalist, Bismarck and Andrassy signed in Gastein the treaty which allied Austria to Germany (September 1879). As Rumania's interests were identical with those of Austria—wrote Count Andrassy privately to Prince Carol a few months later—namely, to prevent the fusion of the northern and the southern Slavs, she had only to express her willingness to become at a given moment the third party in the compact. In 1883 King Carol accepted a secret treaty of defensive alliance from Austria. In return for promises relating to future political partitions in the Balkans, the monarch pledged himself to oppose all developments likely to speed the democratic evolution, of Rumania. Though the treaty was never submitted to parliament for ratification, and notwithstanding a tariff war and a serious difference with Austria on the question of control of the Danube navigation, Rumania was, till the Balkan wars, a faithful 'sleeping partner' of the Triple Alliance.

All through that externally quiet period a marked discrepancy existed and developed between that line of policy and the trend of public opinion. The interest of the Rumanians within the kingdom centred increasingly on their brethren in Transylvania, the solution of whose hard case inspired most of the popular national movements. Not on account of the political despotism of the Magyars, for that of the Russians was in no way behind it. But whilst the Rumanians of Bessarabia were, with few exceptions, illiterate peasants, in Transylvania there was a solidly established and spirited middle class, whose protests kept pace with the oppressive measures. Many of them—and of necessity the more turbulent—migrated to Rumania, and there kept alive the 'Transylvanian Question'. That the country's foreign policy has nevertheless constantly supported the Central Powers is due, to some extent, to the fact that the generation most deeply impressed by the events of 1878 came gradually to the leadership of the country; to a greater extent to the increasing influence of German education,* and the economic and financial supremacy which the benevolent passivity of England and France enabled Germany to acquire; but above all to the personal influence of King Carol. Germany, he considered, was at the beginning of her development and needed, above all, peace; as Rumania was in the same position the wisest policy was to follow Germany, neglecting impracticable national ideals. King Carol

---

* Many prominent statesmen like Sturdza, Maiorescu, Carp, &c. were educated in Germany, whereas the school established by the German community *(Evangelische Knaben und Realschule)*, and which it under the direct control of the German Ministry of Education, is attended by more pupils than any other school in Bucarest.

outlined his views clearly in an interview which he had in Vienna with the Emperor Franz Joseph in 1883: 'No nation consents to be bereaved of its political aspirations, and those of the Rumanians are constantly kept at fever heat by Magyar oppression. But this was no real obstacle to a friendly understanding between the two neighbouring states.'

Such was the position when the Balkan peoples rose in 1912 to sever the last ties which bound them to the decadent Turkish Empire. King Carol, who had, sword in hand, won the independence of his country, could have no objection to such a desire for emancipation. Nor to the Balkan League itself, unfortunately so ephemeral; for by the first year of his reign he had already approached the Greek Government with proposals toward such a league, and toward freeing the Balkans from the undesirable interference of the powers.* It is true that Rumania, like all the other states, had not foreseen the radical changes which were to take place, and which considerably affected her position in the Near East. But she was safe as long as the situation was one of stable equilibrium and the league remained in existence. 'Rumania will only be menaced by a real danger when a Great Bulgaria comes into existence,' remarked Prince Carol to Bismarck in 1880, and Bulgaria had done nothing since to allay Rumanian suspicions. On the contrary, the proviso of the Berlin Convention that all fortifications along the Rumania frontier should be razed to the ground had not been carried out by the Bulgarian Government. Bulgarian official publications regarded the Dobrudja as a 'Bulgaria Irredenta', and at the outset of the first Balkan war a certain section of the Bulgarian press speculated upon the Bulgarian character of the Dobrudja.

The Balkan League having proclaimed, however, that their action did not involve any territorial changes, and the maintenance of the *status quo* having been insisted upon by the European Concert, Rumania declared that she would remain neutral. All this jugglery of mutual assurances

---

*   See Augenzeuge, op. cit., i. 178

broke down with the unexpected rout of the Turks; the formula 'the Balkans to the Balkan peoples' made its appearance, upon which Bulgaria was at once notified that Rumania would insist upon the question of the Dobrudja frontier being included in any fundamental alteration of the Berlin Convention. The Bulgarian Premier, M. Danev, concurred in this point of view, but his conduct of the subsequent London negotiations was so 'diplomatic' that their only result was to strain the patience of the Rumanian Government and public opinion to breaking point. Nevertheless, the Rumanian Government agreed that the point in dispute should be submitted to a conference of the representatives of the great powers in St. Petersburg, and later accepted the decision of that conference, though the country considered it highly unsatisfactory.

The formation of the Balkan League, and especially the collapse of Turkey, had meant a serious blow to the Central Powers' policy of peaceful penetration. Moreover, 'for a century men have been labouring to solve the Eastern. Question. On the day when it shall be considered solved, Europe will inevitably witness the propounding of the Austrian Question.'* To prevent this and to keep open a route to the East Austro-German diplomacy set to work, and having engineered the creation of Albania succeeded in barring Serbia's way to the Adriatic; Serbia was thus forced to seek an outlet in the south, where her interests were doomed to clash with Bulgarian aspirations. The atmosphere grew threatening. In anticipation of a conflict with Bulgaria, Greece and Serbia sought an alliance with Rumania. The offer was declined; but, in accordance with the policy which Bucharest had already made quite clear to Sofia, the Rumanian army was ordered to enter Bulgaria immediately that country attacked her former allies. The Rumanians advanced unopposed to within a few miles of Sofia, and in order to save the capital Bulgaria declared her willingness to comply with their claims. Rumania having refused, however, to conclude a separate peace, Bulgaria had to give way,

---

*   Albert Sorel, op, cit., p. 266.

and the Balkan premiers met in conference at Bucarest to discuss terms. The circumstances were not auspicious. The way in which Bulgaria had conducted previous negotiations, and especially the attack upon her former allies, had exasperated the Rumanians and the Balkan peoples, and the pressure of public opinion hindered from the outset a fair consideration of the Bulgarian point of view. Moreover, cholera was making great ravages in the ranks of the various armies, and, what threatened to be even more destructive, several great powers were looking for a crack in the door to put their tails through, as the Rumanian saying runs. So anxious were the Balkan statesmen to avoid any such interference that they agreed between themselves to a short time limit: on a certain day, and by a certain hour, peace was to be concluded, or hostilities were to start afresh. The treaty was signed on August 10, 1913, Rumania obtaining the line Turtukai-Dobrich-Balchik, this being the line already demanded by her at the time of the London negotiations. The demand was put forth originally as a security against the avowed ambitions of Bulgaria; it was a strategical necessity, but at the same time a political mistake from the point of view of future relations. The Treaty of Bucarest, imperfect arrangement as it was, had nevertheless a great historical significance. 'Without complicating the discussion of our interests, which we are best in a position to understand, by the consideration of other foreign, interests,' remarked the President of the Conference, 'we shall have established for the first time by ourselves peace and harmony amongst our peoples.' Dynastic interests and impatient ambitions, however, completely subverted this momentous step towards a satisfactory solution of the Eastern Question.

The natural counter-effect of the diplomatic activity of the Central Powers was a change in Rumanian policy. Rumania considered the maintenance of the Balkan equilibrium a vital question, and as she had entered upon a closer union with Germany against a Bulgaria subjected to Russian influence, so she now turned to Russia as a guard against a Bulgaria under German influence. This breaking away from the 'traditional'

259

policy of adjutancy-in-waiting to the Central Powers was indicated by the visit of Prince Ferdinand—now King of Rumania—to St. Petersburg, and the even more significant visit which Tsar Nicholas afterwards paid to the late King Carol at Constanza. Time has been too short, however, for those new relations so to shape themselves as to exercise a notable influence upon Rumania's present attitude.

8.

Rumania and the Present War

(a) The Rumanians outside the Kingdom

The axis on which Rumanian foreign policy ought naturally to revolve is the circumstance that almost half the Rumanian nation lives outside Rumanian territory. As the available official statistics generally show political bias it is not possible to give precise figures; but roughly speaking there are about one million Rumanians in Bessarabia, a quarter of a million in Bucovina, three and a half millions in Hungary, while something above half a million form scattered colonies in Bulgaria, Serbia, and Macedonia. All these live in more or less close proximity to the Rumanian frontiers.

That these Rumanian elements have maintained their nationality is due to purely intrinsic causes. We have seen that the independence of Rumania in her foreign relations had only recently been established, since when the king, the factor most influential in foreign politics, had discouraged nationalist tendencies, lest the country's internal development might be compromised by friction with neighbouring states. The Government exerted its influence against any active expression of the national feeling, and the few 'nationalists' and the 'League for the cultural unity of all

Rumanians' had been, as a consequence, driven to seek a justification for their existence in antisemitic agitation.

The above circumstances had little influence upon the situation in Bucovina. This province forms an integral part of the Habsburg monarchy, with which it was incorporated as early as 1775. The political situation of the Rumanian principalities at the time, and the absence of a national cultural movement, left the detached population exposed to Germanization, and later to the Slav influence of the rapidly expanding Ruthene element. That language and national characteristics have, nevertheless, not been lost is due to the fact that the Rumanian population of Bucovina is peasant almost to a man—a class little amenable to changes of civilization.

This also applies largely to Bessarabia, which, first lost in 1812, was incorporated with Rumania in 1856, and finally detached in 1878. The few Rumanians belonging to the landed class were won over by the new masters. But while the Rumanian population was denied any cultural and literary activities of its own, the reactionary attitude of the Russian Government towards education has enabled the Rumanian peasants to preserve their customs and their language. At the same time their resultant ignorance has kept them outside the sphere of intellectual influence of the mother country.

The Rumanians who live in scattered colonies south of the Danube are the descendants of those who took refuge in these regions during the ninth and tenth centuries from the invasions of the Huns. Generally known as Kutzo-Vlakhs, or, among themselves, as Aromuni, they are—as even Weigand, who undoubtedly has Bulgarophil leanings, recognizes—the most intelligent and best educated of the inhabitants of Macedonia. In 1905 the Rumanian Government secured from the Porte official recognition of their separate cultural and religious organizations on a national basis. Exposed as they are to Greek influence, it will be difficult to prevent their final assimilation with that people. The interest taken in them of late by the Rumanian Government arose out of the necessity to secure them against pan-Hellenic propaganda, and to preserve one of the factors entitling Rumania to participate in the settlement of Balkan affairs.

I have sketched elsewhere the early history of the Rumanians of Transylvania, the cradle of the Rumanian nation. As already mentioned, part of the Rumanian nobility of Hungary went over to the Magyars, the remainder migrating over the mountains. Debarred from the support of the noble class, the Rumanian peasantry lost its state of autonomy, which changed into one of serfdom to the soil upon which they toiled. Desperate risings in 1324, 1437, 1514, 1600, and 1784 tended to case the Hungarian oppression, which up to the nineteenth century strove primarily after a political and religious hegemony. But the Magyars having failed in 1848 in their attempt to free themselves from Austrian domination (defeated with the assistance of a Russian army at Villagos, 1849), mainly on account of the fidelity of the other nationalities to the Austrian Crown, they henceforth directed their efforts towards strengthening their own position by forcible assimilation of those nationalities. This they were able to do, however, only after Koeniggraetz, when a weakened Austria had to give way to Hungarian demands. In 1867 the Dual Monarchy was established, and Transylvania, which up to then formed a separate duchy enjoying full political rights, was incorporated with the new Hungarian kingdom. The Magyars were handicapped in their imperialist ambitions by their numerical inferiority. As the next best means to their end, therefore, they resorted to political and national oppression, class despotism, and a complete disregard of the principles of liberty and humanity.* Hungarian was made compulsory in the administration, even in districts where the bulk

---

*   The Rumanians inhabit mainly the province of Transylvania, Banat, Crishiana, and Maramuresh. They represent 46.2 per cent. of the total population of these provinces, the Magyars 32.5 per cent., the Germans 11.5 per cent., and the Serbs 4.5 per cent. These figured are taken from official Hungarian statistics, and it may therefore be assumed that the Rumanian percentage represents a minimum.

of the population did not understand that language. In villages completely inhabited by Rumanians so-called 'State' schools were founded, in which only Hungarian was to be spoken, and all children upwards of three years of age had to attend them. The electoral regulations were drawn up in such a manner that the Rumanians of Transylvania, though ten times more numerous than the Magyars, sent a far smaller number than do the latter to the National Assembly. To quash all protest a special press law was introduced for Transylvania. But the Rumanian journalists being usually acquitted by the juries a new regulation prescribed that press offences should be tried only at Kluj (Klausenburg)—the sole Transylvanian town with a predominating Hungarian population—a measure which was in fundamental contradiction to the principles of justice.* In 1892 the Rumanian grievances were embodied in a memorandum which was to have been presented to the emperor by a deputation. An audience was, however, refused, and at the instance of the Hungarian Government the members of the deputation were sentenced to long terms of imprisonment for having plotted against the unity of the Magyar state.

Notwithstanding these disabilities the Rumanians of Transylvania enjoyed a long period of comparative social and economic liberty at a time when Turkish and Phanariote domination was hampering all progress in Rumania. Office under the Government growing increasingly difficult to obtain, the Rumanians in Transylvania turned largely to commercial and the open professions, and, as a result, a powerful middle class now exists. In their clergy, both of the Orthodox and the Uniate Church— which last, while conducting its ritual in the vernacular, recognizes papal supremacy—the Rumanians have always found strong moral support, while the national struggle tends to unite the various classes. The Rumanians of Hungary form by far the sanest element in the Rumanian

---

* Over a period of 22 years (1886-1908) 850 journalists were charged, 367 of whom were Rumanians; the sentences totalling 216 years of imprisonment, the fines amounting to Fcs. 138,000.

nation. From the Rumanians within the kingdom they have received little beside sympathy. The important part played by the country at the Peace of Bucarest, and her detachment from Austria-Hungary, must necessarily have stimulated the national consciousness of the Transylvanians; while at the same time all hope for betterment from within must have ceased at the death of Archduke Francis Ferdinand, an avowed friend of the long-suffering nationalities. It is, therefore, no mere matter of conjecture that the passive attitude of the Rumanian Government at the beginning of the present conflict must have been a bitter disappointment to them.

(b) Rumania's Attitude

The tragic development of the crisis in the summer of 1914 threw Rumania into a vortex of unexpected hopes and fears. Aspirations till then considered little else than Utopian became tangible possibilities, while, as suddenly, dangers deemed far off loomed large and near. Not only was such a situation quite unforeseen, nor had any plan of action been preconceived to meet it, but it was in Rumania's case a situation unique from the number of conflicting considerations and influences at work within it. Still under the waning influence of the thirty years quasi-alliance with Austria, Rumania was not yet acclimatized to her new relations with Russia. Notwithstanding the inborn sympathy with and admiration for France, the Rumanians could not be blind to Germany's military power. The enthusiasm that would have sided with France for France's sake was faced by the influence of German finance. Sympathy with Serbia existed side by side with suspicion of Bulgaria. Popular sentiment clashed with the views of the king; and the bright vision of the 'principle of nationality' was darkened by the shadow of Russia as despot of the Near East.

One fact in the situation stood out from the rest, namely, the unexpected opportunity of redeeming that half of the Rumanian nation which was still under foreign rule; the more so as one of the parties in the conflict had given the 'principle of nationality' a prominent place in its programme. But the fact that both Austria-Hungary and Russia had a large Rumanian population among their subjects rendered a purely national policy impossible, and Rumania could do nothing but weigh which issue offered her the greater advantage.

Three ways lay open: complete neutrality, active participation on the side of the Central Powers, or common cause with the Triple Entente. Complete neutrality was advocated by a few who had the country's material security most at heart, and also, as a *pis aller*, by those who realized that their opinion that Rumania should make common cause with the Central Powers had no prospect of being acted upon.

That King Carol favoured the idea of a joint action with Germany is likely enough, for such a policy was in keeping with his faith in the power of the German Empire. Moreover, he undoubtedly viewed with satisfaction the possibility of regaining Bessarabia, the loss of which must have been bitterly felt by the victor of Plevna. Such a policy would have met with the approval of many Rumanian statesmen, notably of M. Sturdza, sometime leader of the Liberal party and Prime Minister; of M. Carp, sometime leader of the Conservative party and Prime Minister; of M. Maiorescu, ex-Prime Minister and Foreign Secretary, who presided at the Bucarest Conference of 1913; of M. Marghiloman, till recently leader of the Conservative party, to name only the more important. M. Sturdza, the old statesman who had been one of King Carol's chief coadjutors in the making of modern Rumania, and who had severed for many years his connexion with active politics, again took up his pen to raise a word of warning. M. Carp, the political aristocrat who had retired from public life a few years previously, and had professed a lifelong contempt for the 'Press and all its works', himself started a daily paper *(Moldova)* which, he intended should expound his views. Well-known writers like

M. Radu Rosetti wrote* espousing the cause favoured by the king, though not for the king's reasons: Carol had faith in Germany, the Rumanians mistrusted Russia. They saw no advantage in the dismemberment of Austria, the most powerful check to Russia's plans in the Near East. They dreaded the idea of seeing Russia on the Bosphorus, as rendering illusory Rumania's splendid position at the mouth of the Danube. For not only is a cheap waterway absolutely necessary for the bulky products forming the chief exports of Rumania; but these very products, corn, petroleum, and timber, also form the chief exports of Russia, who, by a stroke of the pen, may rule Rumania out of competition, should she fail to appreciate the political leadership of Petrograd. Paris and Rome were, no doubt, beloved sisters; but Sofia, Moscow, and Budapest were next-door neighbours to be reckoned with.

Those who held views opposed to those, confident in the righteousness of the Allies' cause and in their final victory, advocated immediate intervention, and to that end made the most of the two sentiments which animated public opinion: interest in the fate of the Transylvanians, and sympathy with France. They contended that though a purely national policy was not possible, the difference between Transylvania and Bessarabia in area and in number and quality of the population was such that no hesitation was admissible. The possession of Transylvania was assured if the Allies were successful; whereas Russia would soon recover if defeated, and would regain Bessarabia by force of arms, or have it once more presented to her by a Congress anxious to soothe her 'sentiment de dignite blessee'. A Rumania enlarged in size and population had a better chance of successfully withstanding any eventual pressure from the north, and it was clear that any attempt against her independence would be bound to develop into a European question. Rumania could not forget what she owed to France; and if circumstances had made the

---

*   See R. Rosetti, *Russian Politics at Work in the Rumanian Countries*, facts compiled from French official documents, Bucarest, 1914.

Transylvanian question one 'a laquelle on pense toujours et dont on ne parle jamais', the greater was the duty, now that a favourable opportunity had arisen, to help the brethren across the mountains. It was also a duty to fight for right and civilization, proclaimed M. Take Ionescu, the exponent of progressive ideas in Rumanian politics; and he, together with the prominent Conservative statesman, M. Filipescu, who loathes the idea of the Rumanians being dominated by the inferior Magyars, are the leaders of the interventionist movement. It was due to M. Filipescu's activity, especially, that M. Marghiloman was forced by his own party to resign his position as leader on account of his Austrophil sentiments— an event unparalleled in Rumanian politics.

These were the two main currents of opinion which met in conflict at the Crown Council—a committee *ad hoc* consisting of the Cabinet and the leaders of the Opposition—summoned by the king early in August 1914, when Rumania's neutrality was decided upon. The great influence which the Crown can always wield under the Rumanian political system was rendered the more potent in the present case by the fact that the Premier, M. Bratianu, is above all a practical man, and the Liberal Cabinet over which he presides one of the most colourless the country ever had: a Cabinet weak to the point of being incapable of realizing its own weakness and the imperative necessity at this fateful moment of placing the helm in the hands of a national ministry. M. Bratianu considered that Rumania was too exposed, and had suffered too much in the past for the sake of other countries, to enter now upon such an adventure without ample guarantees. There would always be time for her to come in. This policy of opportunism he was able to justify by powerful argument. The supply of war material for the Rumanian army had been completely in the hands of German and Austrian arsenals, and especially in those of Krupp. For obvious reasons Rumania could no longer rely upon that source; indeed, Germany was actually detaining contracts for war and sanitary material placed with her before the outbreak of the war. There was the further consideration that, owing to the nature of Rumania's foreign policy in the past, no due attention had been given to the defence of the Carpathians, nor to those branches of the service dealing with mountain warfare. On the other hand, a continuous line of fortifications running from Galatz to Focshani formed, together with the lower reaches of the Danube, a strong barrier against attack from the north. Rumania's geographical position is such that a successful offensive from Hungary could soon penetrate to the capital, and by cutting the country in two could completely paralyse its organization. Such arguments acquired a magnified importance in the light of the failure of the negotiations with Bulgaria, and found many a willing ear in a country governed by a heavily involved landed class, and depending almost exclusively in its banking organization upon German and Austrian capital.

From the point of view of practical politics only the issue of the conflict will determine the wisdom or otherwise of Rumania's attitude. But, though it is perhaps out of place to enlarge upon it here, it is impossible not to speak of the moral aspect of the course adopted. By giving heed to the unspoken appeal from Transylvania the Rumanian national spirit would have been quickened, and the people braced to a wholesome sacrifice. Many were the wistful glances cast towards the Carpathians by the subject Rumanians, as they were being led away to fight for their oppressors; but, wilfully unmindful, the leaders of the Rumanian state buried their noses in their ledgers, oblivious of the fact that in these times of internationalism a will in common, with aspirations in common, is the very life-blood of nationality. That sentiment ought not to enter into politics is an argument untenable in a country which has yet to see its national aspirations fulfilled, and which makes of these aspirations definite claims. No Rumanian statesman can contend that possession of Transylvania is necessary to the existence of the Rumanian state. What they can maintain is that deliverance from Magyar oppression is vital to the existence of the Transylvanians. The right to advance such a claim grows out of their very duty of watching over the safety of the subject Rumanians. 'When there are squabbles in the household of my brother-in-law,' said the late Ioan Bratianu when speaking on the Transylvanian question, 'it is no affair of mine; but when he raises a knife against his wife, it is not merely my right to intervene, it is my duty.' It is difficult to account for the obliquity of vision shown by so many Rumanian politicians. 'The whole policy of such a state [having a large compatriot population living in close proximity under foreign domination] must be primarily influenced by anxiety as to the fate of their brothers, and by the duty of emancipating them,' affirms one of the most ardent of Rumanian nationalist orators; and he goes on to assure us that 'if Rumania waits, it is not from hesitation as to her duty, but simply in order that she may discharge it more completely'.* Meantime, while Rumania waits, regiments composed almost completely of Transylvanians have been repeatedly and of set purpose placed in the forefront of the battle, and as often annihilated. Such could never be the simple-hearted Rumanian peasant's conception of his duty, and here, as in so many other cases in the present conflict, the nation at large must not be judged by the policy of the few who hold the reins.

Rumania's claims to Transylvania are not of an historical nature. They are founded upon the numerical superiority of the subject Rumanians in Transylvania, that is upon the 'principle of nationality', and are morally strengthened by the treatment the Transylvanians suffer at the hands of the Magyars. By its passivity, however, the Rumanian Government has sacrificed the prime factor of the 'principle of nationality' to the attainment of an object in itself subordinate to that factor; that is, it has sacrificed the 'people' in order to make more sure of the 'land'. In this way the Rumanian Government has entered upon a policy of acquisition; a policy which Rumania is too weak to pursue save under the patronage of one or a group of great powers; a policy unfortunate inasmuch as it will deprive her of freedom of action in her external politics. Her policy will, in its consequences, certainly react to the detriment of the position

---

*   *Quarterly Review*, London, April, 1915, pp. 449-50.

acquired by the country two years ago, when independent action made her arbiter not only among the smaller Balkan States, but also among those and her late suzerain, Turkey.

Such, indeed, must inevitably be the fate of Balkan politics in general. Passing from Turkish domination to nominal Turkish suzerainty, and thence to independence within the sphere of influence of a power or group of powers, this gradual emancipation of the states of south-eastern Europe found its highest expression in the Balkan League. The war against Turkey was in effect a rebellion against the political tutelage of the powers. But this emancipation was short-lived. By their greed the Balkan States again opened up a way to the intrusion of foreign diplomacy, and even, as we now see, of foreign troops. The first Balkan war marked the zenith of Balkan political emancipation; the second Balkan war was the first act in the tragic *debacle* out of which the present situation developed. The interval between August 1913 (Peace of Bucarest) and August 1914 was merely an armistice during which Bulgaria and Turkey recovered their breath, and German and Austrian diplomacy had time to find a pretext for war on its own account.

'Exhausted but not vanquished we have had to furl our glorious standards in order to await better days,' said Ferdinand of Bulgaria to his soldiers after the conclusion of the Peace of Bucarest; and Budapest, Vienna, and Berlin have no doubt done their best to keep this spirit of revenge alive and to prevent a renascence of the Balkan Alliance. They have succeeded. They have done more: they have succeeded in causing the 'principle of nationality'—that idea which involves the disruption of Austria—to be stifled by the very people whom it was meant to save. For whilst the German peoples are united in this conflict, the majority of the southern Slavs, in fighting the German battles, are fighting to perpetuate the political servitude of the subject races of Austria-Hungary.

However suspicious Rumania may be of Russia, however bitter the quarrels between Bulgars, Greeks, and Serbs, it is not, nor can it ever be natural, that peoples who have groaned under Turkish despotism for centuries should, after only one year of complete liberation, join hands with an old and dreaded enemy not only against their fellow sufferers, but even against those who came 'to die that they may live'. These are the Dead Sea fruits of dynastic policy. Called to the thrones of the small states of the Near East for the purpose of creating order and peace, the German dynasties have overstepped their function and abused the power entrusted to them. As long as, in normal times, political activities were confined to the diplomatic arena there was no peril of rousing the masses out of their ignorant indolence; but, when times are abnormal, it is a different and a dangerous thing to march these peoples against their most intimate feelings. When, as the outcome of the present false situation, sooner or later the dynastic power breaks, it will then be for the powers who are now fighting for better principles not to impose their own views upon the peoples, or to place their own princes upon the vacant thrones. Rather must they see that the small nations of the Near East are given a chance to develop in peace and according to their proper ideals; that they be not again subjected to the disintegrating influence of European diplomacy; and that, above all, to the nations in common, irrespective of their present attitude, there should be a just application of the 'principle of nationality'.

TURKEY.

Turkey is no better name for the Osmanli dominion or any part of it than Normandy would be for Great Britain. It is a mediaeval error of nomenclature sanctioned by long usage in foreign mouths, but without any equivalent in the vernacular of the Osmanlis themselves. The real 'Turkey' is Turkestan, and the real Turks are the Turcomans. The Osmanlis are the least typical Turks surviving. Only a very small proportion of them have any strain of Turkish blood, and this is diluted till it is rarely perceptible in their physiognomy: and if environment rather than blood is to be held responsible for racial features, it can only be said that the territory occupied by the Osmanlis is as unlike the homeland of the true Turks as it can well be, and is quite unsuited to typically Turkish life and manners.

While of course it would be absurd to propose at this time of day any change in the terms by which the civilized world unanimously designates the Osmanlis and their dominion, it is well to insist on their incorrectness, because, like most erroneous names, they have bred erroneous beliefs. Thanks in the main to them, the Ottoman power is supposed to have originated in an overwhelming invasion of Asia Minor by immense numbers of Central Asiatic migrants, who, intent, like the early Arab armies, on offering to Asia first and Europe second the choice of apostasy or death, absorbed or annihilated almost all the previous populations, and swept forward into the Balkans as single-minded apostles of Islam. If the composition and the aims of the Osmanlis had been these, it would pass all understanding how they contrived, within a century of their appearance on the western scene, to establish in North-west Asia and South-east Europe the most civilized and best-ordered state of their time. Who, then, are the Osmanlis in reality? What have they to do with true Turks? and in virtue of what innate qualities did they found and consolidate their power?

1.
Origin of the Osmanlis

We hear of Turks first from Chinese sources. They were then the inhabitants, strong and predatory, of the Altai plains and valleys: but later on, about the sixth century A.D., they are found firmly established in what is still called Turkestan, and pushing westwards towards the Caspian Sea. Somewhat more than another century passes, and, reached by a missionary faith of West Asia, they come out of the Far Eastern darkness into a dim light of western history. One Boja, lord of Kashgar and Khan of what the Chinese knew as the people of Thu-Kiu—probably the same name as 'Turk'—embraced Islam and forced it on his Mazdeist subjects; but other Turkish tribes, notably the powerful Uighurs, remained intolerant of the new dispensation, and expelled the Thu-Kiu *en masse* from their holding in Turkestan into Persia. Here they distributed themselves in detached hordes over the north and centre. At this day, in some parts of Persia, e.g. Azerbaijan, Turks make the bulk of the population besides supplying the reigning dynasty of the whole kingdom. For the Shahs of the Kajar house are not Iranian, but purely Turkish.

This, it should be observed, was the western limit of Turkish expansion in the mass. Azerbaijan is the nearest region to us in which Turki blood predominates, and the westernmost province of the true Turk homeland. All Turks who have passed thence into Hither Asia have come in comparatively small detachments, as minorities to alien majorities. They have invaded as groups of nomads seeking vacant pasturage, or as bands of military adventurers who, first offering their swords to princes of the elder peoples, have subsequently, on several occasions and in several localities, imposed themselves on their former masters. To the first category belong all those Turcoman, Avshar, Yuruk, and other Turki tribes, which filtered over the Euphrates into unoccupied or sparsely inhabited parts of Syria and Asia Minor from the seventh century onwards, and survive to this day in isolated patches, distinguished from the mass of the local populations, partly by an ineradicable instinct for nomadic life, partly by retention of the pre-Islamic beliefs and practices of the first immigrants. In the second category—military adventurers—fall, for example, the Turkish praetorians who made and unmade not less than four caliphs at Bagdad in the ninth century, and that bold *condottiere*, Ahmed ibn Tulun, who captured a throne at Cairo. Even Christian emperors availed themselves of these stout fighters. Theophilus of Constantinople anticipated the Ottoman invasion of Europe by some five hundred years when he established Vardariote Turks in Macedonia.

The most important members of the second category, however, were the Seljuks. Like the earlier Thu-Kiu, they were pushed out of Turkestan late in the tenth century to found a power in Persia. Here, in Khorasan, the mass of the horde settled and remained: and it was only comparatively small section which went on westward as military adventurers to fall upon Bagdad, Syria, Egypt, and Asia Minor. This first conquest was little better than a raid, so brief was the resultant tenure; but a century later two dispossessed nephews of Melek Shah of Persia set out on a military adventure which had more lasting consequences. Penetrating with, a small following into Asia Minor, they seized Konia, and instituted there a kingdom nominally feudatory to the Grand Seljuk of Persia, but in reality independent and destined to last about two centuries. Though numerically weak, their forces, recruited from the professional soldier class which had bolstered up the Abbasid Empire and formed the Seljukian kingdoms of Persia and Syria, were superior to any Byzantine troops that could be arrayed in southern or central Asia Minor. They constituted indeed the only compact body of fighting men seen in these regions for some generations. It found reinforcement from the scattered Turki groups introduced already, as we have seen, into the country; and even from native Christians, who, descended from the Iconoclasts of two centuries before, found the rule of Moslem image-haters more congenial, as it was certainly more effective, than that of Byzantine emperors. The creed of the Seljuks was Islam of an Iranian type. Of Incarnationist colour, it repudiated the dour illiberal spirit of the early Arabian apostles which latter-day Sunnite orthodoxy has revived. Accordingly its professors, backed by an effective force and offering security and privilege, quickly won over the aborigines—Lycaonians, Phrygians, Cappadocians, and Cilicians—and welded them into a nation, leaving only a few detached communities here and there to cherish allegiance to Byzantine Christianity. In the event, the population of quite two-thirds of the Anatolian peninsula had already identified itself with a ruling Turki caste before, early in the thirteenth century, fresh Turks appeared on the scene—those Turks who were to found the Ottoman Empire.

They entered Asia Minor much as the earlier Turcomans had entered it—a small body of nomadic adventurers, thrown off by the larger body of Turks settled in Persia to seek new pastures west of the Euphrates. There are divers legends about the first appearance and establishment of these particular Turks: but all agree that they were of inconsiderable number—not above four hundred families at most. Drifting in by way of Armenia, they pressed gradually westward from Erzerum in hope of finding some unoccupied country which would prove both element and fertile. Byzantine influence was then at a very low ebb. With Constantinople itself in Latin hands, the Greek writ ran only along the north Anatolian coast, ruled from two separate centres, Isnik (Nicaea) and Trebizond: and the Seljuk kingdom was run in reality much more vigorous. Though apparently without a rival, it was subsisting by consent, on the prestige of its past, rather than on actual power. The moment of its dissolution was approaching, and the Anatolian peninsula, two-thirds Islamized, but ill-organised and very loosely knit, was becoming once more a fair field for any adventurer able to command a small compact force.

The newly come Turks were invited finally to settle on the extreme north-western fringe of the Seljuk territory—in a region so near Nicaea that their sword would be a better title to it than any which the feudal authority of Konia could confer. In fact it was a debatable land, an angle pushed up between the lake plain of Nicaea on the one hand and the plain of Brusa on the other, and divided from each by not lofty heights, Yenishehr, its chief town, which became the Osmanli chief Ertogrul's residence, lies, as the crow flies, a good deal less than fifty miles from the Sea of Marmora, and not a hundred miles from Constantinople itself. Here Ertogrul was to be a Warden of the Marches, to hold his territory for the Seljuk and extend it for himself at the expense of Nicaea if he could. If he won through, so much the better for Sultan Alaeddin; if he failed, *vile damnum!*

Hardly were his tribesmen settled, however, among the Bithynians and Greeks of Yenishehr, before the Seljuk collapse became a fact. The Tartar storm, ridden by Jenghis Khan, which had overwhelmed Central Asia, spent its last force on the kingdom of Konia, and, withdrawing, left the Seljuks bankrupt of force and prestige and Anatolia without an overlord. The feudatories were free everywhere to make or mar themselves, and they spent the last half of the thirteenth century in fighting for whatever might be saved from the Seljuk wreck before it foundered for ever about 1300 A.D. In the south, the centre, and the east of the peninsula, where Islam had long rooted itself as the popular social system, various Turki emirates established themselves on a purely Moslem basis—certain of these, like the Danishmand emirate of Cappadocia, being restorations of tribal jurisdictions which had existed before the imposition of Seljuk overlordship.

In the extreme north-west, however, where the mass of society was still Christian and held itself Greek, no Turkish, potentate could either revive a pre-Seljukian status or simply carry on a Seljukian system

276

in miniature. If he was to preserve independence at all, he must rely on a society which was not yet Moslem and form a coalition with the 'Greeks', into whom the recent recovery of Constantinople from the Latins had put fresh heart. Osman, who had succeeded Ertogrul in 1288, recognized where his only possible chance of continued dominion and future aggrandizement lay. He turned to the Greeks, as an element of vitality and numerical strength to be absorbed into his nascent state, and applied himself unremittingly to winning over and identifying with himself the Greek feudal seigneurs in his territory or about its frontiers. Some of these, like Michael, lord of Harmankaya, readily enough stood in with the vigorous Turk and became Moslems. Others, as the new state gained momentum, found themselves obliged to accept it or be crushed. There are to this day Greek communities in the Brusa district jealously guarding privileges which date from compacts made with their seigneurs by Osman and his son Orkhan.

It was not till the Seljuk kingdom was finally extinguished, in or about 1300 A.D. that Osman assumed at Yenishehr the style and title of a sultan. Acknowledged from Afium Kara Hissar, in northern Phrygia, to the Bithynian coast of the Marmora, beside whose waters his standards had already been displayed, he lived on to see Brusa fall to his son Orkhan, in 1326, and become the new capital. Though Nicaea still held out, Osman died virtual lord of the Asiatic Greeks; and marrying his son to a Christian girl, the famous Nilufer, after whom the river of Brusa is still named, he laid on Christian foundations the strength of his dynasty and his state. The first regiment of professional Ottoman soldiery was recruited by him and embodied later by Orkhan, his son, from Greek and other Christian-born youths, who, forced to apostatize, were educated as Imperial slaves in imitation of the Mamelukes, constituted more than a century earlier in Egypt, and now masters where they had been bondmen. It is not indeed for nothing that Osman's latest successor, and all who hold by him, distinguish themselves from other peoples by his name. They are Osmanlis (or by a European use of the more correct form

Othman, 'Ottomans'), because they derived their being as a nation and derive their national strength, not so much from central Asia as from the blend of Turk and Greek which Osman promoted among his people. This Greek strain has often been reinforced since his day and mingled with other Caucasian strains.

It was left to Orkhan to round off this Turco-Grecian realm in Byzantine Asia by the capture first of Ismid (Nicomedia) and then of Isnik (Nicaea); and with this last acquisition the nucleus of a self-sufficient sovereign state was complete. After the peaceful absorption of the emirate of Karasi, which added west central Asia Minor almost as far south as the Hermus, the Osmanli ruled in 1338 a dominion of greater area than that of the Greek emperor, whose capital and coasts now looked across to Ottoman shores all the way from the Bosphorus to the Hellespont.

2.
Expansion of the Osmanli Kingdom

If the new state was to expand by conquest, its line of advance was already foreshadowed. For the present, it could hardly break back into Asia Minor, occupied as this was by Moslem principalities sanctioned by the same tradition as itself, namely, the prestige of the Seljuks. To attack these would be to sin against Islam. But in front lay a rich but weak Christian state, the centre of the civilization to which the popular element in the Osmanli society belonged. As inevitably as the state of Nicaea had desired, won, and transferred itself to, Constantinople, so did the Osmanli state of Brusa yearn towards the same goal; and it needed no invitation from a Greek to dispose an Ottoman sultan to push over to the European shore.

Such an invitation, however, did in fact precede the first Osmanli crossing in force. In 1345 John Cantacuzene solicited help of Orkhan against the menace of Dushan, the Serb. Twelve years later came a second invitation. Orkhan's son, Suleiman, this time ferried a large army over the Hellespont, and, by taking and holding Gallipoli and Rodosto, secured a passage from continent to continent, which the Ottomans would never again let go.

Such invitations, though they neither prompted the extension of the Osmanli realm into Europe nor sensibly precipitated it, did nevertheless divert the course of the Ottoman arms and reprieve the Greek empire till Timur and his Tartars could come on the scene and, all unconsciously, secure it a further respite. But for these diversions there is little doubt Constantinople would have passed into Ottoman hands nearly a century earlier than the historic date of its fall. The Osmanli armies, thus led aside to make the Serbs and not the Greeks of Europe their first objective, became involved at once in a tangle of Balkan affairs from which they only extricated themselves after forty years of incessant fighting in almost every part of the peninsula except the domain of the Greek emperor. This warfare, which in no way advanced the proper aims of the lords of Brusa and Nicaea, not only profited the Greek emperor by relieving him of concern about his land frontier but also used up strength which might have made head against the Tartars. Constantinople then, as now, was detached from the Balkans. The Osmanlis, had they possessed themselves of it, might well have let the latter be for a long time to come. Instead, they had to battle, with the help now of one section of the Balkan peoples, now of another, till forced to make an end of all their feuds and treacheries by annexations after the victories of Kosovo in 1389 and Nikopolis in 1396.

Nor was this all. They became involved also with certain peoples of the main continent of Europe, whose interests or sympathies had been affected by those long and sanguinary Balkan wars. There was already bad blood and to spare between the Osmanlis on the one hand, and Hungarians, Poles, and Italian Venetians on the other, long before any second opportunity to attack Constantinople occurred: and the Osmanlis were in for that age-long struggle to secure a 'scientific frontier' beyond the Danube, whence the Adriatic on the one flank and the Euxine on the other could be commanded, which was to make Ottoman history down to the eighteenth century and spell ruin in the end.

It is a vulgar error to suppose that the Osmanlis set out for Europe, in the spirit of Arab apostles, to force their creed and dominion on all the world. Both in Asia and Europe, from first to last, their expeditions and conquests have been inspired palpably by motives similar to those active among the Christian powers, namely, desire for political security and the command of commercial areas. Such wars as the Ottoman sultans, once they were established at Constantinople, did wage again and again with knightly orders or with Italian republics would have been undertaken, and fought with the same persistence, by any Greek emperor who felt himself strong enough. Even the Asiatic campaigns, which Selim I and some of his successors, down to the end of the seventeenth century, would undertake, were planned and carried out from similar motives. Their object was to secure the eastern basin of the Mediterranean by the establishment of some strong frontier against Iran, out of which had come more than once forces threatening the destruction of Ottoman power. It does not, of course, in any respect disprove their purpose that, in the event, this object was never attained, and that an unsatisfactory Turco-Persian border still illustrates at this day the failures of Selim I and Mohammed IV.

By the opening of the fifteenth century, when, all unlooked for, a most terrible Tartar storm was about to break upon western Asia, the Osmanli realm had grown considerably, not only in Europe by conquest, but also in Asia by the peaceful effect of marriages and heritages. Indeed it now comprised scarcely less of the Anatolian peninsula than the last Seljuks had held, that is to say, the whole of the north as far as the Halys river beyond Angora, the central plateau to beyond Konia, and all the western coast-lands. The only emirs not tributary were those of Karamania, Cappadocia, and Pontus, that is of the southern and eastern fringes; and one detached fragment of Greek power survived in the last-named country, the kingdom of Trebizond. As for Europe, it had become the main scene of Osmanli operations, and now contained the administrative capital, Adrianople, though Brusu kept a sentimental primacy. Sultan Murad, who some years after his succession in 1359 had definitely transferred the centre of political gravity to Thrace, was nevertheless carried to the Bithynian capital for burial, Bulgaria, Serbia, and districts of both Bosnia and Macedonia were now integral parts of an empire which had come to number at least as many Christian as Moslem subjects, and to depend as much on the first as on the last. Not only had the professional Osmanli soldiery, the Janissaries, continued to be recruited from the children of native Christian races, but contingents of adult native warriors, who still professed Christianity, had been invited or had offered themselves to fight Osmanli battles—even those waged against men of the True Faith in Asia. A considerable body of Christian Serbs had stood up in Murad's line at the battle of Konia in 1381, before the treachery of another body of the same race gave him the victory eight years later at Kosovo. So little did the Osmanli state model itself on the earlier caliphial empires and so naturally did it lean towards the Roman or Byzantine imperial type.

And just because it had come to be in Europe and of Europe, it was able to survive the terrible disaster of Angora in 1402. Though the Osmanli army was annihilated by Timur, and an Osmanli sultan, for the first and last time in history, remained in the hands of the foe, the administrative machinery of the Osmanli state was not paralysed. A new ruler was proclaimed at Adrianople, and the European part of the realm held firm. The moment that the Tartars began to give ground, the Osmanlis began to recover it. In less than twenty years they stood again in Asia as they were before Timur's attack, and secure for the time on the east, could return to restore their prestige in the west, where the Tartar victory had bred unrest and brought both the Hungarians and the Venetians on the Balkan scene. Their success was once more rapid and astonishing: Salonika passed once and for all into Ottoman hands: the Frank seigneurs and the despots of Greece were alike humbled; and although Murad II failed to crush the Albanian, Skanderbey, he worsted his most dangerous foe, John Hunyadi, with the help of Wallach treachery at the second battle of Kosovo. At his death, three years later, he left the Balkans quiet and the field clear for his successor to proceed with the long deferred but inevitable enterprise of attacking all that was left of Greek empire, the district and city of Constantinople.

The doom of New Rome was fulfilled within two years. In the end it passed easily enough into the hands of those who already had been in possession of its proper empire for a century or more. Historians have made more of this fall of Constantinople in 1453 than contemporary opinion seems to have made of it. No prince in Europe was moved to any action by its peril, except, very half-heartedly, the Doge. Venice could not feel quite indifferent to the prospect of the main part of that empire, which, while in Greek hands, had been her most serious commercial competitor, passing into the stronger hands of the Osmanlis. Once in Constantinople, the latter, long a land power only, would be bound to concern themselves with the sea also. The Venetians made no effort worthy of their apprehensions, though these were indeed exceedingly well founded; for, as all the world knows, to the sea the Osmanlis did at once betake themselves. In less than thirty years they were ranging all the eastern Mediterranean and laying siege to Rhodes, the stronghold of one of their most dangerous competitors, the Knights Hospitallers.

In this consequence consists the chief historic importance of the Osmanli capture of Constantinople. For no other reason can it he called an epoch-marking event. If it guaranteed the Empire of the East against passing into any western hands, for example, those of Venice or Genoa, it did not affect the balance of power between Christendom and Islam; for the strength of the former had long ceased to reside at all in Constantinople. The last Greek emperor died a martyr, but not a champion.

3.

Heritage and Expansion of Byzantine Empire

On the morrow of his victory, Mohammed the Conqueror took pains to make it clear that his introduction of a new heaven did not entail a new earth. As little as might be would be changed. He had displaced a Palaeologus by an Osmanli only in order that an empire long in fact Osmanli should henceforth be so also *de jure*. Therefore he confirmed the pre-existing Oecumenical patriarch in his functions and the Byzantine Greeks in their privileges, renewed the rights secured to Christian foreigners by the Greek emperors, and proclaimed that, for his accession to the throne, there should not be made a Moslem the more or a Christian the less. Moreover, during the thirty years left to him of life, Mohammed devoted himself to precisely those tasks which would have fallen to a Greek emperor desirous of restoring Byzantine power. He thrust back Latins wherever they were encroaching on the Greek sphere, as were the Venetians of the Morea, the Hospitallers of Rhodes, and the Genoese of the Crimea: and he rounded off the proper Byzantine holding by annexing, in Europe, all the Balkan peninsula except the impracticable Black Mountain, the Albanian highlands, and the Hungarian fortress of Belgrade; and, in Asia, what had remained independent in the Anatolian peninsula, the emirates of Karamania and Cappadocia.

Before Mohammed died in 1481 the Osmanli Turco-Grecian nation may be said to have come into its own. It was lord *de facto et de jure belli* of the eastern or Greek Empire, that is of all territories and seas grouped geographically round Constantinople as a centre, with only a few exceptions unredeemed, of which the most notable were the islands of Cyprus, Rhodes, and Krete, still in Latin hands. Needless to say, the Osmanlis themselves differed greatly from their imperial predecessors. Their official speech, their official creed, their family system were all foreign to Europe, and many of their ideas of government had been learned in the past from Persia and China, or were derived from the original tribal organization of the true Turks. But if they were neither more nor less Asiatics than the contemporary Russians, they were quite as much Europeans as many of the Greek emperors had been—those of the Isaurian dynasty, for instance. They had given no evidence as yet of a fanatical Moslem spirit—this was to be bred in them by subsequent experiences—and their official creed had governed their policy hardly more than does ours in India or Egypt. Mohammed the Conqueror had not only shown marked favour to Christians, whether his *rayas* or not, but encouraged letters and the arts in a very un-Arabian spirit. Did he not have himself portrayed by Gentile Bellini? The higher offices of state, both civil and military, were confided (and would continue so to be for a century to come) almost exclusively to men of Christian origin. Commerce was encouraged, and western traders recognized that their facilities were greater now than they had been under Greek rule. The Venetians, for example, enjoyed in perfect liberty a virtual monopoly of the Aegean and Euxine trade. The social condition of the peasantry seems to have been better than it had been under Greek seigneurs, whether in Europe or in Asia, and better than it was at the moment in feudal Christendom. The Osmanli military organization was reputed the best in the world, and its fame attracted adventurous spirits from all over Europe to learn war in the first school of the age. Ottoman armies, it is worth while to remember, were the only ones then attended by efficient medical and commissariat services, and may be said to have introduced to Europe these alleviations of the horrors of war.

Had the immediate successors of Mohammed been content—or, rather, had they been able—to remain within his boundaries, they would have robbed Ottoman history of one century of sinister brilliance, but might have postponed for many centuries the subsequent sordid decay; for the seeds of this were undoubtedly sown by the three great sultans who followed the taker of Constantinople. Their ambitions or their necessities led to a great increase of the professional army which would entail many evils in time to come. Among these were praetorianism in the capital and the great provincial towns; subjection of land and peasantry to military seigneurs, who gradually detached themselves from the central control; wars undertaken abroad for no better reason than the employment of soldiery feared at home; consequent expansion of the territorial empire beyond the administrative capacity of the central government; development of the 'tribute-children' system of recruiting into a scourge of the *rayas* and a continual offence to neighbouring states, and the supplementing of that system by acceptance of any and every alien outlaw who might offer himself for service: lastly, revival of the dormant crusading spirit of Europe, which reacted on the Osmanlis, begetting in them an Arabian fanaticism and disposing them to revert to the obscurantist spirit of the earliest Moslems. To sum the matter up in other words: the omnipotence and indiscipline of the Janissaries; the contumacy of 'Dere Beys' ('Lords of the Valleys,' who maintained a feudal independence) and of provincial governors; the concentration of the official mind on things military and religious, to the exclusion of other interests; the degradation and embitterment of the Christian elements in the empire; the perpetual financial embarrassment of the government with its inevitable consequence of oppression and neglect of the governed; and the constant provocation in Christendom of a hostility which was always latent and recurrently active—all these evils, which combined to push the empire nearer and nearer to ruin from the seventeenth century onwards, can be traced to the brilliant epoch of Osmanli history associated with the names of Bayezid II, Selim I, and Suleiman the Magnificent.

At the same time Fate, rather than any sultan, must be blamed. It was impossible to forgo some further extension of the empire, and very difficult to arrest extension at any satisfactory static point. For one thing, as has been pointed out already, there were important territories in the proper Byzantine sphere still unredeemed at the death of Mohammed. Rhodes, Krete, and Cyprus, whose possession carried with it something like superior control of the Levantine trade, were in Latin hands. Austrian as well as Venetian occupation of the best harbours was virtually closing the Adriatic to the masters of the Balkans. Nor could the inner lands of the Peninsula be quite securely held while the great fortress of Belgrade, with the passage of the Danube, remained in Hungarian keeping, Furthermore, the Black Sea, which all masters of the Bosphorus have desired to make a Byzantine lake, was in dispute with the Wallachs and the Poles; and, in the reign of Mohammed's successor, a cloud no bigger than a man's hand came up above its northern horizon—the harbinger of the Muscovite.

As for the Asiatic part of the Byzantine sphere, there was only one little corner in the south-east to be rounded off to bring all the Anatolian peninsula under the Osmanli. But that corner, the Cilician plain, promised trouble, since it was held by another Islamic power, that of the Egyptian Mamelukes, which, claiming to be at least equal to the Osmanli, possessed vitality much below its pretensions. The temptation to poach on it was strong, and any lord of Constantinople who once gave way to this, would find himself led on to assume control of all coasts of the easternmost Levant, and then to push into inland Asia in quest of a scientific frontier at their back—perilous and costly enterprise which Rome had essayed again and again and had to renounce in the end. Bayezid II took the first step by summoning the Mameluke to evacuate certain forts near Tarsus, and expelling his garrisons *vi et armis*. Cilicia passed to the Osmanli; but for the moment he pushed no farther. Bayezid, who was under the obligation always to lead his army in person, could make but one campaign at a time; and a need in Europe was the more pressing. In quitting Cilicia, however, he left open a new question in Ottoman politics—the Asiatic continental question—and indicated to his successor a line of least resistance on which to advance. Nor would this be his only dangerous legacy. The prolonged and repeated raids into Adriatic lands, as far north as Carniola and Carinthia, with which the rest of Bayezid's reign was occupied, brought Ottoman militarism at last to a point, whose eventual attainment might have been foreseen any time in the past century—the point at which, strong in the possession of a new arm, artillery, it would assume control of the state.

Bayezid's seed was harvested by Selim. First in a long series of praetorian creatures which would end only with the destroyer of the praetorians themselves three centuries later, he owed his elevation to a Janissary revolt, and all the eight bloody years of his reign were to be punctuated by Janissary tumults. To keep his creators in any sort of order and contentment he had no choice but to make war from his first year to his last. When he died, in 1520, the Ottoman Empire had been swelled to almost as wide limits in Asia and Africa as it has ever attained since his day. Syria, Armenia, great part of Kurdistan, northern Mesopotamia, part of Arabia, and last, but not least, Egypt, were forced to acknowledge Osmanli suzerainty, and for the first time an Osmanli sultan had proclaimed himself caliph. True that neither by his birth nor by the manner of his appointment did Selim satisfy the orthodox caliphial tradition; but, besides his acquisition of certain venerated relics of the Prophet, such as the *Sanjak i-sherif* or holy standard, and besides a yet more important acquisition—the control of the holy cities of the faith—he could base a claim on the unquestioned fact that the office was vacant, and the equally certain fact that he was the most powerful Moslem prince in the world. Purists might deny him if they dared: the vulgar Sunni mind was impressed and disposed to accept. The main importance, however, of Selim's assumption of the caliphate was that it consecrated Osmanli militarism to a religious end—to the original programme of Islam. This was a new thing, fraught with dire possibilities from that day forward. It marked the supersession of the Byzantine or European ideal by the Asiatic in Osmanli policy, and introduced a phase of Ottoman history which has endured to our own time.

The inevitable process was continued in the next reign. Almost all the military glories of Suleiman—known to contemporary Europe as 'the Magnificent' and often held by historians the greatest of Osmanli sultans—made for weakening, not strengthening, the empire. His earliest operations indeed, the captures of Rhodes from the Knights and of Belgrade and [)S]abac from the Hungarians, expressed a legitimate Byzantine policy; and the siege of Malta, one of his latest ventures, might also be defended as a measure taken in the true interests of Byzantine commerce. But the most brilliant and momentous of his achievements bred evils for which military prestige and the material profits to be gained from the oppression of an irreconcilable population were inadequate compensation. This was the conquest of Hungary. It would result in Buda and its kingdom remaining Ottoman territory for a century and a half, and in the principalities of Wallachia and Moldavia abiding under the Ottoman shadow even longer, and passing for all time out of the central European into the Balkan sphere; but also it would result in the Osmanli power finding itself on a weak frontier face to face at last with a really strong Christian race, the Germanic, before which, since it could not advance, it would have ultimately to withdraw; and in the rousing of Europe to a sense of its common danger from Moslem activity. Suleiman's failure to take Vienna more than made good the panic which had followed on his victory at Mohacs. It was felt that the Moslem, now that he had failed against the bulwark of central Europe, was to go no farther, and that the hour of revenge was near.

It was nearer than perhaps was expected. Ottoman capacity to administer the overgrown empire in Europe and Asia was strained already almost to breaking-point, and it was in recognition of this fact that Suleiman made the great effort to reorganize his imperial system, which has earned him his honourable title of *El Kanun*, the Regulator. But if he could reset and cleanse the wheels of the administrative machine, he could not increase its capacity. New blood was beginning to fail for the governing class just as the demands on it became greater. No longer could it be manned exclusively from the Christian born. Two centuries of recruiting in the Balkans and West Asia had sapped their resources. Even the Janissaries were not now all 'tribute-children'. Their own sons, free men Moslem born, began to be admitted to the ranks. This change was a vital infringement of the old principle of Osmanli rule, that all the higher administrative and military functions should be vested in slaves of the imperial household, directly dependent on the sultan himself; and once breached, this principle could not but give way more and more. The descendants of imperial slaves, free-born Moslems, but barred from the glory and profits of their fathers' function, had gradually become a very numerous class of country gentlemen distributed over all parts of the empire, and a very malcontent one. Though it was still subservient, its dissatisfaction at exclusion from the central administration was soon to show itself partly in assaults on the time-honoured system, partly in assumption of local jurisdiction, which would develop into provincial independence.

The overgrowth of his empire further compelled Suleiman to divide the standing army, in order that more than one imperial force might take the field at a time. Unable to lead all his armies in person, he elected, in the latter part of his reign, to lead none, and for the first time left the Janissaries to march without a sultan to war. Remaining himself at the centre, he initiated a fashion which would encourage Osmanli sultans to lapse into half-hidden beings, whom their subjects would gradually invest with religious character. Under these conditions the ruler, the governing class (its power grew with this devolution), the dominant population of the state, and the state itself all grew more fanatically Moslem.

In the early years of the seventeenth century, Ahmed I being on the throne, the Ottoman Empire embraced the widest territorial area which it was ever to cover at any one moment. In what may be called the proper Byzantine field, Cyprus had been recovered and Krete alone stood out. Outside that field, Hungary on the north and Yemen (since Selim's conquest in 1516) on the south were the frontier provinces, and the Ottoman flag had been carried not only to the Persian Gulf but also far upon the Iranian plateau, in the long wars of Murad III, which culminated in 1588 with the occupation of Tabriz and half Azerbaijan.

4.

Shrinkage and Retreat

The fringes of this vast empire, however, none too surely held, were already involving it in insoluble difficulties and imminent dangers. On the one hand, in Asia, it had been found impossible to establish military fiefs in Arabia, Kurdistan, or anywhere east of it, on the system which had secured the Osmanli tenure elsewhere. On the other hand, in Europe, as we have seen, the empire had a very unsatisfactory frontier, beyond which a strong people not only set limits to further progress but was prepared to dispute the ground already gained. In a treaty signed at Sitvatorok, in 1606, the Osmanli sultan was forced to acknowledge definitely the absolute and equal sovereignty of his northern neighbour, Austria; and although, less than a century later, Vienna would be attacked once more, there was never again to be serious prospect of an extension of the empire in the direction of central Europe.

Moreover, however appearances might be maintained on the frontiers, the heart of the empire had begun patently to fail. The history of the next two centuries, the seventeenth and eighteenth, is one long record of praetorian tumults at home; and ever more rarely will these be compensated by military successes abroad. The first of these centuries had not half elapsed ere the Janissaries had taken the lives of two sultans, and brought the Grand Vizierate to such a perilous pass that no ordinary holder of it, unless backed by some very powerful Albanian or other tribal influence, could hope to save his credit or even his life. During this period indeed no Osmanli of the older stocks ever exercised real control of affairs. It was only among the more recently assimilated elements, such as the Albanian, the Slavonic, or the Greek, that men of the requisite character and vigour could be found. The rally which marked the latter half of the seventeenth century was entirely the work of Albanians or of other generals and admirals, none of whom had had a Moslem grandfather.

Marked by the last Osmanli conquest made at the expense of Europe—that of Krete; by the definite subjugation of Wallachia; by the second siege of Vienna; by the recovery of the Morea from Venice; and finally by an honourable arrangement with Austria about the Danube frontier—it is all to be credited to the Kuprili 'dynasty' of Albanian viziers, which conspicuously outshone the contemporary sovereigns of the dynasty of Osman, the best of them, Mohammed IV, not excepted. It was, however, no more than a rally; for greater danger already threatened from another quarter. Agreement had not been reached with Austria at Carlowitz, in 1699, before a new and baleful planet swam into the Osmanli sky.

It was, this time, no central European power, to which, at the worst, all that lay north of the proper Byzantine sphere might be abandoned; but a claimant for part of that sphere itself, perhaps even for the very heart of it. Russia, seeking an economic outlet, had sapped her way south to the Euxine shore, and was on the point of challenging the Osmanli right to that sea. The contest would involve a vital issue; and if the Porte did not yet grasp this fact, others had grasped it. The famous 'Testament of Peter the Great' may or may not be a genuine document; but, in either case, it proves that certain views about the necessary policy of Russia in the Byzantine area, which became commonplaces of western political thinkers as the eighteenth century advanced, were already familiar to east European minds in the earlier part of that century.

Battle was not long in being joined. In the event, it would cost Russia about sixty years of strenuous effort to reduce the Byzantine power of the Osmanlis to a condition little better than that in which Osman had found the Byzantine power of the Greeks four centuries before. During the first two-thirds of this period the contest was waged not unequally. By the Treaty of Belgrade, in 1739, Sultan Mahmud I appeared for a moment even to have gained the whole issue, Russia agreeing to her own exclusion from the Black Sea, and from interference in the Danubian principalities. But the success could not be sustained. Repeated effort was rapidly exhausting Osmanli strength, sapped as it was by increasing internal disease: and when a crisis arrived with the accession of the Empress Catherine, it proved too weak to meet it. During the ten years following 1764 Osmanli hold on the Black Sea was lost irretrievably. After the destruction of the fleet at Chesme the Crimea became untenable and was abandoned to the brief mercies of Russia: and with a veiled Russian protectorate established in the Danubian principalities, and an open Russian occupation in Morean ports, Constantinople had lost once more her own seas. When Selim III was set on a tottering throne, in 1787, the wheel of Byzantine destiny seemed to have come again almost full circle: and the world was expecting a Muscovite succession to that empire which had acknowledged already the Roman, the Greek, and the Osmanli.

Certainly history looked like repeating itself. As in the fourteenth century, so in the eighteenth, the imperial provinces, having shaken off almost all control of the capital, were administering themselves, and happier for doing so. Mesopotamia, Syria, Egypt, and Trebizond acknowledged adventurers as virtually independent lords. Asia Minor, in general, was being controlled, in like disregard of imperial majesty, by a group of 'Dere Beys', descended, in different districts, from tribal chieftains or privileged tax-farmers, or, often, from both. The latter part of the eighteenth century was the heyday of the Anatolian feudal families—of such as the Chapanoghlus of Yuzgad, whose sway stretched from Pontus to Cilicia, right across the base of the peninsula, or the Karamanoghlus of Magnesia, Bergama, and Aidin, who ruled as much territory as the former emirs of Karasi and Sarukhan, and were recognized by the representatives of the great trading companies as wielding the only effective authority in Smyrna. The wide and rich regions controlled by such families usually contributed neither an *asper* to the sultan's treasury nor a man to the imperial armies.

On no mountain of either Europe or Asia—and mountains formed a large part of the Ottoman empire in both—did the imperial writ run. Macedonia and Albania were obedient only to their local beys, and so far had gone the devolution of Serbia and Bosnia to Janissary aghas, feudal beys, and the Beylerbey of Rumili, that these provinces hardly concerned themselves more with the capital. The late sultan, Mustapha III, had lost almost the last remnant of his subjects' respect, not so much by the ill success of his mutinous armies as by his depreciation of the imperial coinage. He had died bankrupt of prestige, leaving no visible assets to his successor. What might become of the latter no one in the empire appeared to care. As in 1453, it waited other lords.

5.

Revival

It has been waiting, nevertheless, ever since—waiting for much more than a century; and perhaps the end is not even yet. Why, then, have expectations not only within but without the empire been so greatly at fault? How came Montesquieu, Burke, and other confident prophets since their time to be so signally mistaken? There were several co-operating causes, but one paramount. Constantinople was no longer, as in 1453, a matter of concern only to itself, its immediate neighbours, and certain trading republics of Italy. It had become involved with the commercial interests of a far wider circle, in particular of the great trading peoples of western Europe, the British, the French, and the Dutch, and with the political interests of the Germanic and Russian nations. None of these could be indifferent to a revolution in its fortunes, and least of all to its passing, not to a power out of Asia, but to a rival power among themselves. Europe was already in labour with the doctrine of the Balance of Power. The bantling would not be born at Vienna till early in the century to come: but even before the end of the eighteenth century it could be foreseen that its life would be bound up with the maintenance of Constantinople in independence of any one of the parent powers—that is, with the prolongation of the Osmanli phase of its imperial fortunes. This doctrine,

293

consistently acted upon by Europe, has been the sheet anchor of the Ottoman empire for a century. Even to this day its Moslem dynasty has never been without one powerful Christian champion or another.

There were, however, some thirty years still to elapse after Selim's accession before that doctrine was fully born: and had her hands been free, Russia might well have been in secure possession of the Byzantine throne long before 1815. For, internally, the Osmanli state went from bad to worse. The tumultuous insubordination of the Janissaries became an ever greater scandal. Never in all the long history of their riots was their record for the years 1807-9 equalled or even approached. Never before, also, had the provinces been so utterly out of hand. This was the era of Jezzar the Butcher at Acre, of the rise of Mehemet Ali in Egypt, of Ali Pasha in Epirus, and of Pasvanoghlu at Vidin. When Mahmud II was thrust on to the throne in 1809, he certainly began his reign with no more personal authority and no more imperial prestige or jurisdiction than the last Greek emperor had enjoyed on his accession in 1448.

The great European war, however, which had been raging intermittently for nearly twenty years, had saved Mahmud an empire to which he could succeed in name and try to give substance. Whatever the Osmanlis suffered during that war, it undoubtedly kept them in Constantinople. Temporary loss of Egypt and the small damage done by the British attack on Constantinople in 1807 were a small price to pay for the diversion of Russia's main energies to other than Byzantine fields, and for the assurance, made doubly sure when the great enemy did again attack, that she would not be allowed to settle the account alone. Whatever Napoleon may have planned and signed at Tilsit, the aegis of France was consistently opposed to the enemies of the Osmanlis down to the close of the Napoleonic age.

Thus it came about that those thirty perilous years passed without the expected catastrophe. There was still a successor of Osman reigning in Constantinople when the great Christian powers, met in conclave at Vienna, half unconsciously guaranteed the continued existence of the

Osmanli Empire simply by leaving it out of account in striking a Balance of Power in Europe. Its European territory, with the capital within it, was of quite enough importance to disturb seriously the nice adjustment agreed at Vienna; and, therefore, while any one's henceforth to take or leave, it would become always some one's to guard. A few years had yet to pass before the phrase, the Maintenance of the Integrity of the Ottoman Empire, would be a watchword of European diplomacy: but, whether formulated thus or not, that principle became a sure rock of defence for the Osmanli Empire on the birthday of the doctrine of the Balance of Power.

Secure from destruction by any foes but those of his own household, as none knew better than he, the reigning Osmanli was scheming to regain the independence and dignity of his forefathers. Himself a creature of the Janissaries, Mahmud had plotted the abolition of his creators from the first year of his reign, but making a too precipitate effort after the conclusion of peace with Russia, had ignominiously failed and fallen into worse bondage than ever. Now, better assured of his imperial position and supported by leading men of all classes among his subjects, he returned not only to his original enterprise but to schemes for removing other checks on the power of the sovereign which had come into being in the last two centuries—notably the feudal independence of the Dere Beys, and the irresponsibility of provincial governors.

Probably Mahmud II—if he is to be credited with personal initiation of the reforms always associated with his name—was not conscious of any purpose more revolutionary than that of becoming master in his own house, as his ancestors had been. What he ultimately accomplished, however, was something of much greater and more lasting moment to the Osmanli state. It was nothing less than the elimination of the most Byzantine features in its constitution and government. The substitution of national forces for mercenary praetorians: the substitution of direct imperial government of the provinces for devolution to seigneurs, tribal chiefs, and irresponsible officers: the substitution of direct collection for tax-farming: and the substitution of administration by bureaucrats for administration by household officers—these, the chief reforms carried through under Mahmud, were all anti-Byzantine. They did not cause the Osmanli state to be born anew, but, at least, they went far to purge it of original sin.

That Mahmud and his advisers could carry through such reforms at all in so old a body politic is remarkable: that they carried them through amid the events of his reign is almost miraculous. One affront after another was put on the Sultan, one blow after another was struck at his empire. Inspired by echoes of the French Revolution and by Napoleon's recognition of the rights of nationalities, first the Serbs and then the Greeks seized moments of Ottoman disorder to rise in revolt against their local lords. The first, who had risen under Selim III, achieved, under Mahmud, autonomy, but not independence, nothing remaining to the sultan as before except the fortress of Belgrade with five other strongholds. The second, who began with no higher hopes than the Serbs, were encouraged, by the better acquaintance and keener sympathy of Europe, to fight their way out to complete freedom. The Morea and central Greece passed out of the empire, the first provinces so to pass since the Osmanli loss of Hungary. Yet it was in the middle of that fatal struggle that Mahmud settled for ever with the Janissaries, and during all its course he was settling one after another with the Dere Beys!

When he had thus sacrificed the flower of his professional troops and had hardly had time to replace the local governments of the provinces by anything much better than general anarchy, he found himself faced by a Russian assault. His raw levies fought as no other raw levies than the Turkish can, and, helped by manifestations of jealousy by the other powers, staved off the capture of Constantinople, which, at one moment, seemed about to take place at last. But he had to accept humiliating terms, amounting virtually, to a cession of the Black Sea. Mahmud recognized that such a price he must pay for crossing the broad stream between Byzantinism and Nationalism, and kept on his way.

Finally came a blow at the hands of one of his own household and creed. Mehemet Ali of Egypt, who had faithfully fought his sovereign's battles in Arabia and the Morea, held his services ill requited and his claim to be increased beyond other pashas ignored, and proceeded to take what had not been granted. He went farther than he had intended—more than half-way across Asia Minor—after the imperial armies had suffered three signal defeats, before he extorted what he had desired at first: and in the end, after very brief enjoyment, he had to resign all again to the mandate, not of his sovereign, but of certain European powers who commanded his seas. Mahmud, however, who lived neither to see himself saved by the *giaur* fleets, nor even to hear of his latest defeat, had gone forward with the reorganization of the central and provincial administration, undismayed by Mehemet Ali's contumacy or the insistence of Russia at the gate of the Bosphorus.

As news arrived from time to time in the west of Mahmud's disasters, it was customary to prophesy the imminent dissolution of his empire. We, however, looking backward now, can see that by its losses the Osmanli state in reality grew stronger. Each of its humiliations pledged some power or group of powers more deeply to support it: and before Mahmud died, he had reason to believe that, so long as the European Concert should ensue the Balance of Power, his dynasty would not be expelled from Constantinople. His belief has been justified. At every fresh crisis of Ottoman fortunes, and especially after every fresh Russian attack, foreign protection has unfailingly been extended to his successors.

It was not, however, only in virtue of the increasing solicitude of the powers on its behalf that during the nineteenth century the empire was growing and would grow stronger, but also in virtue of certain assets within itself. First among these ranked the resources of its Asiatic territories, which, as the European lands diminished, became more and more nearly identified with the empire. When, having got rid of the old army, Mahmud imposed service on all his Moslem subjects, in theory, but in effect only on the Osmanlis (not the Arabs, Kurds, or other half assimilated nomads and hillmen), it meant more than a similar measure would have meant in a Christian empire. For, the life of Islam being war, military service binds Moslems together and to their chiefs as it binds men under no other dispensation; therefore Mahmud, so far as he was able to enforce his decree, created not merely a national army but a nation. His success was most immediate and complete in Anatolia, the homeland of the Osmanlis. There, however, it was attained only by the previous reduction of those feudal families which, for many generations, had arrogated to themselves the levying and control of local forces. Hence, as in Constantinople with the Janissaries, so in the provinces with the Dere Beys, destruction of a drastic order had to precede construction, and more of Mahmud's reign had to be devoted to the former than remained for the latter.

He did, however, live to see not only the germ of a nation emerge from chaos, but also the framework of an organization for governing it well or ill. The centralized bureaucracy which he succeeded in initiating was, of course, wretchedly imperfect both in constitution and equipment. But it promised to promote the end he had in view and no other, inasmuch as, being the only existent machine of government, it derived any effective power it had from himself alone. Dependent on Stambul, it served to turn thither the eyes and prayers of the provincials. The naturally submissive and peaceful population of Asia Minor quickly accustomed itself to look beyond the dismantled strongholds of its fallen beys. As for the rest—contumacious and bellicose beys and sheikhs of Kurdish hills and Syrian steppes—their hour of surrender was yet to come.

The eventual product of Mahmud's persistency was the 'Turkey' we have seen in our own time—that Turkey irretrievably Asiatic in spirit under a semi-European system of administration, which has governed despotically in the interests of one creed and one class, with slipshod, makeshift methods, but has always governed, and little by little has extended its range. Knowing its imperfections and its weakness, we have watched with amazement its hand feeling forward none the less towards one remote frontier district after another, painfully but surely getting its grip, and at last closing on Turcoman chiefs and Kurdish beys, first in the Anatolian and Cilician hills, then in the mountains of Armenia, finally in the wildest Alps of the Persian borderland. We have marked its stealthy movement into the steppes and deserts of Syria, Mesopotamia, and Arabia—now drawn back, now pushed farther till it has reached and held regions over which Mahmud could claim nothing but a suzerainty in name. To judge how far the shrinkage of the Osmanli European empire has been compensated by expansion of its Asiatic, one has only to compare the political state of Kurdistan, as it was at the end of the eighteenth century, and as it has been in our own time.

It is impossible to believe that the Greek Empire, however buttressed and protected by foreign powers, could ever have reconstituted itself after falling so low as it fell in the fourteenth century and as the Osmanli Empire fell in the eighteenth; and it is clear that the latter must still have possessed latent springs of vitality, deficient in the former. What can these have been? It is worth while to try to answer this question at the present juncture, since those springs, if they existed a hundred years ago, can hardly now be dry.

In the first place it had its predominant creed. This had acted as Islam acts everywhere, as a very strong social bond, uniting the vast majority of subjects in all districts except certain parts of the European empire, in instinctive loyalty to the person of the padishah, whatever might be felt about his government. Thus had it acted with special efficacy in Asia Minor, whose inhabitants the Osmanli emperors, unlike the Greek, had always been at some pains to attach to themselves. The sultan, therefore, could still count on general support from the population of his empire's heart, and had at his disposal the resources of a country which no administration, however improvident or malign, has ever been able to exhaust.

In the second place the Osmanli 'Turks', however fallen away from the virtues of their ancestors, had not lost either 'the will to power' or their capacity for governing under military law. If they had never succeeded in learning to rule as civilians they had not forgotten how to rule as soldiers.

In the third place the sultanate of Stambul had retained a vague but valuable prestige, based partly on past history, partly on its pretension to religious influence throughout a much larger area than its proper dominions; and the conservative population of the latter was in great measure very imperfectly informed of its sovereign's actual position.

In the fourth and last place, among the populations on whose loyalty the Osmanli sultan could make good his claim, were several strong unexhausted elements, especially in Anatolia. There are few more vigorous and enduring peoples than the peasants of the central plateau of Asia Minor, north, east, and south. With this rock of defence to stand upon, the sultan could draw also on the strength of other more distant races, less firmly attached to himself, but not less vigorous, such, for example, as the Albanians of his European mountains and the Kurds of his Asiatic. However decadent might be the Turco-Grecian Osmanli (he, unfortunately, had the lion's share of office), those other elements had suffered no decline in physical or mental development. Indeed, one cannot be among them now without feeling that their day is not only not gone, but is still, for the most part, yet to be.

Such were latent assets of the Osmanli Empire, appreciated imperfectly by the prophets of its dissolution. Thanks to them, that empire continued not only to hold together throughout the nineteenth century but, in some measure, to consolidate itself. Even when the protective fence, set up by European powers about it, was violated, as by Russia several times—in 1829, in 1854, and in 1877—the nation, which Mahmud had made, always proved capable of stout enough resistance to delay the enemy till European diplomacy, however slow of movement, could come to its aid, and ultimately to dispose the victor to accept terms consistent with its continued existence. It was an existence, of course, of sufferance, but one which grew better assured the longer it lasted. By an irony of the Osmanli position, the worse the empire was administered, the stronger became its international guarantee. No better example can be cited than the effect of its financial follies. When national bankruptcy, long contemplated by its Government, supervened at last, the sultan had nothing more to fear from Europe. He became, *ipso facto*, the cherished protege of every power whose nationals had lent his country money.

Considering the magnitude of the change which Mahmud instituted, the stage at which he left it, and the character of the society in which it had to be carried out, it was unfortunate that he should have been followed on the throne by two well-meaning weaklings, of whom the first was a voluptuary, the second a fantastic spendthrift of doubtful sanity. Mahmud, as has been said, being occupied for the greater part of his reign in destroying the old order, had been able to reconstruct little more than a framework. His operations had been almost entirely forcible—of a kind understood by and congenial to the Osmanli character—and partly by circumstances but more by his natural sympathies, he had been identified from first to last with military enterprises. Though he was known to contemplate the eventual supremacy of civil law, and the equality of all sorts and conditions of his subjects before it, he did nothing to open this vista to public view. Consequently he encountered little or no factious opposition. Very few held briefs for either the Janissaries or the Dere Beys; and fewer regretted them when they were gone. Osmanli society identified itself with the new army and accepted the consequent reform of the central or provincial administration. Nothing in these changes seemed to affect Islam or the privileged position of Moslems in the empire.

It was quite another matter when Abdul Mejid, in the beginning of his reign, promulgated an imperial decree—the famous Tanzimat or Hatti Sherif of Gulkhaneh—which, amid many excellent and popular provisions for the continued reform of the administration, proclaimed the equality of Christian and Moslem subjects in service, in reward, and before the law. The new sultan, essentially a civilian and a man of easy-going temperament, had been induced to believe that the end of an evolution, which had only just begun, could be anticipated *per saltum*, and that he and all his subjects would live happily together ever after. His counsellors had been partly politicians, who for various reasons, good and bad, wished to gain West European sympathy for their country, involved in potential bondage to Russia since the Treaty of Unkiar Skelessi (1833), and recently afflicted by Ibrahim Pasha's victory at Nizib; and they looked to Great Britain to get them out of the Syrian mess. Partly also Abdul Mejid had been influenced by enthusiasts, who set more store by ideas or the phrases in which they were expressed, than by the evidence of facts. There were then, as since, 'young men in a hurry' among the more Europeanized Osmanlis. The net result of the sultan's precipitancy was to set against himself and his policy all who wished that such it consummation of the reform process might never come and all who knew it would never come, if snatched at thus—that is, both the 'Old Turks' and the moderate Liberals; and, further, to change for the worse the spirit in which the new machine of government was being worked and in which fresh developments of it would be accepted.

To his credit, however, Abdul Mejid went on with administrative reform. The organization of the army into corps—the foundation of the existing system—and the imposition of five years' service on all subjects of the empire (in theory which an Albanian rising caused to be imperfectly realized in fact), belong to the early part of his reign; as do also, on the civil side, the institution of responsible councils of state and formation of ministries, and much provision for secondary education. To his latest years is to be credited the codification of the civil law. He had the advantage of some dozen initial years of comparative security from external foes, after the Syrian question had been settled in his favour by Great Britain and her allied powers at the cheap price of a guarantee of hereditary succession to the house of Mehemet Ali. Thanks to the same support, war with Persia was avoided and war with Russia postponed.

But the provinces, even if quiet (which some of them, e.g. the Lebanon in the early 'forties', were not), proved far from content. If the form of Osmanli government had changed greatly, its spirit had changed little, and defective communications militated against the responsibility of officials to the centre. Money was scarce, and the paper currency—an ill-omened device of Mahmud's—was depreciated, distrusted, and regarded as an imperial betrayal of confidence. Finally, the hostility of Russia, notoriously unabated, and the encouragement of aspiring *rayas* credited to her and other foreign powers made bad blood between creeds and encouraged opposition to the execution of the pro-Christian Tanzimat. When Christian turbulence at last brought on, in 1854, the Russian attack which developed into the Crimean War, and Christian allies, though they frustrated that attack, made a peace by which the Osmanlis gained nothing, the latter were in no mood to welcome the repetition of the Tanzimat, which Abdul Mejid consented to embody in the Treaty of Paris. The reign closed amid turbulence and humiliations—massacre and bombardment at Jidda, massacre and Franco-British coercion in Syria—from all of which the sultan took refuge with women and wine, to meet in 1861 a drunkard's end.

His successor, Abdul Aziz, had much the same intentions, the same civilian sympathies, the same policy of Europeanization, and a different, but more fatal, weakness of character. He was, perhaps, never wholly sane; but his aberration, at first attested only by an exalted conviction of his divine character and inability to do wrong, excited little attention until it began to issue in fantastic expenditure. By an irony of history, he is the one Osmanli sultan upon the roll of our Order of the Garter, the right to place a banner in St, George's Chapel having been offered to this Allah-possessed caliph on the occasion of his visit to the West in 1867.

Despite the good intentions of Abdul Aziz himself—as sincere as can be credited to a disordered brain—and despite more than one minister of outstanding ability, reform and almost everything else in the empire went to the bad in this unhappy reign. The administration settled down to lifeless routine and lapsed into corruption: the national army was starved: the depreciation of the currency grew worse as the revenue declined and the sultan's household and personal extravagance increased. Encouraged by the inertia of the imperial Government, the Christians of the European provinces waxed bold. Though Montenegro was severely handled for contumacy, the Serbs were able to cover their penultimate stage towards freedom by forcing in 1867 the withdrawal of the last Ottoman garrisons from their fortresses. Krete stood at bay for three years and all but won her liberty. Bosnia rose in arms, but divided against herself. Pregnant with graver trouble than these, Bulgaria showed signs of waking from long sleep. In 1870 she obtained recognition as a nationality in the Ottoman Empire, her Church being detached from the control of the Oecumenical Patriarch of the Greeks and placed under an Exarch. Presently, her peasantry growing ever more restive, passed from protest to revolt against the Circassian refugee-colonists with whom the Porte was flooding the land. The sultan, in an evil hour, for lack of trained troops, let loose irregulars on the villages, and the Bulgarian atrocities, which they committed in 1875, sowed a fatal harvest for his successor to reap. His own time was almost fulfilled. The following spring a dozen high officials, with the assent of the Sheikh-ul-Islam and the active dissent of no one, took Abdul Aziz from his throne to a prison, wherein two days later he perished, probably by his own hand. A puppet reigned three months as Murad V, and then, at the bidding of the same king-makers whom his uncle had obeyed, left the throne free for his brother Abdul Hamid, a man of affairs and ability, who was to be the most conspicuous, or rather, the most notorious Osmanli sultan since Suleiman.

6.

Relapse

The new sultan, who had not expected his throne, found his realm in perilous case. Nominally sovereign and a member of the Concert of Europe, he was in reality a semi-neutralized dependant, existing, as an

304

undischarged bankrupt, on sufferance of the powers. Should the Concert be dissolved, or even divided, and any one of its members be left free to foreclose its Ottoman mortgages, the empire would be at an end. Internally it was in many parts in open revolt, in all the rest stagnant and slowly rotting. The thrice-foiled claimant to its succession, who six years before had denounced the Black Sea clause of the Treaty of Paris and so freed its hands for offence, was manifestly preparing a fresh assault. Something drastic must be done; but what?

This danger of the empire's international situation, and also the disgrace of it, had been evident for some time past to those who had any just appreciation of affairs; and in the educated class, at any rate, something like a public opinion, very apprehensive and very much ashamed, had struggled into being. The discovery of a leader in Midhat Pasha, former governor-general of Bagdad, and a king-maker of recent notoriety, induced the party of this opinion to take precipitate action. Murad had been deposed in August. Before the year was out Midhat presented himself before Abdul Hamid with a formal demand for the promulgation of a Constitution, proposing not only to put into execution the pious hopes of the two Hatti Sherifs of Abdul Mejid but also to limit the sovereign and govern the empire by representative institutions. The new sultan, hardly settled on his uneasy throne, could not deny those who had deposed his two predecessors, and, shrewdly aware that ripe facts would not be long in getting the better of immature ideas, accepted. A parliament was summoned; an electorate, with only the haziest notions of what it was about, went through the form of sending representatives to Constantinople; and the sittings were inaugurated by a speech from the throne, framed on the most approved Britannic model, the deputies, it is said, jostling and crowding the while to sit, as many as possible, on the right, which they understood was always the side of powers that be.

It is true this extemporized chamber never had a chance. The Russians crossed the Pruth before it had done much more than verify its powers, and the thoughts and energies of the Osmanlis were soon occupied with the most severe and disastrous struggle in which the empire had ever engaged. But it is equally certain that it could not have turned to account any chance it might have had. Once more the 'young men in a hurry' had snatched at the end of an evolution hardly begun, without taking into account the immaturity of Osmanli society in political education and political capacity. After suspension during the war, the parliament was dissolved unregretted, and its creator was tried for his life, and banished. In failing, however, Midhat left bad to become so much worse that the next reformers would inevitably have a more convinced public opinion behind them, and he had virtually destroyed the power of Mahmud's bureaucracy. If the only immediate effect was the substitution of an unlimited autocracy, the Osmanli peoples would be able thenceforward to ascribe their misfortunes to a single person, meditate attack, on a single position, and dream of realizing some day an ideal which had been definitely formulated.

The Russian onslaught, which began in both Europe and Asia in the spring of 1877, had been brought on, after a fashion become customary, by movements in the Slavonic provinces of the Ottoman Empire and in Rumania; and the latter province, now independent in all but name and, in defiance of Ottoman protests, disposing of a regular army, joined the invader. In campaigns lasting a little less than a year, the Osmanli Empire was brought nearer to passing than ever before, and it was in a suburb of Constantinople itself that the final armistice was arranged. But action by rival powers, both before the peace and in the revision of it at Berlin, gave fresh assurance that the end would not be suffered to come yet; and, moreover, through the long series of disasters, much latent strength of the empire and its peoples had been revealed.

When that empire had emerged, shorn of several provinces—in Europe, of Rumania, Serbia, and northern Greece, with Bulgaria also well on the road they had travelled to emancipation, and in Asia, of a broad slice of Caucasia—Abdul Hamid cut his losses, and, under the new guarantee of the Berlin Treaty, took heart to try his hand at reviving

Osmanli power. He and his advisers had their idea, the contrary of the idea of Midhat and all the sultans since Mahmud. The empire must be made, not more European, but more Asiatic. In the development of Islamic spirit to pan-Islamic unity it would find new strength; and towards this end in the early eighties, while he was yet comparatively young, with intelligence unclouded and courage sufficient, Abdul Hamid patiently set himself. In Asia, naturally sympathetic to autocracy, and the home of the faith of his fathers, he set on foot a pan-Islamic propaganda. He exalted his caliphate; he wooed the Arabs, and he plotted with extraneous Moslems against whatever foreign government they might have to endure.

It cannot be denied that this idea was based on the logic of facts, and, if it could be realized, promised better than Midhat's for escape from shameful dependence. Indeed, Abdul Hamid, an autocrat bent on remaining one, could hardly have acted upon any other. By far the greater part of the territorial empire remaining to him lay in Asia. The little left in Europe would obviously soon be reduced to less. The Balkan lands were waking, or already awake, to a sense of separate nationality, and what chance did the Osmanli element, less progressive than any, stand in them? The acceptance of the Ottoman power into the Concert of Europe, though formally notified to Abdul Mejid, had proved an empty thing. In that galley there was no place for a sultan except as a dependent or a slave. As an Asiatic power, however, exerting temporal sway over some eighteen million bodies and religious influence over many times more souls, the Osmanli caliph might command a place in the sun.

The result belied these hopes. Abdul Hamid's failure was owed in the main to facts independent of his personality or statecraft. The expansion of Islam over an immense geographical area and among peoples living in incompatible stages of sophistication, under most diverse political and social conditions, has probably made any universal caliphial authority for ever impossible. The original idea of the caliphate, like that of the *jehad* or holy war of the faithful, presupposed that all Moslems were under governments of their own creed, and, perhaps, under one government.

Moreover, if such a caliph were ever to be again, an Osmanli sultan would not be a strong candidate. Apart from the disqualification of his blood, he being not of the Prophet's tribe nor even an Arab, he is lord of a state irretrievably compromised in purist eyes (as Wahabis and Senussis have testified once and again) by its Byzantine heritage of necessary relations with infidels. Abdul Hamid's predecessors for two centuries or more had been at no pains to infuse reality into their nominal leadership of the faithful. To call a real caliphate out of so long abeyance could hardly have been effected even by a bold soldier, who appealed to the general imagination of Moslems; and certainly was beyond the power of a timid civilian.

When Abdul Hamid had played this card and failed, he had no other; and his natural pusillanimity and shiftiness induced him to withdraw ever more into the depths of his palace, and there use his intelligence in exploiting this shameful dependence of his country on foreign powers. Unable or unwilling to encourage national resistance, he consoled himself, as a weak malcontent will, by setting one power against another, pin-pricking the stronger and blustering to the weaker. The history of his reign is a long record of protests and surrenders to the great in big matters, as to Great Britain in the matter of Egypt in 1881, to Russia in that of Eastern Rumelia in 1885, to France on the question of the Constantinople quays and other claims, and to all the powers in 1881 in the matter of the financial control. Between times he put in such pin-pricks as he could, removing his neighbours' landmarks in the Aden *hinterland* or the Sinaitic peninsula. He succeeded, however, in keeping his empire out of a foreign war with any power for about thirty years, with the single exception of a brief conflict with Greece in 1897. While in the first half of his reign he was at pains to make no European friend, in the latter he fell more and more under the influence of Germany, which, almost from the accession of Kaiser Wilhelm II, began to prepare a southward way for future use, and alone of the powers, never browbeat the sultan.

Internally, the empire passed more and more under the government of the imperial household. Defeated by the sheer geographical difficulty of controlling directly an area so vast and inadequately equipped with means of communication, Abdul Hamid soon relaxed the spasmodic efforts of his early years to better the condition of his subjects; and, uncontrolled and demoralized by the national disgrace, the administration went from bad to much worse. Ministers irresponsible; officials without sense of public obligation; venality in all ranks; universal suspicion and delation; violent remedies, such as the Armenian massacres of 1894, for diseases due to neglect; the peasantry, whether Moslem or Christian, but especially Christian, forced ultimately to liquidate all accounts; impoverishment of the whole empire by the improvidence and oppression of the central power—such phrasing of the conventional results of 'Palace' government expresses inadequately the fruits of Yildiz under Abdul Hamid II.

Pari passu with this disorder of central and provincial administration increased the foreign encroachments on the empire. The nation saw not only rapid multiplication of concessions and hypothecations to aliens, and of alien persons themselves installed in its midst under extra-territorial immunity from its laws, secured by the capitulations, but also whole provinces sequestered, administered independently of the sultan's government, and prepared for eventual alienation. Egypt, Tunisia, Eastern Rumelia, Krete—these had all been withdrawn from Ottoman control since the Berlin settlement, and now Macedonia seemed to be going the same way. Bitter to swallow as the other losses had been—pills thinly sugared with a guarantee of suzerainty—the loss of Macedonia would be more bitter still; for, if it were withdrawn from Ottoman use and profit, Albania would follow and so would the command of the north Aegean and the Adriatic shores; while an ancient Moslem population would remain at Christian mercy.

It was partly Ottoman fault, partly the fault of circumstances beyond Ottoman control, that this district had become a scandal and a reproach. In the days of Osmanli greatness Macedonia had been neglected in favour of provinces to the north, which were richer and more nearly related to the ways into central Europe. When more attention began to be paid to it by the Government, it had already become a cockpit for the new-born Christian nationalities, which had been developed on the north, east, and south. These were using every weapon, material and spiritual, to secure preponderance in its society, and had created chronic disorder which the Ottoman administration now weakly encouraged to save itself trouble, now violently dragooned. Already the powers had not only proposed autonomy for it, but begun to control its police and its finance. This was the last straw. The public opinion which had slowly been forming for thirty years gained the army, and Midhat's seed came to fruit.

By an irony of fate Macedonia not only supplied the spectacle which exasperated the army to revolt, but by its very disorder made the preparation of that revolt possible; for it was due to local limitations of Ottoman sovereignty that the chief promoters of revolution were able to conspire in safety. By another irony, two of the few progressive measures ever encouraged by Abdul Hamid contributed to his undoing. If he had not sent young officers to be trained abroad, the army, the one Ottoman institution never allowed wholly to decay, would have remained outside the conspiracy. If he had never promoted the construction of railways, as he began to do after 1897, the Salonika army could have had no such influence on affairs in Constantinople as it exerted in 1908 and again in 1909. As it was, the sultan, at a mandate from Resna in Macedonia, re-enacted Midhat's Constitution, and, a year later, saw an army from Salonika arrive to uphold that Constitution against the reaction he had fostered, and to send him, dethroned and captive, to the place whence itself had come.

7.
Revolution

Looking back on this revolution across seven years of its consequences, we see plainly enough that it was inspired far less by desire for humane progress than by shame of Osmanli military decline. The 'Liberty, Equality,

Fraternity' programme which its authors put forward (a civilian minority among them, sincerely enough), Europe accepted, and the populace of the empire acted upon for a moment, did not express the motive of the movement or eventually guide its course. The essence of that movement was militant nationalism. The empire was to be regenerated, not by humanizing it but by Ottomanizing it. The Osmanli, the man of the sword, was the type to which all others, who wished to be of the nation, were to conform. Such as did not so wish must be eliminated by the rest.

The revolutionary Committee in Salonika, called 'of Union and Progress', held up its cards at first, but by 1910 events had forced its hand on the table. The definite annexation of Bosnia and Hercegovina by Austria-Hungary in 1908, and the declaration of independence and assumption of the title Tsar by the ruler of Bulgaria, since they were the price to be paid by the revolutionaries for a success largely made in Germany, were opposed officially only *pro forma*; but when uninformed opinion in the empire was exasperated thereby against Christendom, the Committee, to appease reactionaries, had to give premature proof of pan-Osmanli and pro-Moslem intentions by taking drastic action against *rayas*. The Greeks of the empire, never without suspicions, had failed to testify the same enthusiasm for Ottoman fraternity which others, e.g. the Armenians, had shown; now they resumed their separatist attitude, and made it clear that they still aspired, not to Ottoman, but to Hellenic nationality. Nor were even the Moslems of the empire unanimous for fraternity among themselves. The Arab-speaking societies complained of under-representation in the councils and offices of the state, and made no secret of their intention not to be assimilated by the Turk-speaking Osmanlis. To all suggestions, however, of local home-rule and conciliation of particularist societies in the empire, the Committee was deaf. Without union, it believed in no progress, and by union it understood the assimilation of all societies in the empire to the Osmanli.

Logic was on the side of the Committee in its choice of both end and means. In pan-Ottomanism, if it could be effected, lay certainly the single chance of restoring Osmanli independence and power to anything like the position they had once held. In rule by a militarist oligarchy for some generations to come, lay the one hope of realizing the pan-Ottoman idea and educating the resultant nation to self-government. That end, however, it was impossible to realize under the circumstances in which past history had involved the Ottoman Empire. There was too much bad blood between different elements of its society which Osmanli rulers had been labouring for centuries rather to keep apart than to unite; and certain important elements, both Moslem and Christian, had already developed too mature ideas of separate nationality. With all its defects, however, the new order did undoubtedly rest on a wider basis than the old, and its organization was better conceived and executed. It retained some of the sympathy of Europe which its beginnings had excited, and the western powers, regarding its representative institutions as earnests of good government, however ill they might work at the first, were disposed to give it every chance.

Unfortunately the Young Turks were in a hurry to bring on their millennium, and careless of certain neighbouring powers, not formidable individually but to be reckoned with if united, to whom the prospect of regenerated Osmanlis assimilating their nationals could not be welcome. Had the Young Turks been content to put their policy of Ottomanization in the background for awhile, had they made no more than a show of accepting local distinctions of creed and politics, keeping in the meantime a tight rein on the Old Turks, they might long have avoided the union of those neighbours, and been in a better position to resist, should that union eventually be arrayed against themselves.

But a considerable and energetic element among them belonged to the nervous Levantine type of Osmanli, which is as little minded to compromise as any Old Turk, though from a different motive. It elected to deal drastically and at once with Macedonia, the peculiar object not only of European solicitude but also of the interest of Bulgaria, Serbia, and Greece. If ever a province required delicate handling it was this. It did not get it. The interested neighbours, each beset by fugitives of its oppressed nationals, protested only to be ignored or browbeaten. They drew towards one another; old feuds and jealousies were put on one side; and at last, in the summer of 1912, a Holy League of Balkan States, inspired by Venezelos, the new Kretan Prime Minister of Greece, and by Ferdinand of Bulgaria, was formed with a view to common action against the oppressor of Greek, Serbian, and Bulgarian nationals in Macedonia. Montenegro, always spoiling for a fight, was deputed to fire the train, and at the approach of autumn the first Balkan war blazed up.

8.
Balkan War

The course of the struggle is described elsewhere in this volume. Its event illustrates the danger of an alliance succeeding beyond the expectations in which it was formed. The constituent powers had looked for a stiff struggle with the Ottoman armies, but for final success sufficient to enable them, at the best, to divide Macedonia among themselves, at the worst, to secure its autonomy under international guarantee. Neither they nor any one else expected such an Ottoman collapse as was in store. Their moment of attack was better chosen than they knew. The Osmanli War Office was caught fairly in the middle of the stream. Fighting during the revolution, subsequently against Albanians and other recalcitrant provincials, and latterly against the Italians, who had snatched at Tripoli the year before, had reduced the *Nizam*, the first line of troops, far below strength. The *Redif*, the second line, had received hardly more training, thanks to the disorganization of Abdul Hamid's last years and of the first years of the new order, than the *Mustafuz*, the third and last line. Armament, auxiliary services, and the like had been disorganized preparatory to a scheme for thorough reorganization, which had been carried, as yet, but a very little way. A foreign (German) element, introduced into the command, had had time to impair the old spirit of Ottoman soldiers, but not to create a new one. The armies sent against the Bulgarians in Thrace were so many mobs of various arms; those which met the Serbs, a little better; those which opposed the Greeks, a little worse.

It followed that the Bulgarians, who had proposed to do no more in Thrace than block Adrianople and immobilize the Constantinople forces, were carried by their own momentum right down to Chataldja, and there and at Adrianople had to prosecute siege operations when they ought to have been marching to Kavala and Salonika. The Serbs, after hard fighting, broke through not only into Macedonia but into Albania, and reached the Adriatic, but warned off this by the powers, consoled themselves with the occupation of much more Macedonian territory than the concerted plans of the allies had foreseen. The Greeks, instead of hard contests for the Haliacmon Valley and Epirus—their proper Irredenta—pushed such weak forces before them that they got through to Salonika just in time to forestall a Bulgarian column. Ottoman collapse was complete everywhere, except on the Chataldja front. It remained to divide the spoil. Serbia might not have Adriatic Albania, and therefore wanted as much Macedonia as she had actually overrun. Greece wanted the rest of Macedonia and had virtually got it. Remained Bulgaria who, with more of Thrace than she wanted, found herself almost entirely crowded out of Macedonia, the common objective of all.

Faced with division *ex post facto*, the allies found their *a priori* agreement would not resolve the situation. Bulgaria, the predominant partner and the most aggrieved, would neither recognize the others' rights of possession nor honestly submit her claims to the only possible arbiter, the Tsar of Russia. Finding herself one against two, she tried a *coup de main* on both fronts, failed, and brought on a second Balkan war, in which a new determining factor, Rumania, intervened at a critical moment to decide the issue against her. The Ottoman armies recovered nearly all they had lost in eastern and central Thrace, including Adrianople, almost without

314

firing a shot, and were not ill pleased to be quit of a desperate situation at the price of Macedonia, Albania, and western Thrace.

Defeated and impoverished, the Ottoman power came out of the war clinging to a mere remnant of its European empire—one single mutilated province which did not pay its way. With the lost territories had gone about one-eighth of the whole population and one-tenth of the total imperial revenue. But when these heavy losses had been cut, there was nothing more of a serious nature to put to debit, but a little even to credit. Ottoman prestige had suffered but slightly in the eyes of the people. The obstinate and successful defence of the Chataldja lines and the subsequent recovery of eastern Thrace with Adrianople, the first European seat of the Osmanlis, had almost effaced the sense of Osmanli disgrace, and stood to the general credit of the Committee and the individual credit of its military leader, Enver Bey. The loss of some thousands of soldiers and much material was compensated by an invaluable lesson in the faultiness of the military system, and especially the *Redif* organization. The way was now clearer than before for re-making the army on the best European model, the German. The campaign had not been long, nor, as wars go, costly to wage. In the peace Turkey gained a new lease of life from the powers, and, profligate that she was, the promise of more millions of foreign money.

Over and above all this an advantage, which she rated above international guarantees, was secured to her—the prospective support of the strongest military power in Europe. The success of Serbia so menaced Germano-Austrian plans for the penetration of the Balkans, that the Central Powers were bound to woo Turkey even more lavishly than before, and to seek alliance where they had been content with influence. In a strong Turkey resided all their hope of saving from the Slavs the way to the Mediterranean. They had kept this policy in view for more than twenty years, and in a hundred ways, by introduction of Germans into the military organization, promotion of German financial enterprise, pushing of German commerce, pressure on behalf of German concessions which would entail provincial influence (for example, the construction of a transcontinental railway in Asia), those powers had been manifesting their interest in Turkey with ever-increasing solicitude. Now they must attach her to themselves with hoops of steel and, with her help, as soon as might be, try to recast the Balkan situation.

The experience of the recent war and the prospect in the future made continuance and accentuation of military government in the Ottoman Empire inevitable. The Committee, which had made its way back to power by violent methods, now suppressed its own Constitution almost as completely as Abdul Hamid had suppressed Midhat's parliament. Re-organization of the military personnel, accumulation of war material, strengthening of defences, provision of arsenals, dockyards, and ships, together with devices for obtaining money to pay for all these things, make Ottoman history for the years 1912-14. The bond with Germany was drawn lighter. More German instructors were invited, more German engineers commissioned, more munitions of war paid for in French gold. By 1914 it had become so evident that the Osmanlis must array themselves with Austro-Germany in any European war, that one wonders why a moment's credit was ever given to their protestations of neutrality when that war came at last in August 1914. Turkey then needed other three months to complete her first line of defences and mobilize. These were allowed to her, and in the late autumn she entered the field against Great Britain, France, and Russia, armed with German guns, led by German officers, and fed with German gold.

9.
The Future

Turkey's situation, therefore, in general terms has become this. With the dissolution of the Concert of Europe the Ottoman Empire has lost what had been for a century its chief security for continued existence. Its fate now depends on that of two European powers which are at war with the rest of the former Concert. Among the last named are Turkey's two principal creditors, holding together about seventy-five per cent. of her public debt. In the event of the defeat of her friends, these creditors will be free to foreclose, the debtor being certainly in no position to meet her obligations. Allied with Christian powers, the Osmanli caliph has proved no more able than his predecessors to unite Islam in his defence; but, for what his title is worth, Mohammed V is still caliph, no rival claim having been put forward. The loyalty of the empire remains where it was, pending victory or defeat, the provinces being slow to realize, and still slower to resent, the disastrous economic state to which the war is reducing them.

The present struggle may leave the Osmanli Empire in one of three situations: (1) member of a victorious alliance, reinforced, enlarged, and lightened of financial burdens, as the wages of its sin; (2) member of a defeated alliance, bound to pay the price of blood in loss of territory, or independence, or even existence; (3) party to a compromise under which its territorial empire might conceivably remain Ottoman, but under even stricter European tutelage than of old.

The first alternative it would be idle to discuss, for the result of conditions so novel are impossible to foresee. Nor, indeed, when immediate events are so doubtful an at the present moment, is it profitable to attempt to forecast the ultimate result of any of the alternatives. Should, however, either the second or the third become fact, certain general truths about the Osmanlis will govern the consequences; and these must be borne in mind by any in whose hands the disposal of the empire may lie.

The influence of the Osmanlis in their empire to-day resides in three things: first, in their possession of Constantinople; second, in the sultan's caliphate and his guardianship of the holy cities of Islam; third, in certain qualities of Osmanli character, notably 'will to power' and courage in the field.

What Constantinople means for the Osmanlis is implied in that name *Roum* by which the western dominions of the Turks have been known ever since the Seljuks won Asia Minor. Apart from the prestige of their own early conquests, the Osmanlis inherited, and in a measure retain in the Near East, the traditional prestige of the greatest empire which ever held it. They stand not only for their own past but also for whatever still lives of the prestige of Rome. Theirs is still the repute of the imperial people *par excellence*, chosen and called to rule.

That this repute should continue, after the sweeping victories of Semites and subsequent centuries of Ottoman retreat before other heirs of Rome, is a paradox to be explained only by the fact that a large part of the population of the Near East remains at this day in about the same stage of civilization and knowledge as in the time of, say, Heraclius. The Osmanlis, be it remembered, were and are foreigners in a great part of their Asiatic empire equally with the Greeks of Byzantium or the Romans of Italy; and their establishment in Constantinople nearly five centuries ago did not mean to the indigenous peoples of the Near East what it meant to Europe—a victory of the East over the West—so much as a continuation of immemorial 'Roman' dominion still exercised from the same imperial centre. Since Rome first spread its shadow over the Near East, many men of many races, whose variety was imperfectly realised, if realised at all, by the peasants of Asia Minor, Syria, Mesopotamia, and Egypt, have ruled in its name; the Osmanlis, whose governmental system was in part the Byzantine, made but one more change which meant the same old thing. The peasants know, of course, about those Semitic victories; but they know also that if the Semite has had his day of triumph and imposed, as was right and proper, his God and his Prophet on Roum—even on all mankind as many believed, and some may be found in remoter regions who still believe—he has returned to his own place south of Taurus; and still Roum is Roum, natural indefeasible Lord of the World.

318

Such a belief is dying now, of course; but it dies slowly and hard. It still constitutes a real asset of the Osmanlis, and will not cease to have value until they lose Constantinople. On the possession of the old imperial city it depends for whatever vitality it has. You may demonstrate, as you will, and as many publicists have done since the Balkan War and before, what and how great economic, political, and social advantages would accrue to the Osmanlis, if they could bring themselves to transfer their capital to Asia. Here they would be rid of Rumelia, which costs, and will always cost them, more than it yields. Here they could concentrate Moslems where their co-religionists are already the great majority, and so have done with the everlasting friction and weakness entailed in jurisdiction over preponderant Christian elements. Here they might throw off the remnants of their Byzantinism as a garment and, no longer forced to face two ways, live and govern with single minds as the Asiatics they are.

Vain illusion, as Osmanli imperialists know! It is their empire that would fall away as a garment so soon as the Near East realized that they no longer ruled in the Imperial City. Enver Pasha and the Committee were amply justified in straining the resources of the Ottoman Empire to cracking-point, not merely to retain Constantinople but also to recover Adrianople and a territory in Europe large enough to bulk as Roum. Nothing that happened in that war made so greatly for the continuation of the old order in Asiatic Turkey as the reoccupation of Adrianople. The one occasion on which Europeans in Syria had reason to expect a general explosion was when premature rumours of the entry of the Bulgarian army into Stambul gained currency for a few hours. That explosion, had the news proved true or not been contradicted in time, would have been a panic-stricken, ungovernable impulse of anarchy—of men conscious that an old world had passed away and ignorant what conceivable new world could come to be.

But the perilous moment passed, to be succeeded by general diffusion of a belief that the inevitable catastrophe was only postponed. In the breathing-time allowed, Arabs, Kurds, and Armenians discussed and

319

planned together revolt from the moribund Osmanli, and, separately, the mutual massacre and plundering of one another. Arab national organizations and nationalist journals sprang to life at Beirut and elsewhere. The revival of Arab empire was talked of, and names of possible capitals and kings were bandied about. One Arab province, the Hasa, actually broke away. Then men began to say that the Bulgarians would not advance beyond Chataldja: the Balkan States were at war among themselves: finally, Adrianople had been re-occupied. And all was as in the beginning. Budding life withered in the Arab movement, and the Near East settled down once more in the persistent shadow of Roum.

Such is the first element in Osmanli prestige, doomed to disappear the moment that the Ottoman state relinquishes Europe. Meanwhile there it is for what it is worth; and it is actually worth a tradition of submission, natural and honourable, to a race of superior destiny, which is instinctive in some millions of savage simple hearts.

∗ ∗ ∗ ∗ ∗

What of the second element? The religious prestige of the Ottoman power as the repository of caliphial authority and trustee for Islam in the Holy Land of Arabia, is an asset almost impossible to estimate. Would a death struggle of the Osmanlis in Europe rouse the Sunni world? Would the Moslems of India, Afghanistan, Turkestan, China, and Malaya take up arms for the Ottoman sultan as caliph? Nothing but the event will prove that they would. Jehad, or Holy War, is an obsolescent weapon difficult and dangerous for Young Turks to wield: difficult because their own Islamic sincerity is suspect and they are taking the field now as clients of *giaur* peoples; dangerous because the Ottoman nation itself includes numerous Christian elements, indispensable to its economy.

Undoubtedly, however, the Ottoman sultanate can count on its religious prestige appealing widely, overriding counteracting sentiments, and, if it rouses to action, rousing the most dangerous temper of all. It is futile to ignore the caliph because he is not of the Koreish, and owes his dignity to a sixteenth-century transfer. These facts are either unknown or not borne in mind by half the Sunnites on whom he might call, and weigh far less with the other half than his hereditary dominion over the Holy Cities, sanctioned by the prescription of nearly four centuries.

One thing can be foretold with certainty. The religious prestige of an Ottoman sultan, who had definitely lost control of the Holy Places, would cease as quickly and utterly as the secular prestige of one who had evacuated Constantinople: and since the loss of the latter would probably precipitate an Arab revolt, and cut off the Hejaz, the religious element in Ottoman prestige may be said to depend on Constantinople as much as the secular. All the more reason why the Committee of Union and Progress should not have accepted that well-meant advice of European publicists! A successful revolt of the Arab-speaking provinces would indeed sound the death-knell of the Ottoman Empire. No other event would be so immediately and surely catastrophic.

* * * * *

The third element in Osmanli prestige, inherent qualities of the Osmanli 'Turk' himself, will be admitted by every one who knows him and his history. To say that he has the 'will to power' is not, however, to say that he has an aptitude for government. He wishes to govern others; his will to do so imposes itself on peoples who have not the same will; they give way to him and he governs them indifferently, though often better than they can govern themselves. For example, bad as, according to our standards, Turkish government is, native Arab government, when not in tutelage to Europeans, has generally proved itself worse, when tried in the Ottoman area in modern times. Where it is of a purely Bedawi barbaric type, as in the emirates of central Arabia, it does well enough; but if the population be contaminated ever so little with non-Arab elements, practices, or ideas, Arab administration seems incapable of producing effective government. It has had chances in the Holy Cities at intervals, and for longer periods in the Yemen. But a European, long resident in the latter country, who has groaned under Turkish administration, where it has always been most oppressive, bore witness that the rule of the native Imam only served to replace oppressive government by oppressive anarchy.

As for the Osmanli's courage as a fighting man, that has often been exemplified, and never better than in the Gallipoli peninsula. It is admitted. The European and Anatolian Osmanlis yield little one to the other in this virtue; but the palm, if awarded at all, must be given to the levies from northern and central Asia Minor.

* * * * *

If Constantinople should be lost, the Arab-speaking parts of the empire would in all likelihood break away, carrying the Holy Cities with them. When the constant risk of this consummation, with the cataclysmic nature of its consequences is considered, one marvels why the Committee, which has shown no mean understanding of some conditions essential to Osmanli empire, should have done so little hitherto to conciliate Arab susceptibilities. Neither in the constitution of the parliament nor in the higher commands of the army have the Arab-speaking peoples been given anything like their fair share; and loudly and insistently have they protested. Perhaps the Committee, whose leading members are of a markedly Europeanized type, understands Asia less well than Europe. Certainly its programme of Ottomanization, elaborated by military ex-attaches, by Jew bankers and officials from Salonika, and by doctors, lawyers, and other *intellectuels* fresh from Paris, was conceived on lines which offered the pure Asiatic very little scope. The free and equal Osmanlis were all to take their cue from men of the Byzantine sort which the European provinces, and especially the city of Constantinople, breed. After the revolution, nothing in Turkey struck one so much as the apparition on the top of things everywhere of a type of Osmanli who has the characteristic qualities of the Levantine Greek. Young officers, controlling their elders, only needed a change of uniform to pass in an Athenian crowd. Spare and dapper officials, presiding in seats of authority over Kurds and Arabs, reminded one of Greek journalists. Osmanli journalists themselves treated one to rhodomontades punctuated with restless gesticulation, which revived memories of Athenian cafes in war-time. It was the Byzantine triumphing over the Asiatic; and the most Asiatic elements in the empire were the least likely to meet with the appreciation or sympathy of the Byzantines.

Are the Arab-speaking peoples, therefore, likely to revolt, or be successful in splitting the Ottoman Empire, if they do? The present writer would like to say, in parenthesis, that, in his opinion, this consummation of the empire is not devoutly to be wished. The substitution of Arab administration for Osmanli would necessarily entail European tutelage of the parts of the Arab-speaking area in which powers, like ourselves, have vital interests—Syria, for example, southern Mesopotamia, and, probably, Hejaz. The last named, in particular, would involve us in so ticklish and thankless a task, that one can only be thankful for the Turkish caretaker there to-day, and loth to see him dismissed.

An Arab revolt, however, might break out whether the Triple Entente desired its success or not. What chance of success would it have? The peoples of the Arab part of the Ottoman Empire are a congeries of differing races, creeds, sects, and social systems, with no common bond except language. The physical character of their land compels a good third of them to be nomadic, predatory barbarians, feared by the other two-thirds. The settled folk are divided into Moslem and Christian (not to mention a large Jewish element), the cleavage being more abrupt than in western Turkey and the tradition and actual spirit of mutual enmity more separative. Further, each of those main creed-divisions is subdivided. Even Islam in this region includes a number of incompatible sects, such as the Ansariye, the Metawali, and the Druses in the Syrian mountains, Shiite Arabs on the Gulf coast and the Persian border, with pagan Kurds and Yezidis in the latter region and north Mesopotamia. As for the Christians, their divisions are notorious, most of these being subdivided again into two or more hostile communions apiece. It is almost impossible to imagine the inhabitants of Syria concerting a common plan or taking common action. The only elements among them which have shown any political sense or capacity for political organization are Christian. The Maronites of the Lebanon are most conspicuous among these; but neither their numbers nor their traditional relations with their neighbours qualify them to form the nucleus of a free united Syria. The 'Arab Movement' up to the present has consisted in little more than talk and journalese. It has not developed any considerable organization to meet that stable efficient organization which the Committee of Union and Progress has directed throughout the Ottoman dominions.

As for the rest of the empire, Asia Minor will stand by the Osmanli cause, even if Europe and Constantinople, and even if the Holy Places and all the Arab-speaking provinces be lost. Its allegiance does not depend on either the tradition of Roum or the caliphate, but on essential unity with the Osmanli nation. Asia Minor is the nation. There, prepared equally by Byzantine domination and by Seljukian influence, the great mass of the people long ago identified itself insensibly and completely with the tradition and hope of the Osmanlis. The subsequent occupation of the Byzantine capital by the heirs of the Byzantine system, and their still later assumption of caliphial responsibility, were not needed to cement the union. Even a military occupation by Russia or by another strong power would not detach Anatolia from the Osmanli unity; for a thing cannot be detached from itself. But, of course, that occupation might after long years cause the unity itself to cease to be.

Such an occupation, however, would probably not be seriously resisted or subsequently rebelled against by the Moslem majority in Asia Minor, supposing Osmanli armaments to have been crushed. The Anatolian population is a sober, labouring peasantry, essentially agricultural and wedded to the soil. The levies for Yemen and Europe, which have gone far to deplete and exhaust it of recent years, were composed of men who fought to order and without imagination, steadily and faithfully, as their fathers had fought. They have no lust for war, no Arabian tradition of fighting for its own sake, and little, if any, fanaticism. Attempts to inspire Anatolian troops with religious rage in the Balkan War were failures. They were asked to fight in too modern a way under too many Teutonic officers. The result illustrated a prophecy ascribed to Ghasri Mukhtar Pasha. When German instructors were first introduced into Turkey, he foretold that they would be the end of the Ottoman army. No, these Anatolians desire nothing better than to follow their plough-oxen, and live their common village life, under any master who will let them be.

Elements of the Christian minority, however, Armenian and Greek, would give trouble with their developed ideas of nationality and irrepressible tendency to 'Europize'. They would present, indeed, problems of which at present one cannot foresee the solution. It seems inevitable that an autonomous Armenia, like an autonomous Poland, must be constituted ere long; but where? There is no geographical unit of the Ottoman area in which Armenians are the majority. If they cluster more thickly in the vilayets of Angora, Sivas, Erzerum, Kharput, and Van, i.e. in easternmost Asia Minor, than elsewhere, and form a village people of the soil, they are consistently a minority in any large administrative district. Numerous, too, in the trans-Tauric vilayets of Adana and Aleppo, the seat of their most recent independence, they are townsmen in the main, and not an essential element of the agricultural population. Even if a considerable proportion of the Armenians, now dispersed through towns of western Asia Minor and in Constantinople, could be induced to concentrate in a reconstituted Armenia (which is doubtful, seeing how addicted they are to general commerce and what may be called parasitic life), they could not fill out both the Greater and the Lesser Armenias of history, in sufficient strength to overbear the Osmanli and Kurdish elements. The widest area which might he constituted an autonomous Armenia with good prospect of self-sufficiency would be the present Russian province, where the head-quarters of the national religion lie, with the addition of the provinces of Erzerum, Van, and Kharput.

But, if Russia had brought herself to make a self-denying ordinance, she would have to police her new Armenia very strongly for some years; for an acute Kurdish problem would confront it, and no concentration of nationals could be looked for from the Armenia Irredenta of Diarbekr, Urfa, Aleppo, Aintab, Marash, Adana, Kaisariyeh, Sivas, Angora, and Trebizond (not to mention farther and more foreign towns), until public security was assured in what for generations has been a cockpit. The Kurd is, of course, an Indo-European as much as the Armenian, and rarely a true Moslem; but it would be a very long time indeed before these facts reconciled him to the domination of the race which he has plundered for three centuries. Most of the Osmanlis of eastern Asia Minor are descendants of converted Armenians; but their assimilation would be slow and doubtful. Islam, more rapidly and completely than any other creed, extinguishes racial sympathies and groups its adherents anew.

The Anatolian Greeks are less numerous but not less difficult to provide for. The scattered groups of them on the plateau—in Cappadocia, Pontus, the Konia district—and on the eastward coast-lands would offer no serious difficulty to a lord of the interior. But those in the western river-basins from Isbarta to the Marmora, and those on the western and north-western littorals, are of a more advanced and cohesive political character, imbued with nationalism, intimate with their independent nationals, and actively interested in Hellenic national politics. What happens at Athens has long concerned them more than what happens at Constantinople; and with Greece occupying the islands in the daily view of many of them, they are coming to regard themselves more and more every day as citizens of Graecia Irredenta. What is to be done with these? What, in particular, with Smyrna, the second city of the Ottoman Empire and the first of 'Magna Graecia'? Its three and a half hundred thousand souls include the largest Greek urban population resident in any one city.

Shall it be united to Greece? Greece herself might well hesitate. It would prove a very irksome possession, involving her in all sorts of continental difficulties and risks. There is no good frontier inland for such an *enclave*. It could hardly be held without the rest of westernmost Asia, from Caria to the Dardanelles, and in this region the great majority of the population is Moslem of old stocks, devotedly attached both to their faith and to the Osmanli tradition.

The present writer, however, is not among the prophets. He has but tried to set forth what may delay and what may precipitate the collapse of an empire, whose doom has been long foreseen, often planned, invariably postponed; and, further, to indicate some difficulties which, being bound to confront heirs of the Osmanlis, will be better met the better they are understood before the final agony—If this is, indeed, to be!

Lightning Source UK Ltd.
Milton Keynes UK
UKHW021828160223
417092UK00004B/327